BLOCKBUSTERS

BLOCKBUSTERS

WHY BIG HITS – AND BIG RISKS – ARE THE FUTURE OF

THE ENTERTAINMENT BUSINESS

ANITA ELBERSE

ff

FABER & FABER

First published in the USA in 2013
by Henry Holt and Company, LLC
175 Fifth Avenue
New York, New York 10010

First published in the UK in 2014 by
Faber & Faber Limited
Bloomsbury House
74–77 Great Russell Street
London WC1B 3DA

Printed in England by CPI Group (UK) Ltd, Croydon CR0 4YY

A CIP record for this book
is available from the British Library

ISBN 978–0–571–30922–1

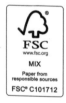

2 4 6 8 10 9 7 5 3 1

To Michael

CONTENTS

BLOCKBUSTERS

SHOW BUSINESS—
A BUSINESS OF BLOCKBUSTERS

I n 1999, Alan Horn, new in his role as president and chief oper- ating officer of the film and television studio Warner Bros., embarked on a high-stakes strategy. Entrusted with the power to decide which movies the studio would make—the coveted "greenlighting" decision—he chose to single out four or five so- called tent-pole or event films—those thought to have the broadest appeal—among its annual output of around twenty-five movies, and support those picks with a disproportionately large chunk of its total production and marketing budget. Other studio heads had produced daring, big-budget movies before, of course, but no one had, as Horn put it, "really pursued it as a strategy"—none had, in other words, dared to make a handful of such big bets each year, at the expense of the attention lavished on a larger number of smaller movies. "In the movie business, the product is the same price to the consumer regardless of the cost of manufacturing it—whether its production budget is $15 million or $150 million. So it may be counterintuitive to spend more money," Horn told me. "But in the end, it is all about getting people to come to the theater. The idea was that movies with greater production value should be more ap- pealing to prospective moviegoers. Audiences respond to movie stars, but those lead to higher costs. Audiences respond to special effects, but those lead to higher costs, too. And you have to let audiences know you are there with your movie—really market it as an event—but that of course further adds to the costs. You can only do so many of those big films in a given year."

Over the next few years, as Horn's strategy played out at Warner Bros., another executive was quickly moving up the ranks at a rival media conglomerate. Jeff Zucker, a former field and executive producer of *The Today Show*, climbed up to president and later chief executive officer of NBC's Television Group, overseeing what was then the number-one-rated television network in the United States. In 2007, after taking the reins at parent company NBC Universal, he led a push to cut the rising costs of programming at the television network—in many ways the exact opposite of Horn's strategy at Warner. "We're managing for margins instead of ratings," asserted Ben Silverman, whom Zucker had appointed as co-chair of NBC Entertainment. Fresh off a career as a high-flying television producer in his own right, Silverman was seemingly taking all the right measures to increase profits and reduce risk in his new role as a network executive: betting less on the most expensive dramatic content and instead focusing on intellectual property and formats that could be acquired at more reasonable prices; relying less on A-list actors and producers who could command fees of sometimes hundreds of thousands of dollars per episode; and cutting back on pilots that often came with a price tag several times that of a regular episode but generally did little to gauge true demand for a new series.

By 2011, Horn could look back on an unparalleled winning streak: under his leadership, Warner Bros. became the only studio in history to surpass $1 billion at the domestic box office for eleven years in a row. All indications are that profits had seen a strong upward trajectory as well, helped by smash hits such as the *Harry Potter* movies, *The Dark Knight*, *The Hangover* and its sequel, *Happy Feet*, *Million Dollar Baby*, *Ocean's 11* and its two sequels, and *Sherlock Holmes*. Alan Horn's stock had risen so high that when Walt Disney in 2012 was looking for a new executive to bring the magic back to its troubled studio, it recruited Horn—only a year after his retirement from Warner Bros.—to take over as Walt Disney Studios' chairman. "He's earned the respect of the industry for driving tremendous, sustained creative and financial success," Disney's chief executive officer Bob Iger said.

And Zucker? His strategy failed miserably, and in 2010 he was asked to leave his high-profile job. But the damage had been done: NBC was farther behind on all the metrics that mattered—including, by all accounts, the profit margins Zucker and Silverman sought most. During Zucker's tenure, NBC fell from its perch as the highest-rated television network to fourth place, behind its three broadcast rivals—ABC, CBS, and FOX—a demise once unthinkable for the network that built its reputation on its "must-see" prime-time lineup. One rival executive labeled Zucker "a case study in the most destructive media executive ever to exist." While that may be too strong a statement, it is clear that his "managing for margins" strategy had disastrous results.

Warner's approach, which is the very strategy that NBC sought to escape, seems to fly in the face of conventional business rules. Why would film or television executives choose to put themselves in a position where their company's overall performance—or even survival—rests on a few big product launches each year, and let spending on those products reach levels that make recovering costs appear almost impossible? Especially in an industry in which audience demand is fickle and the failure rate is so high, would it not be more sensible in the long run to forgo these kinds of outsize investments and instead place a larger number of smaller bets, closely guard costs, and "manage for margins"?

Quite the contrary: what Warner Bros., NBC, and many other entertainment businesses have found out—often the hard way—is that a "blockbuster strategy" works. The leading television networks, film studios, book publishers, music labels, video game publishers, and producers in other sectors of the entertainment industry thrive on making huge investments to acquire, develop, and market concepts with strong hit potential, and they bank on the sales of those to make up for the middling performance of their other content. That is one of the essential lessons I have learned from studying these businesses: rather than spreading resources evenly across product lines (which might seem to be the most effective approach when no one knows for sure which products will catch on) and vigorously trying to save costs in an effort to increase profits, betting heavily on likely blockbusters and spending considerably less on the "also rans" is the surest way to lasting success in show business.

Blockbuster strategies are certainly not free of risk—even the biggest productions supported by the highest advertising budgets can, and sometimes will, fail to create a splash in the market. Just ask the people who thought investing in the 2012 movie *John Carter* was a great idea, or those who felt the television show *Lone Star* would make audiences tune in en masse that same year. In today's fragile economy, a world in which a high-profile business executive's every move is scrutinized by traditional news media and bloggers alike, appearing to play it safe may be a top priority. But content producers can't afford to walk away from big bets—doing so would actually *increase* their chance of failure in the long run. The highest-performing entertainment businesses take their chances on a small group of titles and turn those choices into successes by investing heavily in their development, supporting them with a high level of promotional spending, often well in advance of their release into the marketplace ("coming soon to a theater near you"), and distributing them as widely as possible. It may not look anything like the way products in other sectors of the economy are introduced, but it works.

In this book, I will do more than simply present evidence of the higher returns of blockbuster strategies. I will also try to explain *why* they are so effective and describe what is likely to go wrong when entertainment companies stop playing the blockbuster game and instead shift their focus to what may appear to be more risk-averse strategies, much like NBC did. As a professor at the Harvard Business School, I have studied media, sports, and other entertainment sectors for a decade. Over the years, I have heard all kinds of theories about why the entertainment industry is organized the way it is, or how it can be run better. And with the advent of digital technology that makes it possible for virtually everyone to become a content producer and share their creations with the world, there is much speculation about how the entertainment landscape might change, for the better or for the worse. "Old media" are dead in the water, some say. Studios will learn to stop betting on expensive projects and overpaid actors, instead taking "more shots at goal" with inexpensive ideas. Musicians will be freed from the shackles of record labels. Sports leagues will no longer need the likes of ESPN and will go directly to consumers via the Web. Once consumers are able to consume whatever they want, whenever they want it, they will migrate away from the hits. Or they will opt for the lowest-common-denominator content, ruining our culture. Paying for content is old-fashioned—free is the future. The list goes on and on.

My goal in this book is to separate fact from fiction—to describe how the entertainment industry really works, based on an understanding of why entertainment executives make the decisions they make and on actual data about how those decisions play out in the marketplace. In my role at the Harvard Business School, I am in the fortunate position to have been granted rare access to executives who make these kinds of decisions on a regular basis—sometimes while they are in the process of making them. I have worked on dozens of case studies of companies and people in film, television, music, publishing, sports, and other sectors of entertainment, and have conducted numerous one-on-one interviews and other conversations with practitioners (and spent an inordinate amount of time visiting film premieres, sports events, and other celebrity get-togethers—the kinds of sacrifices one has to make in the name of research). Drawing on my observations from the field, as well as on an expansive body of scholarly research, I will use these pages to try to get to the bottom of why media executives do what they do and how their strategies pan out. (If the word *scholarly* scared you in this last sentence, please don't worry—I promise to avoid all mentions of the fancy econometric and statistical techniques that were used to analyze sales patterns, and to concentrate squarely on the results that matter.)

As it turns out, how executives can best deal with risk is similar across the worlds of film, television, music, book publishing, sports, and other entertainment sectors. The lessons learned about blockbusters in film and television also apply to the rest of the entertainment industry. For instance, as I will show, many of the principles that underlie Warner Bros.' winning streak also explain why Grand Central Publishing could seriously consider making what some dismissed as an outrageously high bid for the rights to a manuscript about a fluffy creature, seemingly giving the publisher little more than an outside shot at recovering its investment. Or how Marvel Entertainment's Spider-Man, The Avengers, and other superheroes could turn into Hollywood executives' safest bets, leading to great riches for the company. And the same lessons capture how a certain Stefani Germanotta, also known as Lady Gaga, could catapult into the public's consciousness and, in just a couple of short years, become one of the planet's biggest celebrities. Or how a small New York–based record label could give rise to best-selling band Maroon 5, scoring one hit after another. Across these case studies, a consistent picture emerges of how businesses that want to maximize revenues and profits can best approach the production and marketing of entertainment products. And even though some cases go back a few years, the underlying issues are as true today as they were then. Anyone who works in show business should take note of these lessons—or, as NBC under Zucker did, ignore them at their peril.

Those who follow the world of entertainment as fans may find learning about these principles worthwhile, too, for they will determine what tomorrow's entertainment offerings will look like. Some of the lessons may be a bit disheartening to consumers who dislike the blockbuster mind-set of established entertainment companies and would rather see them invest in more niche offerings or unproven talent. But the purpose of this book is not to pass judgment on what makes for "good" or "bad" products, or to question purely creative decisions; there's no arguing about taste, after all.

Instead, the focus here is on explaining why entertainment markets work the way they do and what strategies will help build thriving, lasting businesses—the kinds of businesses, in other words, that deliver the types of products that vast numbers of people enjoy.

Zucker and Silverman are long gone at NBC, but the network is still recovering. It has dramatically changed its approach. After Zucker's departure, NBC Universal Television's new chairman, Jeff Gaspin, acknowledged that the "managing-for-margins" strategy had run its course and promised agents, producers, and other television industry insiders that the network would be back in the hunt for the next blockbuster hit. Now "in it to win it," as Gaspin put it, NBC's new goal was to put the best possible programs on the air. The network has been breaking the bank to do so. For the fall 2010 television season, it ordered an almost-unheard-of thirteen new series, including big-budget series from A-list producers like J. J. Abrams, Jerry Bruckheimer, and David E. Kelley. The network spent a rumored $150 million in development costs for that season alone and significantly increased its marketing costs in an effort to win back viewers. The next season, it further upped the ante. Taking cues from FOX and its blockbuster hit *American Idol*, NBC bet big on the talent show *The Voice*, paying more than $2 million per episode—and found a genuine hit of its own. In fact, helped by a favorable placement immediately after the 2012 Super Bowl, in February 2012 *The Voice* displaced *American Idol* as America's top-rated television series, causing NBC executives to crow about "an electricity in the building" at the company's headquarters at Rockefeller Center. One top rating for the network does not mean it has returned to its glory days, but it does appear that NBC's new executives have a better idea of what it might take to get there.

At Warner Bros., NBC, and many other entertainment companies, blockbuster strategies often go hand in hand with huge investments in top creative talent. Movie studios handsomely reward superstar actors such as Johnny Depp, Jennifer Lawrence, Will Smith, Kristen Stewart, and Robert Downey Jr. in hopes of converting fans of those stars into audiences for the studios' productions.

The same goes for television networks, with lead actors on the most successful series earning high six-figure salaries for each episode filmed. *The Voice*, for instance, was stacked with A-listers when it launched: the four judges—Christina Aguilera, CeeLo Green, Maroon 5's Adam Levine, and Blake Shelton—were all established stars in the world of music and could command sizable salaries.

The focus on star talent now extends into virtually all sectors of the entertainment industry. Openly admitting that he was taking a page from the book written by major Hollywood studios a year after Alan Horn started his event-film strategy, a Spanish businessman single-handedly raised the bar for investments in A-list talent in the world of soccer. Bringing a show-business mentality to his renowned soccer club, Real Madrid's president, Florentino Pérez, started pursuing what he called his *Galácticos* strategy, a reference to the star power of the players he sought to recruit. At the height of Galacticism, Englishman David Beckham, one of the sport's biggest icons, joined a team that was already brimming with stars from all over the globe. A marketer's dream, for sure, but also a very expensive dream. Are the high fees paid for star talent justified?

A close look at the market for creative talent and the ways in which studio heads, soccer-club presidents, and other entertainment managers decide on these matters reveals that there are good reasons to pay top dollar for star talent (and, admittedly, some not-so-good reasons). Betting on star talent creates important marketing advantages, drawing audiences and sponsors alike. But the competition for the few stars at the top is so severe that the pressure on entertainment businesses is getting pretty intense: the truth is that often they can barely afford to compete for the most sought-after performers, but at the same time they cannot afford *not* to do so. The tug-of-war between stars and entertainment companies, with each party vying for a bigger piece of the revenues and profits generated by blockbuster products, is one of the most fascinating aspects of today's entertainment economy—and one with great consequences for the future of show business.

As with any tug-of-war, offering accurate predictions about

who ultimately will be victorious requires a thorough understanding of each side's strengths and weaknesses as well as its strategies. Providing such insights is another major objective of this book, which is why I take a close look at the business models of star-focused enterprises like the major Hollywood studios and Real Madrid. I also give considerable attention to companies that take a different approach and instead specialize in developing promising talent into stars. Argentine soccer club Boca Juniors and Real Madrid's archrival FC Barcelona, for example, are both famous for fostering some of the world's best soccer players. And NBC's *Saturday Night Live*, one of television's longest-running shows, has served as a stepping-stone for dozens of A-list comedians, from Eddie Murphy and Adam Sandler to Jimmy Fallon and Tina Fey. One axiom becomes very clear: entertainment companies go to great lengths to gain the upper hand in their ongoing dealings with creative talent.

Such efforts don't come about in a vacuum, of course: superstars and the people who advise them are getting smarter about wielding their power. Recognizing their outsize value, talented actors, musicians, athletes, and other performers are pushing for ever-higher rewards. That, in turn, is putting pressure on the business models of studios, record labels, sports teams, and other content producers. Both sides have gotten ever more creative in their efforts to negotiate favorable agreements. And so it could come to be that, in 2006, even when his status as a star actor was first being challenged, the venerable studio MGM made a stunning move by offering Tom Cruise a part of a movie *studio* rather than a part in a movie—an ownership stake in MGM's United Artists, to be precise. Or that Russian tennis player Maria Sharapova forged lucrative endorsement partnerships with an impressive set of brands, leading her to become the highest-paid female athlete in the world (and beating out a stellar cast of male athletes, too). And that, to the astonishment of many sports-industry insiders (even before his much-debated decision to "take his talents to South Beach," as he described his move to the Miami Heat), basketball superstar LeBron James established his own firm to handle all aspects of his business ventures and marketing activities, taking a highly innovative approach to sports marketing.

My research shows that there is a clear logic to these developments, one that can be grasped by closely studying the characteristics of the market for creative talent as well as the talent's appetite for risk at different stages of their career. It is a logic that those who work in entertainment should be intimately aware of, as it yields lessons about how businesses can best recruit, manage, and reward talent—even if not every decision turns out as well as those involved might have hoped. It also offers important clues to any aspiring musician, actor, author, or athlete who wants to discover the best approach to his or her creative career. For superstars and lesser-known talent alike, knowing when to pursue which opportunities is critical, especially because the careers of most creative people are so short-lived.

All of this now transpires in a media environment that, with the arrival of the YouTube, Twitter, and Facebook era, is of course vastly different from what it was when Alan Horn and Jeff Zucker first dreamed up their strategies, and when Lady Gaga and LeBron James first emerged on the scene. Undoubtedly, the biggest question currently facing entertainment companies is how the rapid rise of digital technology will affect their bets on blockbusters and superstars. Because advances in digital technology substantially lower the cost of doing business, there are good reasons to suspect that far-reaching changes are on the horizon. New technologies, after all, make it easier and cheaper for content producers to offer entertainment goods—just think of the savings that result from distributing a movie online rather than having to transport physical prints to theaters all over the world. At the same time, new technologies, such as sophisticated recommendation engines, make it less of a hassle for consumers to find and purchase the goods they want. These effects are especially apparent in the entertainment sector, where goods like films, television shows, books, and music can be fully digitized.

Some industry insiders have suggested that digital technology will spell the end of blockbusters—and, with that, the effectiveness of blockbuster strategies. Is the rise of online distribution channels a sign that soon the "old" rules of the entertainment business will no longer apply? Looking at the popularity of sites such as YouTube that democratize content production and distribution, one might be tempted to conclude that a "yes" is the only right answer. But a closer look reveals that the reality isn't quite so simple. In fact, in today's markets where, thanks to the Internet, buyers have easy access to millions and millions of titles, the principles of the blockbuster strategy may be more applicable than ever before. As I will describe in the latter half of this book, there are fundamental laws of consumer behavior that explain the strategy's enduring appeal—the kinds of laws everyone with an interest in the entertainment industry should be aware of, in other words. The blockbuster strategy's continuing importance to the success of entertainment companies is made abundantly clear in the enormous amounts of data that online channels generate.

Armed with an understanding of the ways in which digital technology is transforming the markets for entertainment goods, one can easily see why YouTube has struggled to turn its immense popularity into a lucrative and sustainable business, and one can begin to make sense of parent company Google's push into Original Channels. It also becomes evident that NBC's decision to co-fund Hulu, a site focused on offering premium, professionally produced online video, may have been one of the broadcaster's smartest moves in recent years—Zucker deserves some credit for that. (Yes, it may come as a surprise, but this is not one of those black-and-white, heroes-and-villains books. Most entertainment executives have their fair share of successes and failures, and Zucker is no different.) These same underlying principles even help us see how the innovative foray into digital distribution of New York City's Metropolitan Opera—specifically, its decision to simulcast live opera to movie theaters around the world—will affect the market for opera. One critical lesson here becomes clear: blockbusters will become more—not less—relevant to popular culture, and blockbuster strategies will thrive.

A second question triggered by the emergence of online channels is whether these channels will ultimately undercut the role of established content producers and distributors. British band Radiohead made a splash a few years ago with an album they self-released, without the help of a record label or retailer, prompting many industry observers to suggest that other bands could and should release their work on their own, too. Previously unheralded musicians have on occasion developed vast fan bases on YouTube and through social networks, and some self-publishing authors have created huge demand for their writings online. As digital technologies become ever more sophisticated and ubiquitous, will creative talent increasingly seize the opportunity to market their creations directly to consumers? If so, the demise of many established entertainment companies may not be far off. According to my research, however, such an extreme scenario is unlikely: it's virtually impossible for most creative people to thrive without the benefits that these enterprises provide. Still, the rise of do-it-yourself production and distribution raises critical issues for even the largest entertainment businesses.

We can learn a lot from content creators and owners who have used digital channels to deliver their content directly to the consumer. Hulu—co-owned by NBC Universal, News Corp.'s FOX, and Disney's ABC—is an example here, too. But the world of sports has perhaps made even bigger waves. Major League Baseball's digital arm stands out: MLB's executives have embraced the opportunities that digital channels afford the league to interact directly with its fans, scoring with products for a host of different platforms and operating systems. The National Football League has taken a strikingly different approach to digital media, but its strategy has proven just as successful, and the resulting lessons for how markets for entertainment goods are evolving are remarkably consistent. All three cases—Hulu, MLB, and the NFL—show how content producers can use new digital distribution channels to their advantage. And all three again underline the benefits that blockbusters provide in that context.

None of this is to deny how disruptive the advances in technology can be to the world of entertainment. Piracy, fueled by the same low costs of reproduction and distribution that explain digital technology's other effects, is often seen as the main culprit. But other forces—such as consumers' expectations that prices will inevitably come down in digital channels—may be more threatening. The so-called unbundling of goods in digital channels also causes headaches for entertainment businesses. For example, now that all the songs on an album are made available for individual purchase online, the album bundle is increasingly playing second fiddle to the individual song. This inversion was unthinkable in a fully analog world, if only because the costs of separately packaging and shipping songs were prohibitive. Meanwhile, the rise of massive online retailers and content aggregators with ultrathin margins has also put tremendous pressure on entertainment companies' business models.

As a result of all these tumultuous changes, blockbuster strategies will undoubtedly evolve—and what is fascinating is that some superstars seem to be leading the way. In 2010, in an award-winning campaign dreamed up by advertising agency Droga5, hip-hop mogul Jay-Z and his manager explored a partnership with Microsoft for the launch of his memoir, *Decoded*. A year later, Lady Gaga, never afraid to innovate, redefined the concept of a major launch with her *Born This Way* album. In the years to come, many more entertainers will surely follow in their footsteps. That's not a blind guess—as we'll see, it is a logical conclusion if one considers both the disruptive effects of digital technology and the factors that explain the effectiveness of blockbuster bets. Blockbuster strategies may become more difficult to execute in a digital world, but, as counterintuitive as it may sound, their relevance only increases. The future of blockbusters in the entertainment economy shines bright.

And, in fact, blockbuster strategies may increasingly pervade other sectors of the economy, along with other marketing practices borrowed from the world of entertainment. So, to conclude the road map of what's to come, I will end the book by pointing to particularly noteworthy examples I have come across in my research over the years. The nightlife business is a focus here: two of the

sector's most successful impresarios are leading a revolution, transforming the business from one that is all about selling bottles—
high-priced alcohol delivered to "table customers" seated at hot
spots in the club—to one that is just as much about selling tickets
to heavily marketed events featuring superstar DJs. But I'll also
point to other examples, from Apple and its big bets in consumer
electronics, to Victoria's Secret with its angelic-superstar-studded
fashion shows, and to Burberry's success in taking the trench coat
digital. As these will show, many of the lessons to be learned about
blockbusters not only apply across the entertainment industry—
they even extend to the business world at large.

Chapter One

BETTING ON BLOCKBUSTERS

n June 2012, less than two weeks after the news of his appointment as chairman of Walt Disney Pictures had Hollywood insiders buzzing, Alan Horn walked onto the Disney studio lot. The well-liked sixty-nine-year-old executive ("I try to be a nice person almost all the time, but next to Alan Horn I look like a complete jerk," actor Steve Carell had joked during Horn's good-bye party at Warner Bros.) was excited about joining Disney, which he described as "one of the most iconic and beloved entertainment companies in the world." But he also knew he had his work cut out for him, as Disney Pictures had posted disappointing box-office results in recent years. In his new role, Horn would oversee production, distribution, and marketing of live-action and animated films from Disney as well as its units Pixar Animation Studios and Marvel. Horn would have to decide whether the event-film strategy he had pioneered at Warner was the right approach for his new employer as well.

After working for producer Norman Lear early in his career and spending a decade at the helm of Castle Rock Entertainment (a production firm he had co-founded that was known for creating the hit television show *Seinfeld* and films such as *A Few Good Men*,

The Shawshank Redemption, and *When Harry Met Sally*), Horn had moved to Warner and fostered a different attitude toward risk. "Other studios made big movies, but no one was doing this on a consistent basis," he told me. "In fact, they were afraid of it. Because the price for movie tickets was fixed, taking on higher costs seemed a bigger risk."

Described as "a consensus builder," Horn went to great lengths to ensure that his Warner colleagues embraced the event-film strategy. His first event-film pick was *The Perfect Storm,* released in 2000. "George Clooney was not a big star at the time, and neither was Mark Wahlberg, but I really liked the story," Horn recalled. "We wanted to create the best visual experience for audiences, and we spent a lot to showcase those in our marketing campaign. I remember I saw an early cut of the trailer and asked, 'Where is the storm?' I wanted a shot of the boat in the storm, with the high seas. It took half a million dollars, but they made it happen in a week. We wanted everyone to know this was going to be big. So we had to have that shot."

Within a few years, the event-film strategy had taken hold, and Warner was releasing four or five such movies annually. Horn focused on what he called "four-quadrant movies": films appealing to young and old as well as male and female moviegoers. In 2008, the studio's picks included *The Dark Knight, Get Smart, Speed Racer,* and, before its release date was moved to 2009, *Harry Potter and the Half-Blood Prince.* In 2010, Horn's last full year in charge, *Inception, Clash of the Titans,* and *Harry Potter and the Deathly Hallows: Part 1* were among the event films. Each event movie received a higher-than-average production and marketing budget and generally had its release date planned years in advance. "The potential upside for our event films is so enormous that we believed it was worth the risk," declared Horn.

The results proved the wisdom of his strategy: under Horn's twelve-year leadership, Warner Bros. Pictures, the largest of the six major Hollywood studios, became the first studio in history to collect more than $1 billion in theatrical revenues for ten years in a row. In 2010, the studio was the market leader in films with worldwide box-office revenues of $4.8 billion—its biggest haul ever. The eight Harry Potter films, the most successful motion picture franchise in history, collected $7.7 billion at the worldwide box office. Warner Bros.' output during this period also included several other lucrative films, including *300, The Dark Knight, The Departed, Gran Torino, The Hangover* and its sequel, *I Am Legend, Million Dollar Baby, Ocean's 11, 12,* and *13,* and *Sherlock Holmes.*

But Horn's strategy remained controversial precisely because it seemed so risky. "Making monster projects into profit centers is no slam-dunk," wrote one *Wall Street Journal* reporter, expressing a sentiment that was widely shared. "Someday soon, one of these big bets will crash so hard that a studio will be left with a staggering write-off." Disney's own *John Carter* was a recent case in point: it had cost an estimated $250 million to produce and likely lost almost as much, easily making it 2012's biggest flop. Detractors of event-film strategies also loved to point to the western *Heaven's Gate,* otherwise known as "the film that sank a studio." Delayed for months and beset by cost overruns, the 1980 movie cost a then-unprecedented $40 million, only to be roundly rejected by both the press and the public (one influential critic called it "an unqualified disaster"). United Artists sold only $3 million's worth of tickets; as a direct result of the massive box-office flop, the studio collapsed and was sold off to MGM.

Horn acknowledged the downside of his approach. "The problem with event movies is that when we fail, it is a colossal failure." And for all of his successes, Horn also had his share of misses during his long tenure at Warner Bros. "In a good year, a major studio is happy to bat .500," he said. "The real goal is overall profitability." The countless variables involved in the moviemaking process plagued every live-action project he decided on. "When Jo Rowling was selling Harry Potter, she was turned down by a number of publishing companies. And they were reading it in the medium in which it would be released! Making a movie is—it's just ridiculous. We are reading a screenplay, and have to imagine what it will look like with a certain director, a certain cinematography, and a certain cast. You say, 'With Channing Tatum it will look this way, but if we go with Matt Damon it will look a different way.' It is such a gut-level decision that it is impossible to define criteria that can make a studio successful year in, year out."

Now, with his arrival at Disney, all eyes were on Horn to do just that: achieve success year in, year out. It didn't help that Disney's appetite for big risks was low after the *John Carter* debacle; making matters worse, Horn knew he would have to compete head-on with Warner and the very strategy he had invented. "Other Hollywood studios have embraced the event-film strategy, too," he said. "So the competition from other major studios for the best ideas, creative talent, and release dates has only increased in recent years. We will have to go up against other big movies in our release weekends." Could Horn bring the magic back to the Mouse House?

Is the event-film strategy—or, as I called it earlier, the "blockbuster strategy"—really the best approach to making and marketing entertainment? For major studios like Warner Bros. and for other large-scale content producers across the different sectors of the entertainment industry, the answer is an unequivocal "yes." In fact, the strategy that Warner Bros. followed is now a common approach among not just movie studios, but also publishers, television production companies, music labels, video game publishers, and producers in other sectors of the media and entertainment industry. But before we delve into the explanation for why such a seemingly risky approach makes sense even in today's competitive marketplace, let's take a closer look at the approach taken by Horn at Warner Bros. and understand the returns that are associated with it.

Rather than dividing its resources evenly across the products in its portfolio, a movie studio following a blockbuster strategy allocates a disproportionately large share of its production and marketing dollars to a small subset of products in the hope that they will bring in the lion's share of revenues and profits. This idea is illustrated in the chart that follows. Even amid considerable uncertainty, the studio bets heavily on the most likely hits. It makes

A Typical Pattern of Blockbuster Investments and Outcomes

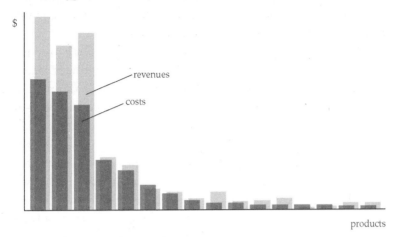

products

"blockbuster bets": big-budget productions aimed at mass audiences. Given the nature of the movie-production process—where the trajectory from acquiring a script or the rights to a property to finally releasing a movie can easily take four years—the studio has to make its picks of the most likely winners at a very early stage. Given the fickle taste of consumers, and given the complexities of a production process that often involves hundreds of people, that's not a simple task. But, the studio's thinking goes, the rewards will be worth the risk.

As a way of examining Warner Bros.' strategy, let's take a look at the year 2010. The studio released twenty-two films that year, spending about $1.5 billion in production costs and upward of $700 million on advertising and other promotional efforts domestically. Warner spent a third of its 2010 production budget on its three biggest titles—$250 million on *Harry Potter and the Deathly Hallows: Part 1*, $175 million on *Inception*, and $125 million on *Clash of the Titans*. Its fourth-biggest investment, the *Sex and the City* sequel, cost another $100 million. Such big bets often feature not only A-list talent but also elaborate visual effects—spectacular sequences, sweeping shots, large-scale sets, multiple locations, and high-tech stunts, for instance—all of which drive up the picture's costs. If the movie is based on a successful property such as a book or a character (as the biggest bets, such as *Harry Potter*, often are), intellectual property rights can also be costly.

"We have made a conscious decision at Warner Bros. to make four to five movies each year that have a shot at reaching $1 billion in revenues," one Warner executive said about the studio's strategy. "And if you commit a large share of your production resources to these few movies, it has implications for your other movies," Horn explained. "You might make a $60 million movie instead of a $90 million movie. It is a balancing act." A television executive I talked to made essentially the same point. "People are under the mistaken impression that studios and networks love all their children equally," he said. "But because there is only a finite amount of production and marketing money available, they have to prioritize."

At Warner Bros. under Alan Horn, the expectation was that those movies with the highest costs would also be the titles with the highest revenues—and the highest profits. In 2010, Warner's results lived up to that expectation. Although the top three biggest bets only accounted for a third of the total production budget, they were responsible for over 40 percent of the domestic and 50 percent of the worldwide box-office revenues generated that year. If we calculate the difference between production expenditures and box-office revenues, it becomes clear that over 60 percent of the year's total surplus came from the studio's top three investments, and nearly 70 percent from its top four movies. At the other extreme, the four least expensive movies released in 2010—*Flipped, Lottery Ticket, The Losers,* and *Splice*—accounted for just under 6 percent of total production spending but only 4 percent of domestic and 1 percent of foreign ticket sales, adding next to nothing to the surplus. Not all of this surplus is profit, of course—for instance, studios like Warner Bros. share close to half of their revenues with the theaters that screen their movies. But the pattern is clear: Warner's biggest investments in 2010 delivered the biggest returns.

So far, so good. But was 2010 just a lucky year, one that happened to be short of one or two big flops that could have seriously

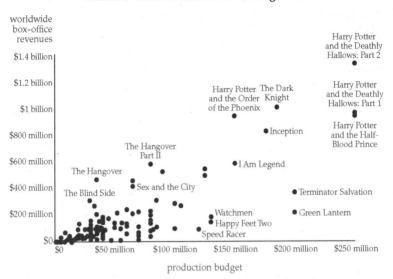

Warner's Movie Bets from 2007 through 2011

The figure plots each of the 119 films that Warner released from 2007 through 2011 (according to research firm Rentrak) by its estimated production budget and worldwide theatrical revenues. For instance, the movie *The Hangover* cost an estimated $35 million to produce and yielded close to $470 million in ticket sales (of which $190 million came in foreign markets).

altered the picture? Are studios like Warner Bros. taking too much risk with their blockbuster bets? The performance of Warner's movies over a longer time horizon certainly does not suggest that to be the case. In fact, the 2010 results reflect a more general phenomenon. Consider the chart above, which shows the returns on Warner's bets from 2007 through 2011, the last five full years of Horn's tenure. During this period, Horn was running his tent-pole strategy at full force, spending $6.5 billion in production costs. But he was also facing strong competition from rival studios that were following his lead with big bets of their own.

At first glance, the chart may look like a random scattering of data points. The messiness of the data reflects the unpredictability of the demand for theatrical films. Warner made substantial investments in a number of well-known franchises, including Harry Potter and the Batman film *The Dark Knight*. While several of those were highly successful, other big bets stumbled at the box office—in particular, the $120 million *Speed Racer* was an unmitigated disaster. (Inspired by a Japanese anime series, starring Emile Hirsch, and released in 2008, it sold well shy of $100 million's worth of tickets across the globe.) As for the smaller investments, they seemed to present the same mix of hits, also-rans, and outright flops. *The Blind Side*, *The Hangover*, and *Gran Torino*, each costing less than $40 million to produce, all made a killing at the box office, while the equally affordable *The Assassination of Jesse James*, *Whiteout*, and *Shorts* never connected with audiences.

But take a look at the next chart, which groups films more systematically by their production budgets. Across all films released over a five-year period, the top 5 percent of films accounted for one-fifth of the total production costs and more than one-quarter of worldwide grosses. The top 10 percent of films consumed roughly a third of the costs but generated more than two-fifths of all revenues—and accounted for nearly half of the difference between production costs and revenues. Warner's biggest investments thus generated disproportionately high returns. On the other end of the spectrum, although they sometimes posted big numbers, smaller investments had little effect on the grand scheme of things. Although the bottom 25 percent of films ranked by their budget (a group that consists of movies made for just below $30 million) accounted for just 6 percent of costs, they generated only 5 percent of ticket sales. And the bottom 10 percent of movies had virtually no impact on sales.

The differences between films at both ends of Warner's portfolio may seem small in relative terms, but they are huge in absolute terms. And in the years of its biggest bets, Warner's total box-office revenues beat those of its main rivals, proving both that a blockbuster focus pays off and that individual blockbusters can significantly lift a content producer's performance. Some critics might say that Warner Bros. would have been far less successful in the mid- to late 2000s if it had not had the *Harry Potter* franchise or *The Dark Knight*. But that is exactly the point: one blockbuster bet can make a year. The best possible outcome of the blockbuster strategy

How Warner's Big Bets Stack Up Against Its Small Bets

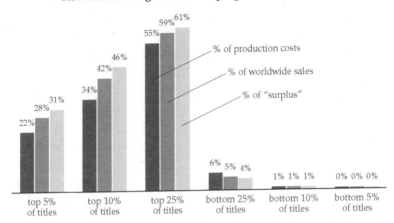

The figure shows how much the 119 movies, when grouped by their production costs, account for Warner's production costs, worldwide box-office sales, and the difference between both (defined as "surplus"). For instance, the top 5 percent most expensive titles account for 22 percent of the production costs, 28 percent of worldwide revenues, and therefore 31 percent of the surplus.

is having a film that lifts the entire bottom line. And the way to get there, my research shows, is by making sizable investments—not by spreading the available budget across a larger number of smaller films.

Horn's motivations for pursuing the event-film strategy are telling. "I was struck by research that shows that the average moviegoer in the US only sees five or six movies a year," he told me in 2012. "And it is even fewer in international territories. Last year, there were over 120 films released by the six major studios, and another 80 by the larger independents such as Summit and The Weinstein Company—that's hundreds of motion-picture viewing opportunities. There is a tough selection process going on," he said. "That is why having something compelling is so important—something of high production value, be it because of the story, or the stars involved, or the special visual effects." The goal, in other words, is to stand out from the competition—to win the battle for attention. That is what the blockbuster strategy is designed to do. "Even the most die-hard fans will not see more than a movie a week," Horn declared. "You have to make sure it is your movie they see."

The success of the blockbuster strategy is even more apparent when marketing costs are included. Making bigger bets results in advertising efficiencies. "The advertising expenditures for a movie that costs $150 million to make are not twice those for a $75 million movie, even if you saturate the market," Horn told me. "You need a certain amount to make sure you can support the film nationally, just to tell audiences you are out there. That makes marketing the $75 million movie expensive. But to give it the extra push you expect for an event movie is not going to cost that much more."

Although Hollywood studio executives are tight-lipped about their advertising spending, data that I obtained from an independent market research company—one that effectively counts the advertisements placed in various media (from television and newspapers to Internet and outdoors) and estimates its value—back up Horn's view. Indeed, when we look at Warner's 2010 movie slate, advertising the bigger productions was disproportionately cheap, as captured in the chart on the next page. The top three movies accounted for a third of the production budget, but those films required only 22 percent of the studio's $700-million-plus advertising budget. Promoting *Inception* ate up the highest number of advertising dollars—just over $60 million, or about a third of the movie's production costs. In contrast, Warner shelled out an extra 75 percent on top of its production budgets to advertise smaller productions like *The Town* and *Life as We Know It*, both made for less than $50 million. Once again, bigger films emerge as relatively smart investments.

With the growing importance of global markets, the relevance of blockbuster bets will only increase. "International box office results are especially strong for event movies," Horn noted. "That's where the real growth is. By 2016, the international box office is projected to be $27 billion, much larger than the domestic box office at a projected $11 billion." Because international theatri-

Production and Advertising Spending:
Why Warner's Big Bets Pay Off More

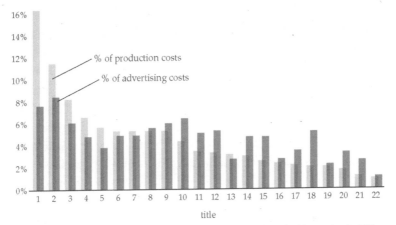

The figure shows, for Warner's 2010 movie slate, how much each title received of Warner's total production and advertising budget. For instance, the second-most-expensive movie released in 2010, *Inception*, used 12 percent of the production budget but only 8 percent of the advertising budget. Ranked number 18 on the list with 2 percent of the production budget, the movie *Cop Out* received as much as 5 percent of the advertising budget.

cal markets are "under-screened"—meaning that when compared to the United States, other countries have relatively few theaters to serve moviegoers—international markets tend to be more selective. "They want four-quadrant movies, and they want stars or characters such as Harry Potter that they know," said Horn. "Those are the movies that travel well."

Movies make much of their revenues outside theaters—from such sources as DVD sales and rentals, streaming rentals, and television—which in theory is a way for smaller movies to make up for the lackluster returns. But in reality, the best predictor of a movie's revenues in subsequent distribution channels (or "windows") is its performance in the theatrical window. "All the ancillary markets are driven by theatrical," Horn said. "The revenues from DVD sales are almost directly proportional to box-office revenues. So those ancillary markets do not bail the smaller movies

out." In fact, when taking into account those other sources of revenues, the effect of bigger investments generating a better payoff is
only magnified.

Properly executing a blockbuster strategy is more than just a
matter of spending more money in order to generate higher revenues, of course—if the game were really that simple, anyone
with deep pockets could be a successful studio head. Instead, it
is about making the right bets. "There is no hope if you just
make a bad movie," Horn declared. "You can try everything you
want with your release strategy, but if the movie is not good
enough, you are done. You have to have a good idea, and execute
it well."

Luck helps as well. Warner Bros. had heaps of it with its biggest blockbuster, *Harry Potter*, as illustrated by the story of how
Warner came to acquire the rights. "We had the rights to *Harry
Potter* even before the book was a success in the UK," Horn told
me. "A woman in the UK happened to buy the book in a store one
day, as a gift for a family member. She liked it so much that she
showed it to her boss, David Heyman, whom she worked for as
an assistant, saying 'You have to read this—this is brilliant.' Now
get this: David had a production deal with Warner Bros. And one
of his childhood friends, Lionel Wigram, was an executive with
us. So he pushed us to option it. But nobody knew what they had
until the book exploded, and off we went." Warner's good fortune did not stop there, Horn recalled: "Before the book became
known, my predecessor offered the *Harry Potter* property to [rival
studio] DreamWorks in a partnership—and they passed. And
then of course it became a hit, a little rocket ship that was taking
off, and they called back and said, 'This was offered to us; we
want to be partners with you.' But I said, 'No, you turned it down,
and the offer is off the table.' I had it in writing. Now isn't that
something?"

Harry Potter aside, have Horn and his team sometimes picked
the wrong titles to focus their attention on? Yes. Each time one of
Warner's big-budget event movies bombed, the studio incurred a
substantial loss. "*Speed Racer* made a bigger dent in our bottom line

than any other movie in 2008," recalled Horn. "The Wachowski siblings wanted to make a family picture, with bright colors, giving it a cartoonish feel. It was very costly and, in the end, too big a leap. But to this day I don't fault them. It could have been the most innovative movie in history. You have to take risks." He added: "You've got to realize that someone walked into somebody's office at Pixar one day, saying they had an idea for an eighty-year-old man and a ten-year-old kid to take off in a house fueled by a balloon. You can see people go 'Wait a minute. . . .' But they made it anyway, and it was a tremendous success." (*Up* grossed well over $700 million at the box office.)

And has Horn greenlighted breakout hits that no one at the studio saw coming? Absolutely. *The Hangover*, for instance, was produced for only $35 million, but it pulled down $470 million in ticket sales, shattering every record for R-rated comedies along the way. Not surprisingly, Warner turned the sequel into a tent-pole movie, with a production and marketing budget set accordingly— this time, the studio took no chances. The same is true for *Sex and the City* and its sequel: the first movie was a small bet that performed much better than expected, and the second got the full tent-pole treatment.

The blockbuster strategy is certainly not risk free, and there are limits as to how much studios can spend on any given film. But what is critical to understand is that a studio would be taking a *greater* risk if it put more emphasis on movies with lower production budgets—if, effectively, it made a larger number of smaller bets. It may sound counterintuitive, but for a studio like Warner Bros. those smaller bets could, in a typical year, actually lose the studio more money than they bring in. Even if some smaller investments do make money, a dollar spent on a big-budget film will average a much higher profit.

Another film studio, Paramount, learned these lessons the hard way—much as NBC did. In the late 1990s, Paramount chose to steer away from what its management saw as a dangerous reliance on big bets. It adopted a philosophy of sticking to mid-range budgets and lesser-known stars, and boasted that it would run its movie production slate "like an actuary chart." But while the mantra on the studio lot was protecting the downside, the studio's cautious strategy ultimately had the opposite effect: by early 2004, Paramount had become known for mostly B-grade films featuring mediocre talent, and its profits had fallen by more than 30 percent. Realizing what was happening, Paramount's executives promptly reversed course, letting the creative community know that the studio was once again willing to pay top dollar for its movies, in part by giving Adam Sandler, Charlize Theron, and other top actors their highest salaries to date to star in upcoming movies. "We intend to relax risk aversion policies and to make more money available to finance more challenging productions," said Sumner Redstone, chairman of Paramount's parent company Viacom, at the time.

Only a mighty studio with significant scale and resources can aggressively pursue a blockbuster strategy—after all, it must be able to absorb an occasional loss the size of a *Speed Racer* or *The Adventures of Pluto Nash*. (The latter was one of the biggest box-office disasters of all time, costing a reported $100 million to produce but generating only $4 million in US theaters in 2002.) Like Warner Bros., Disney's film studio has the resources to invest in blockbusters. So don't expect the studio to dial back its bets on big movies under Horn's leadership.

Some of the reasons why the cost of making movies can run into the hundreds of millions of dollars are easy to understand, but other investments may be more difficult to comprehend. Film studios or television networks paying an actor or actress millions of dollars based on a hunch that audiences will want to see that person star in a movie or show, for instance, especially when there is no shortage of people waiting for their shot to make it in show business. Or producers investing heavily in an untested script just because the subject matter, be it superheroes or vampires, is "hot." Can't entertainment companies consistently avoid such enormous expenses? To find the answer, it's useful to consider why entertainment executives often get caught up in bidding wars. One of the most daring bids in the world of book publishing may be a good place to start.

His charming, unassuming personality easily made up for it, but Dewey Readmore Books, the star of Vicki Myron's *Dewey: The Small-Town Library Cat Who Touched the World*, was one fat cat. A million-dollar cat, in fact. In 2007, the Manhattan-based publishing house Grand Central Publishing shelled out $1.25 million for the rights to the book about the fluffy orange creature, found abandoned as a kitten in the returned-book slot of the Iowa public library in which Myron worked.

Five days before the publisher made the winning bid, Karen Kosztolnyik, then a senior editor at Grand Central Publishing, received a forty-five-page book proposal from Myron's literary agent, Peter McGuigan. Impressed by what she read, Kosztolnyik quickly passed the document on to her boss, Jamie Raab, then senior vice president and publisher of Grand Central, who was hooked on *Dewey* just two pages into the proposal. The following day, they started the bidding process by offering an advance of $300,000, already a significant amount for a book by a first-time author. Author advances in the tens of thousands of dollars were much more common. (Such advances are payments made against an author's royalty, which usually run between 10 percent and 15 percent of the retail price of a hardcover book.) A frantic bidding war ensued, during which McGuigan told Kosztolnyik that a second publisher was shadowing Grand Central's every move. But Raab urged Kosztolnyik to "do everything humanly possible to buy this book," and Grand Central eventually acquired the book in a preemptive strike, a day ahead of a scheduled auction that would have involved other publishers.

Raab and Kosztolnyik had high hopes for *Dewey*, billed as the feline answer to the best-selling *Marley & Me: Life and Love with the World's Worst Dog*, John Grogan's 2005 memoir of his misbehaving Labrador retriever. *Marley & Me* had garnered critical and commercial success, selling over three million copies to date. Dewey was no stranger to the spotlight. Over the course of his nineteen-year life, this unusually resilient cat—named in a contest after the

Dewey Decimal System used in most libraries to catalog books—
became a mascot for the library and the town of Spencer, Iowa. As
his popularity grew, he even started to attract the attention of tour-
ists and filmmakers, appearing in two documentary films. Shortly
after he died in November 2006—in Vicki Myron's arms—his obit-
uary ran in more than 250 publications, including *USA Today* and
the *Washington Post*.

However, this was an unprecedented level of pressure even for
Dewey. When that exceedingly high bid was tendered, the reaction
in many quarters was disbelief. William Morrow, a HarperCollins
imprint, had paid a mere $200,000 for the rights to *Marley & Me*
back in 2004. Grand Central's gamble on *Dewey* immediately
turned the book into one of the publisher's biggest bets for the year
among its annual output of 275 to 300 books. "It's stunning, the
advances being paid. If it might be the next *Da Vinci Code* or the
next *Marley & Me*, the ante just increases, " Robert Miller, the president of rival publisher Hyperion, said. The proposal did not scream
instant success: typically, cat books are not big sellers. According
to Kosztolnyik's records, Peter Gethers's *The Cat Who Went to Paris*
and Stephen Baker's *How to Live with a Neurotic Cat*—next to *Marley
& Me* the two most comparable titles—had sold only around 30,000
and 120,000 paperback units, respectively. And the book's main
character had died—making him unavailable for, say, a publicity-
grabbing appearance on Oprah Winfrey's couch.

"Magical things always happen around Dewey," Myron said
about her furry friend after the bidding. But with more than a year
until the book was published, it would be a while before Grand
Central learned whether its seemingly outrageous bid for the manuscript had been the right move.

The double-or-nothing daring move to acquire *Dewey* was only
one in a string of big bets made by Grand Central and a host of
other leading publishing houses. Like major Hollywood studios,
book publishers, too, have largely adopted a blockbuster strategy.
In the year before the *Dewey* gamble, for instance, Grand Central
spent close to 20 percent of its total adult hardcover acquisition

budget of $40 million on its biggest title alone, and over half of this budget on the five most expensive titles on its list of roughly sixty adult hardcover front-list titles. (A publisher's front list is its catalog of new books; its back list contains books that have already appeared in an initial edition. On average, about 70 percent to 75 percent of a major publisher's sales comes from front-list titles.) Grand Central chose to compete this way in a sector where, like the film industry, the failure rate is high: only about one of every five new books recovers its costs in the marketplace, and retailers reportedly return roughly 30 percent of all publishers' physical book shipments. While exact rates differ across the various sectors and genres, it generally is the case that, for any given title, the most probable outcome is a financial loss.

Grand Central's aggressive pursuit of *Dewey* may prompt a prudent manager in any other industry to wonder what on earth the company was thinking. Faced with such low odds of success, why would Grand Central put itself in the position of having to outsell all cat books released in recent memory to earn back its seven-figure advance and make a decent profit? Rather than putting all their eggs in one basket, wouldn't the executives at Grand Central be smarter to place a larger number of smaller bets on a range of topics or, if the belief in pet books is so strong, commission a number of books on feline or other creatures? Publishers, like movie studios and other entertainment companies, sometimes seem like riverboat gamblers. What explains the prevalence of audacious bets such as the one Grand Central placed on *Dewey*?

The first thing to understand is that, given the variability in execution of books, movies, and television series, and given the constantly shifting tastes of consumers, it is extremely difficult to forecast demand for any individual new title. Speaking about the movie business, screenwriter William Goldman once said, "Nobody knows anything." Executives in the film industry often quote that famous line, and although it may be too strong a statement, Goldman's words accurately reflect the frustration of having to make a prediction based on just a proposal, a script, or even a pilot.

"It *is* guesswork," Jamie Raab told me. "To some extent, we are all just winging it. I have a good track record of picking winners, but it is far from perfect. No one in this industry has a perfect score. It really is a crapshoot, albeit an 'informed' crapshoot." The one useful indicator of potential—and this is a critical notion that drives much of how entertainment industries operate—is a new idea's resemblance along some dimension to an existing hit. But that is an indicator that, by its nature, is evident to any industry player, so there is heavy convergence of interest on certain properties. This, in turn, triggers competitive bidding situations for proposals and soaring fees for the creative people who can bring these properties to the page, the big or small screen, or indeed to any mass entertainment medium.

This was the kind of luck that *Dewey*, in characteristic fashion, stepped into. Soon after the book proposal started to make the rounds, many industry insiders compared *Dewey* to the runaway hit *Marley & Me*. The sixth-highest-selling book (fiction or nonfiction) of 2006, it spawned two related children's titles also written by Grogan about his rambunctious canine (an adaptation for ages eight to twelve, *Marley: A Dog Like No Other*, and the new adventure *Bad Dog, Marley!*), a number of other dog books, and even a Hollywood movie starring Jennifer Aniston and Owen Wilson. Publishers saw essential similarities in Dewey's story: it was a touching story about how an animal could bring out the humanity in people it encountered, featuring an animal that was much more than just an average pet. It would surely appeal to pet lovers, many felt.

While executives at Grand Central were careful about making comparisons between *Dewey* and *Marley*—the world is divided into cat and dog lovers, after all, and every title needs to be judged on its own merits—the similarities undeniably spurred publishers' enthusiasm for the *Dewey* rights. Fearful that the price would reach astronomical heights at auction, Grand Central snapped up the book a day before several other publishers would have had their shot at it. "You can't underestimate the market out there for people who love animals," remarked Kosztolnyik, who would oversee the editorial process. "*Marley & Me* has been a publishing phenomenon. I think there are equally as many cat lovers as there are dog lovers."

These same dynamics also explain why, when the popular television series *Sex and the City* ended in 2004, not one but two shows—*Lipstick Jungle* and *Cashmere Mafia*—sought to fill the gap by building a show around three successful professional women living in New York City. Likewise, the best-selling *Twilight* series sparked a renewed interest in vampires, and we have the smash hit *American Idol* to thank for the onslaught of talent shows—including NBC's *The Voice*—that fill our television screens.

During Alan Horn's tenure at Warner, many of the studio's event films were based on properties that had established their value in other domains. *Harry Potter*, for instance, was a megahit in book form, and *The Dark Knight* was based on the Batman comic-book series. Other event films leaned on formats that had worked in the past, be they sequels to original films that were a resounding success, such as *The Hangover* and *Sex and the City*, or ideas that featured stars, directors, or writers that have previously scored a hit. Even *Speed Racer* fit this pattern, remarked Horn: "The Wachowski siblings had done three *Matrix* movies which were phenomenally successful, and their next film, *V for Vendetta*, also made a fair amount of money. When they, with their track record, said they wanted to do *Speed Racer*, it was hard to say no."

When planning sequels to movie franchises or additional seasons of successful television series, studio executives will strive to leave a "winning formula" unchanged and thus avoid uncertainty about how, say, a switch of a lead actor or talent show judge will pay off. As a result, the costs of production often dramatically increase over time. *American Idol* is an example: in 2009 Simon Cowell was rumored to have pocketed well over $100 million to extend his run as a judge on the show for one more year. (He later launched *X Factor*, a rival talent show, in the United States.)

With so much money invested in their most promising projects, entertainment executives will understandably do everything in their power to make these products a success in the marketplace. For both its fall/winter and spring/summer lists, Grand Central turns a handful of its biggest bets into what Raab calls "focus books," which receive a disproportionately high level of attention and promotional dollars. Of those, a small handful of titles per season are the all-important "make" books. "We pull out all the stops to make those books happen," explained Raab. Focus books will get more attention from the marketing and sales team, more time during meetings (such as those with sales representatives), and a more prominent placement in the publisher's catalog for retailers. At Warner Bros., event films not only receive a higher production and marketing budget; they are also often slotted into the most favorable opening weekends (such as around Memorial Day in the United States), and more efforts are dedicated to these films in dealings with exhibitors, retailers, and other partners. Similarly, television networks' biggest bets are given the most valuable times in the television schedule and more airtime for promotions. The holy grail here is a spot during the Super Bowl, watched in recent years by a hundred million viewers—or, even better, airing an episode immediately after the game, as NBC chose to do in 2012 with a special episode of *The Voice*.

To pursue a more cautious strategy seems foolish. After all, if a product like *Dewey*, *The Dark Knight*, or *The Voice* fails to draw audiences, an entertainment company knows its profitability will be severely hurt. At the same time, the effect is to escalate the company's commitment and increase the size of its bet. With such high stakes and money tied up in a few big projects in the pipeline, the need to score big with a next project becomes more pressing, and the process repeats itself. The result is what I call a "blockbuster trap": a spiral of ever-increasing bets on the most promising concepts.

And so it happens that the expenditures required to procure winning properties can reach bet-the-farm proportions—this explains why NBC and Paramount were inclined to switch away from a blockbuster strategy for a time. When a first-time author can produce a bestseller like *The Art of Fielding* (a much-praised novel by Chad Harbach), when a show like *American Idol* can draw a huge audience after getting its start in an unfavorable summer slot amid decidedly modest expectations, and when a no-name filmmaker with a minuscule budget can produce a major hit like *The Blair Witch Project* or *Paranormal Activity*, it might seem inadvisable to pay so much for material. The race for the next blockbuster can even stifle innovation: the same tendencies that lead to bidding wars for projects that resemble past winners work against other projects that look nothing like them but may have strong merits of their own. Many movie lovers lament the offerings available to them in theaters and speak disapprovingly of a market in which nine of the top ten selling movies in 2011 were sequels of major franchises, and the tenth, *Thor*, was based on a comic-book character.

Yet, as much as managers may crave to reduce the risks that go hand in hand with big bets, and as much as we might want to criticize entertainment executives for single-mindedly chasing after winning formulas, forgoing blockbuster bets altogether likely creates even more problems. What happens if a publisher like Grand Central decides to stop making large bids like the one it tendered for *Dewey*, or when a studio like Warner Bros. forgoes the kinds of investments associated with its event films? And what happens if a content producer of any kind walks away from the most sought-after, and therefore expensive, new properties?

First, when businesses opt out of the blockbuster race, they take themselves out of the market for the most promising new projects. Literary agents will stop sending their most sought-after book proposals and movie scripts to such a producer. "If you are constantly backing out of big-ticket auctions your list is going to hurt," one publishing executive told me. "You are going to get a stigma that you don't play for the big ones, and you are going to get shunned. Say historically you won't bid more than $2 million on a book, but an agent thinks they can get $10 million on a project. Why would they bother letting you into the loop? They will no longer consider you for what they feel are their best projects."

Editors at publishing houses work hard to cultivate working relationships with agents because they tend to be the sources for the lion's share of proposals that eventually are turned into books. Even if a publisher could develop extraordinary competence in

finding gold in the "slush pile" of thousands of pieces of unsolicited material received each year from aspiring authors, the dividends would be limited. After one success, the talent the publisher
has nurtured would discover the value of an agent, driving up the
advance needed to sign the writer's subsequent books. The same
need to build relationships and be "in the market" for the best
projects exists in the film business. "Sometimes this industry is
like the mafia—it's about showing respect," said one Warner Bros.
executive. Similarly, if a television network starts "managing for
margins" rather than aiming for the widest possible audience,
then agents, producers, and writers may quickly stop considering
that network a good destination for their best projects.

In every entertainment business, a strong lineup of projects is
often key to cultivating the next hit. Consider the world of television. Viewership is "sticky": many viewers will not immediately
switch channels after seeing their favorite program, meaning they
may also end up watching the program in the next slot. In addition, networks primarily advertise new shows using promotions
they run on their own channels, so that much of a new program's
viewership is a direct result of the popularity of the other programs on its channel. Even a casual examination of television schedules over the years reveals strong success-breeds-success trends. It
is no coincidence that ABC launched *Grey's Anatomy* and a number
of other successes on a Sunday evening anchored by its breakout
hit *Desperate Housewives*. Likewise, FOX used *American Idol* to boost
House, Lie to Me, and most recently *Glee*. As a result, any smart producer sitting on what he or she believes is the next big idea in television will prefer to do business with the most popular network,
as that increases the chances of market success. So the more content producers focus on saving costs rather than driving sales, the
more they lose their bid to contend for the most promising new
projects.

Second, if a publisher or studio would constantly shy away
from blockbuster bets, the most talented editors, filmmakers, television producers, and other creative talent would leave to work for
a company that would let them pursue the projects they thought

had the highest chances of success. This is not because of the much-discussed "big egos" of creative workers—a factor often named in the aftermath of bidding wars. It's a simple result of the passion that many media and entertainment professionals bring to their work—and the fact that careers are built on blockbusters. Grand Central's publisher and now president Jamie Raab, for example, is known for discovering the best-selling romance novelist Nicholas Sparks. As a result, Raab receives a steady stream of the best new love stories from literary agents.

When you work on a project-by-project basis, as most creative workers do, every project could be your last. Hits buy you extra time and new opportunities in your career. A few misses here and there can be overcome: A-list talent is rarely evaluated on a "hit rate" or "batting average"—the total number of hits, or just the most recent hit, generally matters more. George Clooney, for instance, became a leading man in the 1990s after his star turn on NBC's popular series ER—at the time, everyone seemed to have forgotten that he had previously played parts in more than a dozen television shows that never went anywhere. But people and projects that have "failure" written all over them often receive the cold shoulder.

When, in the mid-2000s, a brave producer named Rob Ahrens wanted to resurrect the 1980 Olivia Newton-John roller-disco film Xanadu—widely seen as one of Hollywood's biggest debacles ever—as a Broadway musical, he encountered strong resistance. Described by influential film critics as "the epic failure to end all epic failures," "the most dreadful, tasteless movie of the decade," and "truly stupendously bad" (one critic simply warned audiences to "Xana-don't!"), Xanadu is credited with inspiring the Golden Raspberry Awards, affectionately known as the "Razzies" and now an annual celebration of Hollywood's worst moviemaking. Not the most likely candidate for a musical adaptation, to say the least.

Although Broadway productions based on box-office hits are common—Spamalot, described by its makers as a musical "lovingly ripped off" from the successful motion picture Monty Python and the Holy Grail, is one example—shows based on Hollywood flops are rare. Not surprisingly, Ahrens faced numerous obstacles during his five-year quest for support. "As soon as you say *Xanadu*," he remarked, "[people] either get it right away, or they look down on you and then they call the police." When Ahrens approached Douglas Carter Beane, his choice for playwright, Beane's first response—"No! Never!"—was not encouraging. "I passed several times, because it's a really bad movie," said Beane, who initially saw the opportunity as "theater suicide wrapped up in a nice box." He added: "My partner said, 'That sounds like a resume stopper.' Another friend of mine said, 'Do you want to keep working in this business we call show?'"

Third, by extension, not bidding for sought-after projects makes it harder to get best efforts from sales and marketing representatives and other employees. After winning the hotly contested rights to a book like *Dewey*, Grand Central executives can forcefully make the case that this book will beat its competitors. ("It's a sure bet to do as well as *Marley & Me*—why else would everyone be after it?") The same principle holds true in the film industry. As Horn put it, "It's really hard to convince marketing people to get behind a project when they have nothing to sell, whether it is a big star or a well-known literary property." Firing up those who will be involved in the development and marketing process is crucial, especially because most media titles have only a short window in which to make money and the lion's share of marketing activity takes place before their launch—when it is still largely unknown how audiences will respond.

Finding and fostering internal champions of projects is an integral part of executing a blockbuster strategy. Raab described their national sales meeting, held twice a year and attended by all salespeople, as a "pep rally." As she told me, "The idea is to have everyone walk out excited. Our job is to create the conditions to make a splash in the market—to get people to buy into our hopeful thinking." Similarly, at Grand Central's launch meetings, during which the company's projects are formally introduced to internal constituents from the editorial, sales, marketing, and other departments, as well as several senior executives of Grand Central's parent company Hachette, "a smart editor will make comparisons with other successful products [so] everyone understands this is going to be a big book," as the director of marketing put it.

Fourth, critically, if entertainment businesses forgo making big bets on likely blockbusters, they will find their channel power waning over time. Retailer support is decisive in most media markets. In the film industry, the number of screens a movie receives from exhibitors in its first few weeks remains the best predictor of its revenues. Exhibitors want to see evidence that a movie is worthy of their scarce resources; they like nothing better than to know that a studio is making a significant push for a film and planning an extensive marketing campaign. A blockbuster strategy helps them to use their resources effectively. "Exhibitors totally embrace the blockbuster philosophy," said Horn. "They don't bear any of the costs—whether the movie costs $20 million or $200 million makes no difference to them. But they do see the benefits of us spending more. What they want to do is sell popcorn. Blockbuster movies put a lot more people in seats, which means they sell more popcorn. That's the beauty of it for them."

In the book business, a large share of products is bought on impulse—surveys show that just under three-quarters of the people entering a bookstore buy a book they did not intend to buy—so securing significant display space with book retailers such Barnes & Noble is particularly important. These "pile 'em high and watch 'em fly" tactics may seem old-fashioned, but they tend to be very effective at triggering sales. For television networks, getting buy-in from local television stations is crucial, and stations often strongly object to cost-cutting measures that may reduce the likely size of a popular show's audience. NBC experienced this firsthand in 2009 when the network announced that it would move Jay Leno's new show to the ten p.m. slot in place of more expensive dramatic content, which station managers believe is a better lead-in for local news programs.

The way in which retailers market entertainment products to consumers is driven by the same forces that made *Dewey* such a pricey creature. This is noticeable even in the smallest details. If you had walked into a Borders bookstore around the time of the book's launch, you might have noticed the "Like This? Try These" signs with one arrow pointing to the bestseller *Marley & Me* and another arrow to several books that were similar to that book: *The Art of Racing in the Rain*, *A Three Dog Life*, and *Merle's Door*, all books about dogs. When *Dewey* hit the shelves, it, too, claimed a spot on that row—as much a "copycat" strategy as one will ever see. And so content producers, in turn, try to cater to the marketing strategies of retailers, sometimes going so far as to copy the look of products. For instance, publishers hoping to speak to the same audience that made Malcolm Gladwell's *The Tipping Point* a huge hit sometimes mimic that book's distinctive cover design. Gladwell himself has had no reason to change his winning formula: it's no coincidence that his more recent books, *Blink* and *Outliers*, look like they belong right next to *The Tipping Point* on the shelf. Many of the biggest blockbusters spawn knockoffs and imitators: in 2012 the erotic novel *Fifty Shades of Grey* prompted the release of such titles as *Fifty Shades of Pleasure* and *The Ninety Days of Genevieve*. (Literary agent Jonny Geller joked that his agency is now seeing so many unsolicited erotica manuscripts, they have renamed the "slush pile" the "blush pile.")

New channels through which consumers buy books work in similar ways: Amazon automatically lists comparable books under the "Customers Who Bought This Item Also Bought" section, which undoubtedly helps drive sales for those titles. By the same token, new films and television programs are often described as being "from the producers that brought you . . ." to highlight similarities with past winners, and promotions and trailers are placed around current hits that resemble them in some important way, be it the story line, central property, or star actor.

The blockbuster-focused marketing of many entertainment companies did not emerge in a vacuum—it mirrors the way consumers make choices among a wealth of competing entertainment offerings. Because people are inherently social, they generally find value in reading the same books and watching the same television shows and movies that others do. People have a taste for winners:

if, say, a book is popular and has been widely discussed in the media, consumers have more reason to read it than they would an otherwise identical book that has not received such attention. Compounding this tendency is the fact that media products are what economists call "experience goods," that is, audiences have trouble evaluating them before having consumed or experienced them. Unable to judge a book by its cover, readers look for cues as to its suitability for them. A prospective purchaser of Vicki Myron's book will thus find it very useful to hear that *Dewey* is "a *Marley & Me* for cat lovers." Just as publishers do, consumers value resemblances to past favorites.

No surprise, then, that the blockbuster strategy seemed to work wonders for Grand Central during the period *Dewey* was published, just as it did for Warner Bros. under Alan Horn. In 2006, the year before the company acquired the book, Grand Central's fall list consisted of sixty-one adult hardcover front-list titles. Just 20 percent of those titles accounted for roughly 80 percent of sales and an even larger share of profits. "The sins of the many are offset by the plentiful of the few," said one of the company's financial executives. As shown in the chart on the next page, the titles on its fall 2006 list with the highest acquisition costs were for the most part the titles that delivered the highest revenues—and the highest profits. Results are even more skewed than for Warner Bros.: the top 10 percent of Grand Central's titles account for 64 percent of its costs, 72 percent of its net sales, and a staggering 126 percent of its profits.

Remarkably, Grand Central made the lion's share of its profits on just one book—and that title was by far its most expensive. The most popular title that fall cost $7.5 million to develop and market. The book generated net sales of just under $12 million, and gross profits of nearly $5 million—out of the nearly $6 million in total gross profits across the entire list. Meanwhile, as the chart on the following page also shows, many of the publisher's small and medium-size bets lost money. For instance, the thirty titles that were cheapest to acquire actually lost an average of $12,000 each. Even the rare winners among Grand Central's least expensive books

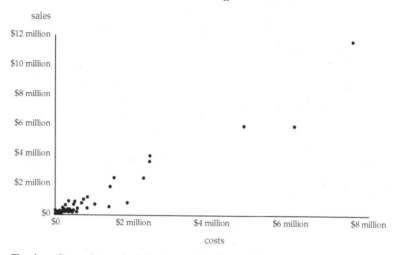

Grand Central Publishing's Bets in 2006

The above figure plots each of the sixty-one hardcover books on Grand Central Publishing's fall 2006 front list by its net sales and (development and marketing) costs. (The publisher asked for the titles not to be identified). The most expensive title on the list cost over $7.5 million and generated $11.6 million in net sales.

contributed very little to the company's profitability. And this particular list is no exception; it is illustrative of the publisher's results in other years as well.

As this example again makes clear, the idea of smaller bets being "safer" is a myth. Blockbuster strategies reliably beat the alternative of more risk-averse strategies: the highest-performing companies in the entertainment and media sector thrive by investing a relatively large proportion of their resources in just a few titles and then turning those choices into successes by giving them a higher level of development and marketing support. It may be partly a self-fulfilling prophecy, but it works. And because the marginal cost of reproducing and distributing entertainment products is relatively low—especially compared to their up-front production expenses—and because of the economies of scale involved in advertising campaigns, the advantage of a bestseller, a box-office champion, or a ratings monster is huge.

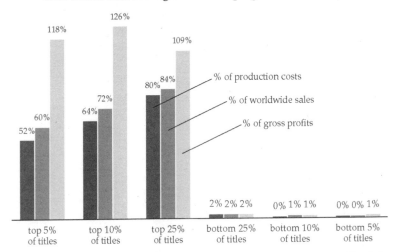

How Grand Central's Big Bets Stack Up Against Its Small Bets

The figure shows how much the fall 2006 hardcover titles, when grouped by their costs, contribute to the publisher's total costs, net sales, and gross profits. For instance, the top 5 percent, the most expensive titles, account for just over half of the development and marketing costs, 60 percent of net sales, and 118 percent of gross profits.

This does not mean media companies can spend without limits, of course—especially given the turbulent markets for their products. Book publishers are experiencing uncertain times with the rise of e-books, broadcast networks see their market shrinking relative to premium cable channels, and film studios can no longer count on DVD sales to be the dependable cash cow they once were. But yielding to an excess of caution and shying away from any attempt to create the next blockbuster with mass appeal may be the surest way for an entertainment company to lose further ground.

As for *Dewey*, how did our fat-cat friend fare? Published in September 2008, the book became one of those blockbuster bets that paid off—and then some. Released at a list price of $19.99, Grand Central's big gamble performed beyond any of the executives' wildest dreams. It captured the number one spot on the *New York Times* hardcover bestseller list and sold 759,000 copies in just over three months, making it the sixth-highest-selling adult nonfiction title that year. It sold another 130,000 hardcover copies in 2009, bringing the total close to 900,000 copies. Having tasted success with cat books, that same year another Hachette imprint published a children's book by Vicki Myron, Bret Witter, and illustrator Steve James. Called *Dewey: There's a Cat in the Library*, it sold 106,000 copies. The next year, Myron and Witter launched another follow-up, *Dewey's Nine Lives: The Legacy of the Small-Town Library Cat Who Inspired Millions*, which offered "nine funny, inspiring, and heart-warming stories about cats." At one point, there was even talk of a movie adaptation starring Meryl Streep as Dewey's caretaker.

Perhaps the key question is not why entertainment executives make blockbuster bets—the real puzzle, it seems, is why they continue to turn out products that are the result of much smaller bets. After all, the financial payoff from these modest investments looks decidedly shaky. If tent-pole films consistently generate the highest returns for Warner Bros., why does the studio also invest in the smaller films that make up the large majority of its annual output? And if Grand Central's expensive "focus" and "make" books consistently outperform the large majority of other titles on its list, why even bother with those smaller investments?

A close look at the way successful entertainment companies operate reveals that both kinds of investments play an important role in their portfolios. Bigger bets tend to generate the highest revenues and profits, bring excitement to the company, help build the brand, and foster future hits. But for a book publisher, a film or television studio, or another type of media producer to carry out a blockbuster strategy, smaller bets are needed, too—for a variety of reasons.

First, smaller investments can serve as test cases. Placing a reasonable number of less expensive bets can help a media producer discover the next big-hit franchise. In the film industry, sequels are seen as one the safest blockbuster bets one can make, and smaller investments may help turn up another film that is ripe for a sequel, much like *The Hangover* and *Sex and the City*. This principle also applies to actors, directors, and other creative workers. Even if studio executives are convinced that a little-known actor is the next Tom Cruise, asking him to star in a $200 million film in his very first assignment seems ill advised. Instead, it is more sensible to commence a collaboration with a promising young actor by giving him a role in a smaller film, one that will allow the studio to learn whether he is truly capable of "carrying a film" and accomplishing all that comes with that responsibility, from performing at a high level on the set every day to fulfilling publicity obligations. Being able to test the appeal of new product formats, from vampire movies to talent shows, is another advantage. Some product types or genres may prove profitable as smaller-scope investments in their own right, as seems to be the case, for instance, with certain ultra-low-budget horror films.

Smaller bets can also help a media producer "fill the pipeline," thereby keeping companies that help sell the producer's output satisfied. For example, a book publisher that delivers a steady stream of new titles to the market will find it easier to build and maintain relationships with retailers. That, in turn, may put the publisher in a position to negotiate steeper discounts, favorable in-store placements, or other marketing advantages. In the film industry, Warner's commitment to producing two dozen movies each year—roughly one Warner Bros. film opens in theaters every other week—helps it to obtain better agreements with theater owners. "Our head of domestic distribution would go out and speak with exhibitors and say, 'I need your best theater on Wilshire Boulevard and I need it for four weeks,'" Horn told me. "The exhibitor might counter that Paramount wants it, too. But then we could say, 'We are Warner Bros., here is our lineup for the year, and this is what we need for this particular movie.' It will always be a back-and-forth in these negotiations, but having the largest number of films gave us weight in the marketplace, which got us better screens, for a longer time, and at a better revenue-sharing rate." Additionally, a larger number of products often leads to volume discounts in media buys: the more products they advertise, the more favorable the advertising rates studios and publishers can secure.

Pursuing a wide range of smaller projects allows studios,

publishers, and other entertainment businesses to form closer links with agents, who are involved in the lion's share of deals for new products and therefore critical gatekeepers in virtually any entertainment sector. Further, a broad portfolio of properties can attract needed financing. For a studio like Warner Bros., which under Horn's leadership relied on co-financing for nearly all of its projects but the surest bets like *Harry Potter*, a broad portfolio can be a useful way to attract outside investors willing to share risk. The studio takes a distribution fee off the top, and then splits revenues with those investors. "Some investors may push back on this model, but they usually don't have the power and the relationships to be an effective distributor, so we have the upper hand in these talks," said Horn. "Again, our scale worked in our favor."

That smaller bets may allow for more flexibility in dealing with these industry partners is an added advantage. For example, it is often easier to move release dates and shift advertising budgets for smaller-scale projects. Large media producers may buy advertising time on television months in advance; having smaller projects to move around can help optimize the use of those resources.

Going for smaller-scale products can enable entertainment companies to build and maintain a favorable critical reputation as well, which in turn can help them attract sought-after A-list talent and their projects. If, say, a film studio wants to cast a superstar actor in an event film, it can be beneficial to have the option of offering that actor the lead in a smaller "passion project," one with the potential to please critics and Academy Award voters. When Warner Bros. agreed to finance Clint Eastwood's *Million Dollar Baby* despite the poor performance of boxing movies in the past—and especially of boxing movies that revolved around female fighters—no one at the studio had any idea it would become a box-office hit. If anyone other than Clint Eastwood had brought the movie to the studio, it likely never would have seen the light of day (or, rather, the darkness of a theater). Fittingly, when Warner threw Horn a good-bye party, George Clooney publicly thanked him for "supporting the things we want to do that studios never want to do." Smart A-list actors remember these sorts of gestures and become allies.

Finally, developing and releasing a number of smaller projects helps producers spread the fixed costs of their production and distribution infrastructures. For the major film studios that have expansive lots and dozens of offices around the world as part of their distribution apparatus, being able to allocate the costs of those resources across a larger number of projects—even if the smaller-scale projects barely break even—can be a huge benefit. For one, it helps them fund their blockbuster bets. "Very few entities in this world can afford to spend $200 million on a movie," noted Horn. "That is our competitive advantage."

Despite the advantages of having a broad and varied portfolio, major studios and other large-scale content producers would probably further tilt their investments toward the bigger projects if they could. But two key constraints make that difficult: raising the funds required to produce blockbusters is a constant challenge, and finding the ideas that lend themselves to bigger-scale production and marketing support is never easy. "We were keen to make more event films, and steadily increased the number over the years," Horn said about his time at Warner. "But there aren't many ideas with global appeal." What competing entertainment businesses do matters, too. As Horn pointed out: "There is a limit on good release dates in a given year."

And so, as a consequence of all these factors, many of today's largest entertainment businesses end up with product portfolios consisting of a few blockbuster investments that require most of their attention as well as a number of smaller bets. That's not to say that no other portfolio approach could possibly work. For example, animated movie house Pixar has an interesting approach: from the outset, it has focused on a very small number of films at any given time. Calling Pixar's strategy a "rifle-shot approach," Horn described its method this way: "They make one movie a year, and really handcraft each one. They are painstaking in their approach, highly self-critical, and work for years on one title before releasing it." That focus has paid off: Pixar has churned out one box-office smash hit after another, from *Toy Story* to *A Bug's Life*; *Monsters, Inc.*; *Finding Nemo*; *The Incredibles*; *Cars*; *Ratatouille*; *WALL-E*; *Up*; and

Brave. But Pixar is not a stand-alone studio: it operates as a unit at Disney and is now Horn's responsibility. Pixar thus can rely on the advantages that come with Disney's wider scale and power—a big plus, for instance, when it comes to distribution—while continuing to lavish attention on each of its films.

Another of Disney's units—Marvel Entertainment—is also a provider of a steady stream of huge hits. In fact, even more so than cats and dogs, comic-book heroes seem to be the favorite targets of Hollywood studios in search of the next blockbuster hit. The people behind the huge splash that the first *Spider-Man* movie made at the box office in 2002—and much of the superhero craze that followed in its footsteps—know a thing or two about creating and monetizing hits. The evolution of their business reveals just how dominant blockbusters have become and underscores many of the lessons learned about effective blockbuster portfolio strategies.

In August 2009, Disney announced a $4 billion purchase of Marvel Entertainment, which owned and managed one of the oldest and most recognizable collections of characters in the entertainment industry. Its proprietary library of thousands of characters, collectively known as the Marvel Universe, includes superheroes such as Spider-Man, X-Men, The Hulk, Daredevil, The Punisher, The Fantastic Four, Captain America, and Thor, all of which were developed for an astonishingly rich trove of comic books dating back to the 1930s.

As Disney's purchase of the company came together, Isaac Perlmutter, Marvel's chief executive officer and at the time its biggest shareholder, and his now former colleagues Avi Arad (who served as chief creative officer) and Peter Cuneo (who preceded Perlmutter as chief executive officer) had every reason to reminisce about a rescue they had staged that none of Marvel's superheroes could have pulled off—that of the company itself. Perlmutter and Arad had made their fortunes as partners in a toy company. With business experience in sectors such as fiberglass, pharmaceuticals, power tools, and electric shavers, Cuneo was as unlikely an entertainment mogul as one can find. But he was an expert at managing turnarounds, and that was his brief at Marvel when he joined the company in July 1999. He succeeded beyond all expectations: exactly a decade after Perlmutter and Arad acquired Marvel out of bankruptcy and hired Cuneo, and nine years after it posted a loss of over $100 million and saw its stock price hover at around $1, the Disney offer valued Marvel at around $50 per share. It was a performance that made the feats of both Spider-Man, with his ability to scamper up the sides of tall buildings, and The Hulk, with his unparalleled power (and greenness), seem decidedly mundane.

During that ten-year period, the executives rebuilt Marvel's original comic-book publishing business into a profitable division, and revamped its toy and licensing operations. Marvel lent its characters to twenty movies, including Sony Pictures' *Spider-Man*, Universal's *The Hulk*, Twentieth Century Fox's *X-Men*, and Lionsgate's *The Punisher*. Many movies recouped their costs by the time they closed out their domestic runs and went on to post big numbers in markets across the globe. Fourteen movies made more than $100 million in US theaters alone, six made more than $200 million, and four made more than $300 million. Remarkably, Marvel's sequels often outperformed its originals. As a result, worldwide grosses collected over a decade hovered close to the $7 billion mark.

Marvel also made licensing deals for a wide range of other products, from video games to apparel and from party items to food. "We contribute our characters and our knowledge of the characters, we work hard to find the right partners, and we approve the products for quality, but we don't contribute any capital," one Marvel executive told me. "We just collect checks." Perlmutter added: "It's a gold mine. Cash just comes in every day."

Within a few years of Cuneo's arrival, early doubts about the company's business model started to disappear. So did fears that the company had milked the best gains from its most prominent characters and might not be capable of further developing lesser-known superheroes such as Ghost Rider, Iron Man, The Punisher, and The Fantastic Four to boost growth. "There is no end to our success—we have a great library of characters," Arad told me in 2004. "I do feel frustrated by all the revenue that we are just giving away," he admitted, pointing to Marvel's relatively modest share of the revenues for its motion pictures. For instance, despite *Spider-Man*'s impressive theatrical box-office gross of over $820 million worldwide and sales of about 7 million $20 DVDs on the day of its release in the United States, Marvel received only about $25 million from Sony Pictures. "We have been focused on activities that require minimal capital investment on our part," said Cuneo at the time. "There are bigger bets to be placed as we move more into the production and distribution of content—but there could be bigger rewards, too."

In 2005, Marvel made its first strides toward that goal by landing $525 million worth of financing courtesy of Merrill Lynch that allowed it to produce its own film slate, and by giving Paramount Pictures the right to distribute those movies. Under the terms of the partnership, Marvel could produce up to ten movies over an eight-year period, with budgets ranging from $45 million to $180 million per film. Marvel received a fee for producing each film and would be able to keep all merchandising revenues, while Paramount collected a distribution fee of 8 percent of the box-office revenues for each film. (The deal also applied to any sequels to these films.) "Marvel has become a marquee entertainment brand," Paramount's chairman and chief executive officer, Brad Grey, said when the agreement was made public. "It speaks to Marvel's strength in the marketplace and the great popularity of its brand and characters that Marvel can obtain such innovative financing for its film slate. We are thrilled to partner with them in this new venture."

Further evidence of Hollywood's interest in Marvel's hit characters and story lines arrived four years later when Disney purchased Marvel. Despite the high purchase price, the agreement required Disney to honor Marvel's ongoing deals with other studios: Sony's right to make movies based on Spider-Man—Marvel's most sought-after character—lasts into perpetuity, and the deal with Paramount locked in several other characters. Yet Disney was undeterred. As Bob Iger, Disney's chief executive officer, put it: "This treasure trove of over 5,000 characters offers Disney the ability to do what we do best."

Marvel's reversal of fortunes over the course of a decade—one of the greatest turnaround stories in the entertainment industry and indeed the business world in general—is a direct result of major movie studios' search for the next blockbuster. Basing a new event film on a Marvel character is now one of the surest bets a Hollywood executive can make. Ironically, the only major studio not mining Marvel's riches is Warner Bros.; its parent company, Time Warner, owns rival comic-book publisher DC Comics, which is known for Batman, Superman, and a host of other characters. Together, Marvel and DC have the market for comic books cornered.

It is too easy to dismiss Marvel as a company that simply got lucky with its *Spider-Man* franchise and since then just banked on that initial success. But the truth is that every studio head knows that the first *Spider-Man*—the highest-grossing film of 2002, and at the time the tenth-highest-grossing movie ever worldwide— single-handedly turned Sony Pictures' otherwise bleak year into a stellar one. In those early years, Marvel relied just as heavily on its biggest blockbuster. By my calculations, in fact, *Spider-Man* accounted for at least half of Marvel's operating income—measured across toys, media licensing, and consumer-products licensing—in 2002 and 2004, and at least a third of the company's operating income in 2003 (when no Spider-Man movie was released).

"It's toys, apparel, school products, games, promotions, pajamas, skateboards, vitamins, lollypops—with Spider-Man, there's virtually no limit," one of Marvel's consumer-products licensing experts told me. Cuneo agreed: "There is nothing close to Spider-Man. He is our number one character, with the widest demographic appeal of any fantasy property. His appeal starts with two-year-old children who wear Spider-Man pajamas and goes up to consumers in their sixties—they all enjoy Spider-Man. I wish all our characters were that broad."

Early successes triggered a superhero craze. As other Marvel movies such as *Daredevil*, *X2* (also known as *X-Men II*), and *The Hulk* performed well at the box office in the years following *Spider-Man*, and especially as the *X-Men* and *Blade* sequels outperformed their originals—a sign of a franchise having staying power or, as industry insiders say, "legs"—Hollywood executives began to compete ever more intensely for new Marvel characters that could be brought to the big screen. Marvel executives let the blockbuster trap work in their favor by pushing for better deal terms in negotiations with studios and other licensing partners. The original deals for *Blade* and *X-Men* stipulated that Marvel would receive a share of studio profits after all expenses had been incorporated. But studios had creative ways of calculating those profits that left only a negligible amount for Marvel—"Hollywood Economics," as Cuneo put it. With a few early movie successes under its belt, however, Marvel was able to negotiate more favorable revenue participation deals that gave it a share, typically between 3 and 7 percent, of box-office grosses for its blockbuster movies. This was still only a fraction of what the partnering studios were able to keep, but a definite improvement.

Meanwhile, Marvel executives created a business model that was specifically designed to minimize product-development and advertising costs—the major financial burdens involved in marketing blockbusters. Minimize those costs for Marvel, that is, and shift expenses to the studios that were licensing Marvel's characters. Here is how it worked. Marvel operated as a mini-conglomerate with divisions focused on comic books, toys, media licensing, and consumer-products licensing. The company developed its characters and story lines in its comic-book division, which effectively served as its research-and-development center, or as its incubator for ideas. And a highly efficient incubator at that, since comic-book publishing is relatively cheap and flexible: a typical print run costs the company only $10,000 to $20,000.

Marvel relied on partnering movie studios to advertise its brands. The company's licensing contracts with studios stipulated that Marvel did not contribute to movie production and marketing expenses. "Usually we get anywhere between thirty million and eighty million dollars in advertising devoted to our movies," Arad told me in 2004. "As a result, the word spreads like wildfire—it leads to worldwide exposure for the Marvel brand and for the specific character." Cuneo explained the resulting positive effect on its brands: "If you have seen our movies, you might get into our comic books, you might get into our video games, you might buy a T-shirt with a Marvel character, or you might buy some of the other consumer products."

How did Marvel make money? Although the partnering studios would undoubtedly have preferred otherwise, Marvel retained full control over merchandising rights, which it used to drive sales in toys and consumer products, the company's main sources of revenues. Consumer-products licensing in particular was—and is—a highly lucrative activity. Costs are incredibly low: at the time Disney made its move, Marvel's consumer media group (which coordinates activities for all consumer products) consisted of just a few salespeople and assistants, supported by a dozen or so legal and product-approval specialists. Contracts specified a minimum guarantee, to be paid to the rights owner regardless of the sales of the licensee's product, and additional royalties if sales exceeded the guarantee. Not surprisingly, the more the character was associated with blockbuster content, the higher both the minimum guarantee and the royalty rate that Marvel could negotiate. No wonder Perlmutter called it "a gold mine."

Marvel's approach to the management of its portfolio of brands was equally clever. Hollywood studio executives—and producers in many other sectors of entertainment—know that strong brands are not created overnight. For every *Finding Nemo*, which introduced a character that immediately resonated with audiences everywhere, there are hundreds of properties such as *Shark Tale* and *Delgo* that disappoint. Marvel's good fortune was that it had an extensive library of tried and tested characters and story lines to exploit, and Perlmutter, Arad, and Cuneo recognized this value. "We don't want to be a regular studio and come up with new ideas for movies," said Arad at the time. "Then we'll be like everybody else in this hit-and-miss business. That's a shot in the dark—we

might as well play blackjack. Somehow the characters have perme-
ated into our culture—that's our marketing advantage."

Blockbusters drove growth for other, lesser-known characters,
building Marvel's portfolio over time. Helped by the fictitious
Marvel Universe, which provided a common historical and contex-
tual background for the company's characters, the executives emphasized the linkages that existed between its hit characters so as
to grow smaller brands. (Elektra, for instance, made an appearance
in the *Daredevil* movie and later starred in a movie of her own.)
Cuneo explained the nature of the content library this way: "You've
got to think of the forty-seven hundred characters not as individuals but as families. We have forty years of Spider-Man stories.
There might be fifty bad guys associated with Spider-Man and
fifty friends. So the Spider-Man family consists of one hundred,
maybe two hundred, properties. The Hulk accounts for another
hundred, while X-Men has about four hundred characters."

The essential natures of Marvel's franchise characters, built up
over decades of appearances in comic books, are remarkably similar. As one Marvel executive put it: "They have some kind of vul-
nerability attached to them. Spider-Man is just a kid with glasses.
Although they have superpowers, our characters are presented as
normal people, with problems that anybody else would have." Because its brands are linked and in many respects similar, Marvel
was in an ideal position to capitalize on Hollywood's search for the
"next big thing" after the *Spider-Man* movie became a hit. Rather
than fight against a blockbuster trap that was gaining momentum,
the major studios helped to further strengthen Marvel's overall
brand by pursuing the film rights to many of the company's other
characters. Some marketing executives even asked for a Marvel-
themed trailer to play just prior to their own films.

Realizing that bigger risks go along with bigger rewards, Marvel executives used their newfound powers to put together the
groundbreaking deal with Paramount and Merrill Lynch—a move
that fit Marvel's desire to capture more of the upside of its movies,
but one that pitted the company directly against some of its other
studio partners. By 2005, just a few short years after the first two

Spider-Man movies had together grossed more than $1.5 billion in worldwide ticket sales, Marvel's characters had become so sought-after that it could negotiate innovative financing: the contracts with Merrill Lynch reportedly stated that an insurer would cover interest payments in case Marvel would not be able to—in return for the movie rights to the central character. Have characters serve as collateral? It is hard to think of a more fitting illustration of the power of the company's blockbuster brands.

Further proving the strength of Marvel's characters, the first films to come out of the company's deal with Paramount—*Iron Man*, *Iron Man 2*, *Thor*, and *Captain America*—performed well, together collecting over $2 billion in global box-office revenues, over three times their estimated production costs. Coming at a time when Disney was struggling to generate hits of its own, Disney's bid for Marvel reflected the major studio's eagerness—or, given the billions of dollars involved in the transaction, some might say desperation—to call some of those blockbusters its own. In October 2010, less than a year after closing the purchase, Disney gained further control of the Marvel portfolio by buying Paramount out of its worldwide marketing and distribution rights for *The Avengers* and *Iron Man 3*, in return for at least $115 million in distribution fees. Before long, no one at Disney had any regrets about the investments: in 2012, the first *Avengers* movie raked in a staggering $1.5 billion in tickets; in 2013, *Iron Man 3* also crossed the $1 billion mark. Whatever the further fortunes of Marvel's resilient superheroes, the evolution of the company and its new life as a subsidiary of Disney underlines Hollywood's reliance on the kind of colossal hits that only Marvel's superheroes and Hollywood's smartest executives can make happen.

Chapter Two

LAUNCHING AND MANAGING BLOCKBUSTERS

Standing backstage at a sold-out concert in Boston's TD Garden in March 2011 during Lady Gaga's smash-hit solo tour, the *Monster Ball*, her manager, Troy Carter, took a moment to take it all in. "When Interscope celebrated its twentieth anniversary last year, Gaga was featured as one of its top acts in the past two decades. . . . It is amazing how far we have come in such a short time," he told me. And he had a point: after emerging on the music scene in 2008—touring as a supporting act for New Kids On The Block, a former boy band beyond their glory years—Lady Gaga hit it big in the fall of 2009. Two short years later, she had become one of the biggest names in entertainment. Along the way, she collected multiple Grammy and MTV Video Music awards, garnering acclaim as both a singer and a songwriter. As Gaga's musical star rose, so did her status in the fashion world, helped by her memorable appearance in a "meat dress" at the 2010 VMAs and, a year later, her red carpet arrival in an egg-shaped vessel held up high by latex-clad dancers. By 2011, *Forbes* ranked her first on its Celebrity 100 list, ahead of Oprah Winfrey.

Working behind the scenes, the thirty-eight-year old Carter had also seen his fortunes dramatically improve. He had been introduced to Gaga by top producer Vincent Herbert a few weeks after Herbert had signed her to his label Streamline Records, a subsidiary of major record company Universal Music Group (to which the flagship Interscope label also belonged). "I wanted someone who shared my vision for Lady Gaga, and Troy understands it. We have been close friends for fifteen years, and I knew he would appreciate this chance," recalled Herbert, who described Carter as "a little kid from Philly with a big heart and a dream to prove himself."

Although he looked much too young to have built a career in entertainment that spanned two decades, Carter had started out in the early 1990s carrying crates of records for Jeffrey Allen Townes and Will Smith, then better known as rap duo DJ Jazzy Jeff & The Fresh Prince. As the hub for all activities related to Lady Gaga ("I think of myself as the air traffic control center—just without the terminals," Carter said about his job as manager), he himself had become a force to be reckoned with in the world of entertainment. Now, after a series of investments and new ventures in Silicon Valley, he was also a rising star in the world of new technology. "The reality of being a talent manager is that I risk my job every week," Carter explained. "Lady Gaga trusts my decisions. We are about breaking boundaries, which means we do something different when we have a chance—we don't just do what worked last time, or what was successful for someone else. But if something doesn't work out, it is my responsibility."

Gaga's ascent to the top may have been swift, but her artistry had been a long time in the making. Born as Stefani Joanne Angelina Germanotta in New York City in 1986, Gaga began playing the piano at age four, composed her first piano ballad when she was thirteen, and played open mike nights at venues around New York one year later. As a student at Covenant of the Sacred Heart, an all-girls Catholic school in Manhattan, she excelled in lead roles in several of the school's musicals. In 2003, she was one of twenty students given early admission to New York University (NYU)'s prestigious Tisch School of the Arts, which allowed her to further develop her singing, playing, and songwriting. A year and a half after arriving, she withdrew from NYU to focus on her music full-time—but not before striking a deal with her father to re-enroll if her music career fizzled: a smart safety net but, needless to say, one that ultimately proved unnecessary.

A day after hearing a recording of Gaga's, Herbert flew her out to Los Angeles. "I knew she was a star," Herbert said. "It was that simple." To Carter, the woman who would go on to sell tens of millions of copies of songs such as *Just Dance*, *Poker Face*, and *Bad Romance* on her first two albums, *The Fame* and *The Fame Monster*, had "being a performer running through her veins." Through a relentless touring schedule—for months on end, she put on seven to eight shows a week, sometimes performing three times per night, in different clubs around the United States and Canada—Gaga had built a fan base with a strong core. "This is not what pop artists usually do," Carter remarked, "but we wanted to build her fan base from the ground up. . . . Once the audience feels they own something, they are going to run with it, and do the work for you."

Gaga heavily relied on Facebook, Twitter, and YouTube to further spread word of mouth and strengthen her connection with her fans—or her "little monsters," as she liked to call them. She turned out to be extraordinarily skilled at doing so: by 2011, Gaga was the most popular living person on Facebook and the most followed person on Twitter. (In typical Gaga fashion, upon receiving the latter distinction, she posted a live video and tweeted, "May you always have soft cuticles while tweeting. May you never have carpal tunnel," to thank her fans for the honor.)

But when Gaga was ready to release her third album, *Born This Way*, Carter and his team decided to rely much less on a grassroots approach to propel sales. Rather, the idea was to support the launch with an intensive marketing effort—"much like opening this as a movie blockbuster in the summer months, like *Avatar*," explained Interscope's vice chairman, Steve Berman. Herbert added: "We can do that because of who she is—she is a part of culture now, and has an enormous platform." But the strategy would be a significant drain on resources, Carter acknowledged: "With an artist of Gaga's caliber, reaching full potential means doing things on an enormous scale." He knew that the launch he had in mind would have to go beyond traditional music-distribution channels and would test the limits of what a record label, even one the size of Universal, could afford.

Now, as Carter made his way through TD Garden's hallways to the stadium floor—"the best place to experience the concert," as he put it—he wondered whether an expensive launch akin to that of a "tent-pole" movie was the right way to capitalize on Gaga's popularity. Or was a more moderate approach—much like the one that Carter had employed so successfully for her first albums—the best way to proceed?

Not only do entertainment businesses make risky bets on the development of a select few products, they often further increase the stakes by investing a great deal of money in distributing and promoting those products as widely as possible, all with an eye toward opening as big as they can. And companies set those marketing budgets at high levels often well before they know how those products will be received in the marketplace. Why? Why would the team behind Lady Gaga want to move away from a word-of-mouth-driven launch that worked so well for them in the past? With Gaga's new album likely to sell like hot cakes, would record label executives not prefer to save on any unnecessary marketing expenditures?

It is hard to argue with anyone who has been as successful as Gaga—when I spoke with Berman, he noted that "she could be a chief marketing officer for a big corporation, because she understands the brand, and how important it is to stand by that brand." All evidence indeed points to team Gaga's approach to releasing *Born This Way* being the wisest course of action. To understand why, it is necessary to take a closer look at the pros and cons of the different ways in which entertainment products are launched—and how, more specifically, media producers decide to allocate their marketing dollars over time.

Most albums, movies, television shows, video games, and

A Limited Release Strategy

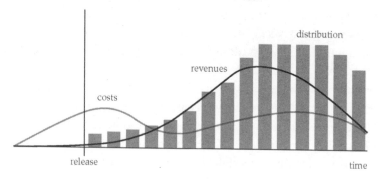

books—and, in fact, the majority of goods *not* produced by entertainment businesses—are launched using what marketers call a "limited" or "grassroots" release strategy, as illustrated in the chart above. The basic idea behind such an approach is to gradually discover what level of marketing spending is most appropriate. It is all about being as efficient as possible with the available resources.

How does this work? When products are introduced using a limited release strategy, initial distribution and advertising levels are relatively low. For instance, in the context of the film industry, this could mean that a film debuts on only a few screens in major cities, and is supported with print and online advertisements in those regions. The primary goal of these efforts is to attract not the largest, but rather the *right* audience to the product, in the hopes that those early customers will in turn spread positive word of mouth and help draw in new audiences. Only if the product takes off—or shows some signs of being on the verge of taking off—will the producer gradually increase the distribution coverage or intensity and support the product with more advertising to further enhance growth. Getting a positive response from the market is critical: if the product fails to impress, the producer will cease to invest, and copies will be pulled from shelves (or, in the case of a movie, from theaters). The principle is to spend sizable amounts of money on the marketing of only those products that are worth it—those that truly have a chance of success in the marketplace.

Some of today's biggest entertainment hits were launched using a limited release strategy. *My Big Fat Greek Wedding* is a classic example: a so-called sleeper movie that originally appeared on only a hundred screens in April 2002, it was initially promoted via a word-of-mouth campaign targeted at Greek communities in the United States. As the film caught on, the executives behind the film slowly expanded its distribution footprint and advertised the film to a wider audience. Not until August of that year was the film shown on a thousand screens—still a low number for a typical release in Hollywood, where films often play on three to four thousand screens at once—and made more than $10 million a week. The film remained in theaters until April 2003, nearly a year after its opening week, and ultimately grossed $240 million domestically. Not a bad haul, given its production costs of only $5 million.

Lady Gaga's first recordings were also released in this fashion. Her first single, *Just Dance*, a glam-influenced pop song co-written with R&B artist Akon and producer RedOne that also featured up-and-coming artist Colby O'Donis, was released in April 2008. Gaining traction proved difficult: "We could not get it played on pop radio," Carter recalled. "Mainstream radio stations told us it was too much of a dance song for them." Bobby Campbell, chief marketing officer at Carter's management firm Atom Factory, chimed in: "Dance music simply was not on the air in Top 40 Radio. Radio stations were saying no to such music." To overcome the problem, Carter followed a release plan that, inspired by successful rap artists' launches, relied on an intense schedule of live performances targeted at communities that seemed especially receptive to her music.

"The gay community seemed to stick to her, and that resonated with her personally. So gay clubs were a natural fit to start the work. We gave them full access to her," explained Campbell. "It was about finding different groups: the gay community, the dance community, the club-going community, the fashion community, the art community, and developing those into a larger pool of Gaga fans. So when Interscope made some headway with radio later on, we had this really strong core of fans who had been following her for months, and who felt they were part of the reason why she was successful."

Most content producers opting for a limited release do so because they lack the funds necessary for a wider rollout. Getting broad distribution for a product tends to be costly, partly because of the additional demands that many retailers make. In the film industry, for example, cinema exhibitors often insist that a film producer or distributor spend a certain amount on marketing before they agree to show a film; these stipulations are frequently a part of the contract between both parties. In the book business, the initial launch of E. L. James's mega-seller *Fifty Shades of Grey*, which the British working mother of two wrote in her spare time, was remarkably modest: lacking the support of a publisher, James published the book's first volume as an e-book and print-on-demand paperback in May 2011. She chose to release the book with a small Australian company called Writers' Coffee Shop, and published two more novels by the same method over the next six months. Excitement about the books soon began to build on blogs and in social media, prompting an executive at major publisher Random House to sign James in early 2012 and give the trilogy a much stronger distribution and marketing push.

Having some control over which audiences become early adopters is another important advantage of a limited release. It is no coincidence that highbrow films are usually released in more upscale neighborhoods in New York City and Los Angeles before they are rolled out to other parts of the country. Producers and distributors know that audiences there are most receptive to those kinds of films, and count on the positive word of mouth from these audiences to then spill over to other markets and help propel sales to greater heights. Jimmy Iovine, Interscope's chairman, talks about capitalizing on "sparks": the idea is that if an entertainment product resonates with audiences in a given market, that market can, with the right kind of support, become a launching pad for a wider rollout. In the case of Gaga's debut album, for instance, Iovine and his colleagues thought initial conditions were most promising in Canada and Australia, which is why they rolled out the album there first—not in the United States.

By their very nature, social networks and video-sharing sites are uniquely suited to enhance any early buzz around a product or artist; indeed, such sites now play a critical role in many grass-roots releases. That certainly was the case for Gaga. "Where other people see digital distribution as a source of cannibalization, we see it as an opportunity," Carter said. "The Beatles, Michael Jackson, and Madonna didn't have Facebook or Twitter. We wanted to use those new tools." Gaga began using both sites in March 2008, right before *Just Dance* was released. Carter and his team arranged for fifty popular music bloggers to interview Gaga in the six months following the *Just Dance* launch; during that period, these interviews alone totaled over ten million impressions.

Using a more novel tactic, Gaga's team also initiated a series of two-minute videos, dubbed *Transmission: Gaga-Vision*, on Gaga's official YouTube channel. "There were fans that discovered her as early as April, and others that came on board months later," recalled Campbell. "Because she is such a visual artist, we felt we had to keep the visual fresh even if we did not release another single. So we put out a series of 'webisodes' that followed her around and gave a peek behind the scenes. It wasn't overly produced, and in fact mostly shot on a flip-cam—the idea was to create intimate moments that make you feel like you were there with her." Atom Factory's digital team worked to syndicate Gaga's content, from her tweets to her music videos, as widely as possible and made sure it got covered by other media.

As is the case with most limited releases, success came gradually. *Just Dance* broke into major charts for dance airplay and club play two months after its release; another two months passed before it entered the Billboard Hot 100, the main singles chart in North America. The song then spent the next five months working its way to the number one spot, which it reached in January 2009. *Just Dance*'s nine-month-long journey up the charts was the second-longest climb to the top spot in Billboard's history. By that time, *Poker Face*, a second single from the album that was marketed in much the same way, was moving up the charts right behind it.

Despite all the advantages that go along with a limited release strategy, however, most blockbuster bets in entertainment are released using what is known as a "wide" or "mainstream" release strategy. Wide releases, as suggested by the chart below, are not designed with efficiency in mind; instead, the goal is to "break through the clutter" and immediately capture the attention of as large an audience as possible.

For products launched in this manner, distribution levels start at a high level, while most promotional activities are concentrated at the time of release—or, to be more precise, in the short period leading up to the release. As a result, sales often peak immediately after launch and then taper off quickly. A successful opening is seen as critical: a failure to reach an acceptably high level of sales early on generally dooms a widely launched new movie, a new recording, or any other type of entertainment product.

Hollywood's event films are perhaps the best example of products launched this way. Major studios have the scale needed to make high up-front investments in advertising and marketing at a time when no sales are being generated. They start promoting a

A Wide Release Strategy

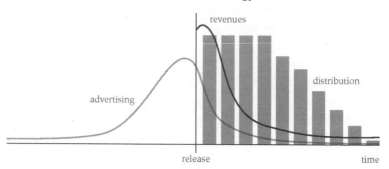

film months—and, if we include teaser trailers, sometimes years—in advance of its opening weekend. Spending ramps up dramatically in the six to eight weeks before release: a studio will spend as much as two-thirds of its marketing budget on television commercials in the final two weeks before a film's opening. And since some of Hollywood's biggest films open on four thousand screens or more across the nation, their first week of release is often also their biggest week in terms of revenues. In 2011, for example, the top hundred films, from *Harry Potter and the Deathly Hallows: Part 2* to *The Iron Lady*, collected 30 percent of their total of $9 billion in domestic theatrical revenues in their first week alone.

As soon as Carter and his team had the opportunity, they opted for a wide release for Lady Gaga's music, too. Released in May 2011, *Born This Way* was shipped to an unprecedented twenty thousand locations across the United States—not just conventional music retailers but also coffee chains like Starbucks, electronics retailers such as RadioShack, and grocery stores and drugstores such as CVS and Walgreens. A long lead time made this possible: in 2010, knowing they would need months to pull off a launch of this scale, Carter and the Interscope executives convinced Gaga to push back the release date. "Normally there is a three- or four-month lead time, but we announced the album release seven months in advance," Berman said. "We wanted to put a stake in the ground." Gaga was initially less than thrilled about this plan, Carter recalled: "I still remember her crying her eyes out at the thought of having to wait this long."

Why put Gaga through this misery? Why do Carter and almost every other executive and manager in the entertainment industry, when given the chance, prefer to push for big openings by spending heavily on advertising and distribution, rather than increasing marketing expenditures more gradually? The reason is simple: all else being equal, the odds of achieving success in the marketplace are higher with a wide release strategy than with a limited release approach. That, in turn, follows from the very nature of entertainment products—and, in fact, from several of the same characteristics that drive major media producers' taste for block-buster portfolio strategies.

First, because people like winners—because they prefer to consume entertainment products that are also chosen by oth-ers—a solid opening is often a huge factor in a rollout. For media products, initial success breeds further success, while a failure to achieve success early on frequently means having no chance to succeed at all. Alan Horn knows all too well how this dynamic works in the film industry. "We always found out how we did on opening weekend," he explained. "For a film released on a Friday, I'd get a call that same night at eleven o'clock saying 'Well, it is over.' And I'd say, 'When you say it is over . . .' but before I could even finish they'd go, 'No, no, it is over!' For some of our event films, they'd tell me, 'We are done. We have just lost $100 million.' " When Disney's $250-million-budget *John Carter* generated a disap-pointing $30 million in revenues in its first weekend, trade maga-zines called it a "fiasco"—a full two days into its run—and audiences fled. Within a week, Disney had issued a report stating it would take a $200 million write-down.

In the film industry, with its tradition of publishing sales fig-ures weekly, each weekend's winner is ensured a great deal of free publicity. Opening-weekend revenues are a quality signal for sub-sequent moviegoers, and most customers (and indeed most report-ers) pay little attention to the fine print, such as how many theaters were necessary to achieve the total grosses, or how much was spent on advertising. By contrast, the movies that, for whatever reason, fail to open well in their first week are immediately considered "losers." They are quickly whisked away to smaller screens at the theaters or disappear from view altogether, only to make room for a new set of movies hoping to capture people's attention from the very start.

But even in sectors where sales figures are harder to come by, we see similar patterns. In book publishing, if new titles fail to catch on, they are often pulled from the shelves in a matter of weeks. Extensive marketing campaigns and the star power of es-tablished authors can help place books in prime spots in bookstores across the country, but they suffer the same fate if they do not open well. On Broadway, underperforming plays, no matter if they cost millions of dollars to produce, are regularly replaced after only a few weeks of disappointing ticket sales. Even Lady Gaga, for all her success, scrambled to release a third song in advance of her album *Born This Way* when the second, *Judas*, underperformed in the market.

Social influence is a powerful force in markets for popular culture. Because we are social beings, people tend to want to listen to the same music that others listen to, read the same books, and see the same movies. Simply put, we repeatedly show a preference for popular products. That tendency, economists have shown, can tip the scales in favor of those products that perform well at the outset—even if the difference between the top performers and the next level down is slight. If one product edges out a rival for the number one position in its first week, that success may become a topic of conversation at the water cooler and ultimately make a huge difference across a product's entire run.

Even products that have no discernible quality differences can, as a result of these forces, experience very different outcomes in the marketplace—luck alone might lead to an early break. The sociologist Duncan Watts has proved this point convincingly. By conducting a set of experiments involving an artificial market for songs, he and his colleagues found that social influence played as large a role in determining the market share of successful songs as actual differences in quality. The experiment was designed to measure varying degrees of social influence: for instance, some respondents could see how many previous participants had downloaded a particular song while others could not, and some respondents saw a list ranked by song popularity while others saw a random listing. In one study, Watts and his colleagues presented respondents with false information—they showed a ranking that was completely inverted from what the download pattern of previous listeners actually looked like. What the study revealed was that while the "best" songs never did very badly and the "worst" songs never did terribly well (even when the rankings began inverted, the very best songs eventually made their way back to the top), any other scenario was possible.

The ultimate success of an entertainment product, Watts and his colleagues revealed, is extremely sensitive to the decisions of a few early-arriving individuals: if consumers making decisions about a product later in its life cycle can see whether that product is popular, they amplify the choices of those early consumers. The result is what Watts calls a "cumulative-advantage process," which helps explain the high unpredictability of the demand for popular-culture goods. Successful songs, movies, books, and artists are not necessarily "better," Watts argues; rather, what people like depends on what they think other people like, and what the market "wants" at any point in time depends on its own history.

Faced with this dynamic, executives will do everything they can to gain the upper hand in a battle with their rivals right from the time of launch—which means opting for a wide release strategy. Achieving scale from the moment of introduction is critical. In the case of *Born This Way*, for instance, it would be very risky to rely primarily on word of mouth: any loss of traction with initial audiences could seriously hinder the album's launch. Especially with a high-profile artist like Lady Gaga, attempting to raise a high level of awareness among the largest possible audience in advance of a new product's release is in fact the safest approach. "We chose a big launch because we could," is how Interscope's Berman put it. "Leave no stone unturned" was Carter's motto ahead of the *Born This Way* campaign: in other words, use every opportunity to make the launch as big as it could be. Similarly, no film-studio executive in his right mind will launch a $200 million movie on a few screens in the hope that word of mouth carries the picture to a wider audience. Smart executives will do what is in their power to create buzz and open big, so as to avoid their products losing the battle for early adopters.

The preference for a so-called push strategy involving wide distribution and high advertising intensity has everything to do with a second characteristic of entertainment products: their experiential nature. This is not to say that consumers will mindlessly choose whatever is put in front of them just because they cannot reliably assess product quality before the moment of consumption, but wide distribution and marketing can make a substantial difference. "In the business, we say 'you can buy an opening weekend,'" Horn said. "You can spend so much that audiences will show up. It will be disappointing for you and for them, but you can get them in those seats."

In the movie industry, study after study has shown that the best predictor of a movie's revenues is the number of screens on which it plays. Sophisticated statistical models (some of which I developed in my own research) that are designed to tease out the tangled effects of factors such as genre, star power, seasonality, competition, and advertising invariably demonstrate that, all else being equal, an increase in the level of distribution is the most effective way to increase sales. Higher advertising expenditures help, too: advertising not only directly increases sales by triggering audiences to buy tickets, it also indirectly drives sales by reassuring theater owners that dedicating screens to a movie will be worth their while. In the music industry, radio airplay—the main way through which new music is promoted—continues to be a critical predictor of recorded-music sales. And in book publishing, distributing a large number of physical books remains a classic tactic.

The fact that entertainment products are experience goods also explains the important role critics can play. Potential customers typically value the opinions of others who have already read, listened to, watched, or otherwise interacted with a product. Because judgments about the quality of these products are inevitably subjective, people tend to trust experts to tell them what to like. But the tastes of regular consumers matter as well, which is why Facebook, Twitter, and other online sharing tools, although mostly associated with grassroots releases, are just as relevant to wide releases. Because social networks make it possible to spread information and opinions about new products across the globe instantaneously, and because entertainment executives are often keen to benefit from that buzz, online sharing mechanisms can fuel ever bigger releases.

A third feature of entertainment goods is that in general they are relatively expensive to produce but cheap to reproduce. The first copy of an album (the "negative") often costs hundreds of thousands, if not millions, of dollars to produce. But once a record label has the first copy in hand, the company has to spend only a fraction of that amount to create more copies and distribute them—each physical record sent to retailers costs a few dollars at most, and even less if the album is distributed online. Not only does this make blockbuster products disproportionately profitable (the more copies sold, the lower the production and distribution costs per copy sold), it also makes media producers eager to earn back their investments sooner rather than later. With so much money tied up in their projects, time is of the essence.

In some entertainment sectors, a wide release also makes it easier for media producers to plan multiple revenue windows, allowing companies to reap further rewards from hit products that carry low marginal costs. In the movie industry contracts between studios and theater owners are often specifically designed with wide releases in mind. Revenues can be shared on a sliding-scale basis, whereby studios receive a higher (and exhibitors a lower) percentage of revenues in the early weeks of a film's release—giving studios yet another reason to aim for big openings. And such launches help protect executives from changes in audiences' tastes in genres, stars, or other product features. The hunger for popular culture items can fade quickly—most are essentially "fads" or "fashions." But some entertainment products are especially perishable or timely—think of a book about a politician running for election, or a new song by an artist who has just won a Grammy Award. For such products, if the necessary resources are available, experienced entertainment executives will favor a big launch over a limited campaign that plays out over many months.

All in all, just as blockbuster bets at first glance seem risky but upon closer examination may in fact be the safer choice, releasing those bets in a manner that emphasizes big openings may seem to only heighten the risk but is often the smartest approach. Such launches are not for the faint of heart because they require huge up-front investments. With a wide release, entertainment executives are effectively doubling down on their investment. But they also increase the probability of achieving mainstream market success—which, of course, is critical to the profitability of blockbuster bets.

For Lady Gaga, the meticulous preparation for a massive launch paid off in spades. Carter and his team used the long buildup to the *Born This Way* launch to take advantage of a series of high-profile, attention-grabbing events to which the superstar had been invited in early 2011, including the Grammy Awards, a taping of *American Idol*, and the season finale of the television mainstay *Saturday Night Live*. And team Gaga worked closely with retailers, super fans, the media, and a variety of other partners in a concerted effort to help grow awareness for the album and make sure that it would be readily available for prospective customers.

Released on a wider scale than any other album in 2011, *Born This Way* sold 1.1 million units in its first week, making it just the seventeenth album to reach the one-million-copies-a-week benchmark since Nielsen SoundScan began tracking such data in 1991. Some say the sales total paints an unfair picture of the album's "true" popularity, as online retailer Amazon sold an estimated 440,000 units for just 99 cents to promote its new cloud-based music service. But those critics overlook the fact that Amazon paid the same wholesale price that other retailers did and fully absorbed the resulting loss—as good an indication as any of Lady Gaga's star power and the level of anticipation for the album. Within a year of its release, the album sold well over two million copies; during the same period, eighteen million copies of the album's songs were sold. Whether Lady Gaga would have sold fewer copies had her team opted for a more gradual release is impossible to say, but her team did not want to risk finding out—and rightly so.

Most creative goods, of course, are released on a much smaller scale than Lady Gaga's album, yet many of these products have made a significant difference in the world of popular culture. The work of a small New York–based label is a case in point: Octone Records is among a select group of music companies that has perfected the art of creating hits with limited resources—and along the way demonstrated the value of a novel "hybrid" model that marries the strengths of both wide and limited releases.

Although he had the deep passion for music required for the job, James Diener never was your typical record-label executive. He mingled with top players in the private-equity sector, read *Harvard Business Review* articles just to keep up with the latest management thinking, and wasn't afraid to try a different model of creating hits in a collaboration with music-industry legend Clive Davis. Diener, who began his career at Columbia Records and rose to the position of vice president of A&R Marketing at the label, had started Octone in 2000 to put a new philosophy on how to launch music to the test. By 2007, after Octone had hit home runs with the first two bands signed—the pop-rock quintet Maroon 5 and the alternative rock band Flyleaf—music-business insiders were following the small label's every move. Initially rejected by the major labels, Maroon 5 had garnered both commercial and critical success, selling ten million copies worldwide of its 2002 debut album *Songs About Jane* and winning the prestigious Grammy Award for "Best New Artist." Flyleaf's first album, meanwhile, had reached gold status with more than five hundred thousand albums sold, and was heading toward the million-units platinum mark.

With Diener in the role of chief executive officer and president, David Boxenbaum—fresh off a career as a strategy consultant at PricewaterhouseCoopers and sporting an Ivy League MBA—as general manager, and Ben Berkman as executive vice president and head of promotion, Octone was based on the belief that once a decision was made to sign an artist, it was the label's job to do everything possible to realize the artist's full potential. The team believed that most major labels were impatient, dropping acts too soon and failing to dedicate sufficient resources and efforts to building their audience. "When I worked at Columbia we signed a lot of acts that didn't get a decent shot," Diener told me. "I wanted to change that."

Octone introduced an innovative model that borrowed the best practices from both independent and major labels. The idea was simple. Octone would focus its efforts on just a few artists each year. Initially, like most independent labels, the company would rely heavily on grassroots marketing campaigns to gradually build its artists' fan bases. But once artists succeeded to the point that they were on the verge of breaking through, the company's distribution and marketing efforts would enter a second, more aggressive phase. To make this phase possible, Octone structured a unique joint-venture model with Sony BMG Music Entertainment, a major label that at the time had revenues of $1.75 billion and the second-highest share of the recorded-music industry (behind Universal Music Group). Diener had successfully pitched the idea of the partnership to Clive Davis and his colleagues at Sony BMG after the famed music executive, responsible for guiding the careers of superstar artists such as Whitney Houston and Bruce Springsteen, courted Diener to leave Columbia Records. Diener took on two roles: he became a full-time senior vice president of A&R and marketing at Sony BMG's J Records while also running Octone.

Under the terms of the partnership, Octone shouldered the initial costs of discovering and promoting its artists. Octone's acts remained exclusively on Octone's profit-and-loss statement until a so-called uplift into the joint venture took place. Artists could get uplifted in three ways, Diener explained. "First, if an artist reaches 75,000 records sold, Octone can elect to uplift the artist into the joint venture, and Sony BMG is required to accommodate this decision. Second, if an artist reaches 125,000 records sold, Sony BMG can compel us to uplift the artist. Third, both parties can mutually agree on a natural time in a project where it becomes appropriate to step in."

Before an artist's uplift, Octone received all revenues and paid the artist's advances, all expenses related to recording the album, manufacturing costs necessary to physically produce the album, tour support, promotion and publicity, and other fees. But after the uplift, Sony BMG was responsible for all new costs, be they distribution, promotion, or sales efforts. From this moment on, Sony BMG and Octone equally split the profits, while Sony BMG covered all losses. Post uplift, Octone continued to provide creative and marketing direction to Sony BMG's efforts, but its options for forcing Sony BMG to action were limited. "The risk in uplifting an album is that you lose total control," said Boxenbaum. "It can be a challenge to manage a relationship with a partner label."

Crucial to the launch of Octone were Laurence Fink, the chief executive officer of investment management firm BlackRock, and Howard Lipson, then senior partner at prominent private equity firm The Blackstone Group. Diener had met Lipson and Fink in 1999 and asked them to fund the proposed new record label. Successful Wall Street financiers and avid music fans, they solicited a group of private equity investors and raised a total of $5 million in initial working capital. "We should have lost all of our money," recalled Fink. "The business conditions in the music industry are very difficult and there are sea changes going on that are seismic. However, Octone shows that you can beat the trends."

"Many independent labels did not have sufficient funds to execute their ideas or were going to run out of money before they could make it," added Lipson. "Therefore, they had to rely on an economic affiliation with a major label in which the major controls everything and the upside for the independent label is limited. Octone was well-capitalized, so we knew we had time to reach a certain level and fulfill our mandate. There was nothing we could do to guarantee success, but we set Octone up so that it could succeed."

For all its success in beating the steep odds of scoring a hit in the music industry—most record companies recovered their investments in only one out of every five or six new albums—Octone had not traveled a perfectly smooth road. Success had proven elusive for the third artist on its roster, Georgia-based singer-songwriter and guitarist Michael Tolcher. Although Octone spent over $750,000 marketing Tolcher's first full album, *I Am*, it sold only one hundred thousand copies, not enough to recover the costs incurred. Now, as they contemplated their next move, Diener and his colleagues faced three options. They could "grind it out," industry parlance for supporting the debut album over a prolonged period by leveraging the small beachhead of fans Tolcher had established on his last US tour in 2006; they could increase the stakes by backing a second album; or they could cut their losses and instead focus on other artists.

Is there a logic behind Octone's efforts to pursue a hybrid model that combines a grassroots with a more mainstream release strategy? Is such a model the answer to the entertainment industry's woes when it comes to consistently creating hits? Finding answers to these questions starts with the realization that, in most entertainment markets, a content producer's scale and its product-release strategy are closely linked. The larger a media company, the more it can afford to put significant marketing efforts behind a product in an attempt to create a hit. But scale also comes with disadvantages. And both those advantages and those disadvantages explain what Octone executives are attempting to do, and whether their model may be here to stay.

Smaller and larger content producers are different in their approaches. First, they vary in terms of the number of products they bring to the market. In the music business, major labels—the industry's biggest powerhouses, such as Sony BMG (now called Sony Music)—tend to have hundreds of artists on their roster, including multiple bestsellers. Alicia Keys, Beyoncé, John Mayer, Britney Spears, and Justin Timberlake were some of the artists on Sony BMG's roster at the time the executives at Octone were trying to determine their next step. Small "indie" labels, on the other hand, tend to have only a few artists. That, in turn, can mean that the success of one artist is essential to the small label's overall fortunes. For all its success, Octone heavily depended on its number one act, Maroon 5: the superstar band brought in more than $10 million in annual profits in North America alone.

Second, while larger players will often prune products quickly after a failed market launch (Sony, for instance, might terminate up to forty underperforming artists in a given year), smaller producers tend to support their products over a relatively long period of time. Larger labels typically do not invest a great deal of time in an album by a new, unproven artist; their strategy often comes down to giving an act one big push to see if the music catches on with fans. Because a major label has abundant resources and several blockbuster artists, it can afford to take a home-run swing and miss. Because of its high overhead costs, a major label also *needs* quick successes: it may not have the patience that is necessary to "break" an act through a series of small victories over a long time horizon. After all, the "next big act" in the label's portfolio is always awaiting its turn.

By contrast, smaller labels like Octone are more committed to developing artists longer. "We tend to stick with our artists," is how Diener described it. Octone both can *and* has to do so because of its smaller roster. It *can* afford to spend more time on its artists. According to Boxenbaum, the label's lower costs—in 2007, it counted only ten employees—and its freedom from the pressure of quarterly earnings reports allow the Octone team to take its time to nurture each project. But it also *has* to make things happen with each of its artists for its model to work: it has limited content to fall back on if one of its new releases were to fail. "We put ourselves in a position of having no choice but to push harder to make our releases work," noted Boxenbaum.

These differences affect how content producers typically release their products. The larger label's wider portfolio and focus on short-term success are suited to a more mainstream release approach built on distribution and marketing strengths. Major labels often stage elaborate marketing campaigns before and around the launch of albums, usually involving a strong push for radio and video airplay and other forms of advertising and securing shelf space in large music and mass-market stores—much like the campaign for Gaga's *Born This Way* album. Meanwhile, smaller labels rely heavily on grassroots marketing techniques, such as using "street teams" of fans who have volunteered to promote the band (and are often recruited via the Internet and at concerts), social-networking techniques, distribution through small record stores (those that do "not just stock but actually *sell* records," as Boxenbaum once put it), and extensive touring to refine an artist's sound and gauge fan interest. These techniques go hand in hand with a gradual rollout of artists and their music, which fits Octone's style of fostering deep connections with fans—much like Lady Gaga originally built a relationship with her fans.

Diener understands the advantages of scale as well as anyone: "Major labels are essentially in the volume business. They have the resources to push artists via mainstream outlets, and they have the ability to achieve economies of scale once sales momentum has been created. There is a reason that the majority of records sold today is distributed by major labels. Most independent labels are not well funded, and most owners or operators of those independent labels do not have the expertise of major labels."

But he also knows that smaller labels can really nurture artists they feel hold artistic promise, even if it means forgoing early profits. "They excel in specialized artist development and marketing strategies, often employed over longer time horizons, that have launched many of today's biggest selling artists," remarked Diener, who pointed out that music that crosses established genres or otherwise does not fit the mainstream mold of the music industry usually comes from smaller labels. Smaller-scale producers may be better positioned to innovate—or, to put it in familiar terms, they may be less likely to fall into the blockbuster trap by spending big on acts that sound just like past winners. It's telling that Adele, who sounds and looks very different from any other artist that dominated the charts before she did, was nurtured by an indie label, XL Recordings. Any music company hoping to copy her phenomenal success will find it has to pay top dollar for artists that could be "the next Adele."

Clearly, then, a partnership between a larger and smaller content producer, when structured in the right way, can bring the best of both worlds together: the smaller producers' ability to innovate, and the larger producers' power to market those products to a mass audience. For a smaller player like Octone, being able to tap into the distribution and marketing strength of a behemoth like Sony BMG brings substantial advantages. As Diener put it: "When artists are on the verge of breaking through, there is nothing like the marketing power of a major label to bring that final push." Boxenbaum agreed: "There are independent labels that have no relationship with major labels. They are just out there plodding along, they are surprised when an album starts to take off, and then they are stuck because they cannot take their campaign to the next level."

Octone's joint venture solves that problem. It helps the label to secure shelf space in retail chains such as Walmart and Target that rarely take risks on new artists, and to get the artists' songs played more on popular radio stations and video networks—the kinds of marketing actions that are commonplace for the major labels. Although borrowing Sony BMG's marketing power comes at a significant cost—half the profits—Octone is banking on sales to be elevated to such an extent that they will make up for the lost share of profits.

That is what seems to have happened with Maroon 5. Signed by Octone to a five-album deal in 2001, the category-blurring band entered the studio that same year. The resulting album, *Songs About Jane*, featured pop rhythms, classic soul melodies, searing guitars, a powerful rock undercurrent, and lead singer Adam Levine's expressive voice. The record was completed in February 2002 and released in the summer of that year. But generating radio airplay and sales proved far from easy. To remedy the situation, later in the summer of 2002, Octone organized a so-called branch tour that enabled invited radio station programmers and regional managers of record retailers to see the band perform, identified a number of retailers that received discounts and marketing support, and set up a tour schedule that ultimately lasted an almost unheard-of three years and involved opening shows for more established bands—it fought a "ground war," as one Octone executive put it. The strategy worked: in the spring of 2003, Maroon 5 fulfilled the uplift requirement.

Sony BMG then stepped in to fund all of the band's promotion, sales, and marketing activities and helped bring the band into more mainstream record stores, radio stations, and concert venues. From that moment forward, sales of the album took off. Helped by the marketing push, the record rapidly ascended the charts—domestically and internationally. At the height of its success, in December 2004, *Songs About Jane* sold well over 100,000 copies in a single week. It also yielded four hit singles, including *This Love* and *She Will Be Loved*, which together topped the charts for ten weeks in 2004. The album ultimately achieved quadruple platinum status in the United States, and reached gold or platinum status in over thirty-five countries.

The partnership wasn't just worthwhile to Octone; Sony BMG benefited, too. For them, the partnership reduced risk. "The dollars spent by Octone, prior to uplift, are the riskiest in the project," Diener said. "Those spent by Sony BMG at the moment of the uplift are some of the surest dollars spent in the music business." In the early stages of an act's career, it's difficult to know how the group's music will be received in the marketplace. By the time Sony BMG enters the picture, the band has already shown its ability to sell records. This is market feedback a label executive can rely on, thus making any further investments in the band safer than those in any untested new act. The lowered risk comes not just from the level of sales achieved; it is also the result of having a base of dedicated fans, name recognition, and greater sophistication about how to handle the media. "By the time of the uplift, Sony BMG can be confident that our artists have done two hundred photo shoots and two hundred interviews, and know how to tell their story to the press. They also have improved a great deal as performers and know how to connect with an audience either in a large concert hall or in a more intimate venue such as a club," Boxenbaum explained.

Are these gains worth the trouble for Sony BMG? Could a major label not establish one or more separate divisions that function much like Octone does, each being responsible for a small roster of artists, so as to avoid having to share half of the upside of an uplifted artist? That surely is a possibility. But fully merging the cultures of a major label and a smaller one can prove challenging, and managing the costs of such "R&D divisions" can be tricky— Sony BMG would have to have a high rate of success in developing and nurturing artists in order for this strategy to be effective. A partnership like the one with Octone encourages Sony BMG to be more disciplined in making development and marketing investments: Octone's efforts allow Sony BMG to pick its battles.

The worth of Octone's model to major labels became apparent in early 2007, when Universal Music Group's Jimmy Iovine proposed to buy out Sony BMG's share in the joint venture and so bring Octone over to Universal. The offer established Octone's valuation at approximately $70 million. Diener's team accepted the proposal and soon relaunched their label as A&M/Octone under the Universal banner.

Lacking the necessary resources to support a product on the verge of taking off is a key problem for many smaller content producers. But there's an issue they struggle with far more often that could ultimately prove more costly—that of not knowing when it is wise to stop investing in a product that is *not* quite catching on. Octone was experiencing that problem firsthand with its third act, Michael Tolcher.

An artist who hailed from Lovejoy, Georgia, Tolcher was in the midst of a string of cross-country gigs in clubs, bars, coffeehouses, and parties when Octone's executives discovered him in July 2002. They liked what they heard of a subsequent demo recording but still found him to be a little unpolished. "Some bands are very slick from the get-go and they have a lot of experience with production equipment and studio boards, but Michael was different," Boxenbaum recalled. "We didn't want to rush out a commercial recording before he was ready." Octone sought to strengthen Tolcher's fan base by arranging opening shows for such established artists as

Crosby, Stills and Nash, Sister Hazel, and Everclear, and by creating opportunities to play in small clubs and bars.

Tolcher's time on the road inspired many of the songs on his
first full album, *I Am*, which was released in May 2004. By 2006,
Tolcher was back on the road, touring extensively and accompanying Michelle Branch, Maroon 5, Gavin DeGraw, and numerous
other acts. He also made television appearances on *Jimmy Kimmel*,
Last Call with Carson Daly, and several network morning shows.
Tolcher's single, *Mission Responsible*, received some airplay on the
radio but the attention proved short-lived. By early 2007, *I Am* had
sold a total of a little less than one hundred thousand copies, a
lackluster performance given that he had been uplifted after the
album achieved seventy-five thousand in cumulative sales. Worse,
Octone's losses on the artist now totaled around $800,000—and
they were increasing every day.

Octone's predicament with Tolcher illustrates the difficulty in
knowing when to stop investing in a product or artist launched
using grassroots techniques. That's the critical issue with such
limited releases: success could be just around the corner, in which
case investing more seems the right thing to do, as it was with Maroon 5. But it is also possible that success may never come, in which
case each additional dollar spent is a waste. Because the signals
coming back from the market are noisy at best, it is virtually impossible to determine the right course of action. Boxenbaum, with
all his experience in the music industry, realizes this all too well:
"The great artists and the bad artists are easy—it is the good artists that can kill you. With the great artists you just keep putting
fuel in their tank. With the bad artists, you realize your mistake
quickly and cut your losses. It is the good artists that bankrupt you
because they are good enough to make you think they are about to
turn the corner and therefore keep you spending."

Octone—by then A&M/Octone—ultimately decided to give
the artist one last push. The label released a new single, supported
by heavy online and video promotions. However, the efforts did
not generate the market response the executives hoped for, and in

2008 Tolcher was released from his contract. Knowing when to pull the plug on an investment, Diener and Boxenbaum have found out, can sometimes be the most critical decision of all. This is especially important in the entertainment business, where the odds of success for any given product are so low.

Fortunately, the label's blockbuster act Maroon 5 fared much better. Relying on Universal's distribution and marketing resources, A&M/Octone released the group's second album, *It Won't Be Soon Before Long*, in the spring of 2007. Featuring a duet with pop star Rihanna, the album debuted at number one on the Billboard album chart and went on to sell over four million units worldwide, earning the band two more Grammy Awards. The band's third album, *Hands All Over*, got off to a more modest start, but received a huge boost from the success of its fourth single, *Moves Like Jagger*, which became the ninth best-selling digital single of 2011 with worldwide sales of seven million copies. Lead singer Adam Levine's turn as a star judge on NBC's *The Voice* further propelled the band—and its appropriately named fourth album, *Overexposed*, released in 2012—into the mainstream market.

Meanwhile, Diener and his colleagues continued doing what they do best: helping a select roster of new artists find an audience. And thanks to their partnership with Universal, the A&M/Octone executives can be confident that they can ramp up quickly the moment they strike gold.

Chapter Three

INVESTING IN SUPERSTARS

n June 2009, Florentino Pérez, president of renowned Spanish soccer club Real Madrid, finally got his wish—and so did the object of his desire, the reigning world player of the year, Cristiano Ronaldo. Completing what Pérez described as a "dream move," Real Madrid purchased the twenty-four-year-old Ronaldo for a record transfer fee of $125 million, to be paid to his previous club, Manchester United, and the promise of a rumored annual salary of more than $10 million. Earlier that month, the Madrid club had acquired Brazilian midfielder Kaká for a lower but still jaw-dropping amount—$92 million—from AC Milan. But Ronaldo, who had racked up an impressive tally of well over one hundred goals in nearly three hundred games for Manchester United, had long been Pérez's top target.

The recruitment of Ronaldo was in many respects a return to what Pérez had termed his *Galácticos* strategy, a forceful effort to attract some of the world's biggest stars to his club. Galacticism reached its peak when twenty-eight-year-old David Beckham, one of the sport's towering names, was added to an already star-studded team that consisted of the Brazilians Roberto Carlos and Ronaldo Luís Nazário de Lima (commonly known simply as Ronaldo and not to be confused with Cristiano Ronaldo, the Portuguese soccer star), Frenchman Zinedine Zidane, Portuguese Luís Figo, and the Spanish forward Raúl and goalkeeper Iker Casillas. Over a thousand journalists attended the press conference during which Beckham was presented to the public as a new Madrid player. And the event was held at eleven a.m. local time to make the evening news broadcasts in Asia where Beckham was particularly popular. (The UK's *Sun* newspaper, meanwhile, set up a help line for distraught British fans.) The star-focused strategy was so ingrained in the club's thinking that in business presentations Real Madrid's executives named individual seasons after the Galáctico the club had landed that year: Zidane in 2001, Ronaldo in 2002, and Beckham in 2003.

Pérez's approach had brought Real Madrid a great windfall off the field, triggering strong growth each year and turning the soccer club into the world's biggest as measured by revenues. Founded in 1902 and proclaimed royal (*"real"*) in 1920 by the king of Spain, the club attracted eighty thousand enthusiastic supporters to each of its home games in the Bernabéu Stadium, and had an estimated one hundred million fans around the globe. Real Madrid had risen to global prominence in the 1950s when it won the first five European Cup competitions. But the club's fortunes declined in the 1970s, a slump that lasted two decades. In 2000, Pérez ran for club president on a campaign promise to woo superstar Figo from arch-rival FC Barcelona. (Real Madrid is owned by its members, and its president is elected by those members to a four-year term.) Once in office, Pérez not only made good on his promise, but also worked with his team of professional managers to turn around the club's precarious financial situation and extend its brand around the world. In Pérez's second season, Real Madrid captured a victory in the European Champions League—by then the most prominent international competition for club teams. Madrid's on-field performance in subsequent seasons, however, largely failed to live up to the huge expectations.

Prompted by an unprecedented three seasons without any trophy, the Galácticos strategy was scaled back under Ramón Calderón, elected as president at the start of the 2006–2007 season. "We don't necessarily need players who do well with the media—we need players who are good for the team," Calderón told me at the time, in an obvious dig at the Galácticos strategy in general and Beckham in particular. "We put less emphasis on the stars, and more on the team as a whole." Another club executive I spoke with agreed: "The model worked very well initially—we have become the standard in international football. But we suffered on the sports side." The director of Calderón's cabinet offered an especially acute analysis: "The true art of managing a football club is knowing how to strike the balance between business and sports. In the Florentino Pérez years, we were too focused on marketing, and not enough on sports. Pérez's idea of bringing in the most talented players and emphasizing the 'show business' aspect of soccer was very innovative. It made it a true spectacle. However, it was extremely difficult to manage: the accumulation of stars produced excesses that we could not correct. It led to big egos, commitments we had to make to our stars, and jealousy among players who were not ready to share the spotlight. So we try to balance that more now."

But Calderón could not see his "Beyond the Galácticos" strategy through; he was forced to resign in 2009 following allegations of rigging votes for a budget proposal. Within months, Pérez was back in the saddle. And with the acquisition of Cristiano Ronaldo, one of Pérez's first major moves, it appeared that Galacticism was back with a vengeance. Now that the returning president had his second chance, friends and foes alike wondered whether Pérez's investments in global superstar players would continue to pay off—both on and off the field—even as the competition for talent was getting more intense.

The key question here—does betting on A-list talent make sense?—goes to the core of how a wide range of entertainment companies operate, and is crucial to their blockbuster strategies. Granted, professional soccer clubs are far from regular businesses, especially those that, like Real Madrid, are member-owned and led by an elected president. But that does not mean that the challenges confronting soccer clubs when recruiting and managing talent are different from those experienced by other entertainment businesses. In fact, we can learn a lot about effective talent strategies from soccer clubs, especially from European teams that have relatively few regulations to interfere with free market principles. (Their American counterparts in soccer, football, basketball, and baseball are all characterized by a redistribution of wealth and talent that rewards underperforming teams in the hopes of fostering a healthy dose of competition on the field.) European soccer clubs live and die by the same kinds of market economies that affect businesses in many other sectors of the entertainment industry: even within the premier European leagues, clubs can differ greatly in their wealth and prestige, and therefore in their ability to afford superstar talent.

Real Madrid, now one of the world's largest franchises in all of sports, has put a huge bet down on its strategy of signing superstars. Its approach is akin to—and in fact was inspired by—film studios, television networks, and other media businesses that invest enormous sums in A-list talent. "We began to think of ourselves as content providers," said one executive as he reflected on Pérez's first term. Another executive, making a direct comparison to the film business, added: "The players and the games—that is the content. The 'movie' we are selling is worth more if, say, Tom Cruise is in the lead." To understand successful models of content exploitation, club executives looked closely at how Disney's movie studio commercialized its biggest hits. "To transform Real Madrid we went partly against what experts were used to," explained one of Pérez's close confidants. "Soccer is over 100 years old, and it takes a while to change the rules of the game."

Evaluating the wisdom of Pérez's approach—and assessing the superstar strategy more generally—requires that we understand a couple of important features of the market for creative talent in which content producers like Real Madrid compete. First, the few performers and other creative workers who have risen to the highest level in their field (professional athletes, A-list movie stars, best-selling authors, and Grammy-winning pop singers) often earn extremely high fees while a much larger group of also-rans in these sectors barely earn a living. The differences between the "haves" and the "have nots" can be staggering. Cristiano Ronaldo's eight-figure annual salary is one case in point. Paychecks in Hollywood also illustrate the disparity vividly. In 1995, Jim Carrey famously became the first star to command $20 million for his role in *The Cable Guy* as the dementedly overeager cable repairman. Tom Cruise reportedly earned more than $70 million—a 22 percent share of total box-office receipts—for *Mission: Impossible*, and another $92 million for its sequel. Most members of the Screen Actors Guild, the union to which virtually all working film actors belong, are less fortunate: two-thirds make less than $1,000 a year (yes, a *year*).

Even within teams of entertainers, athletes, and other creative workers, the differences can be stark. When David Beckham joined the Los Angeles Galaxy after leaving Real Madrid in 2007, he signed on for a guaranteed salary of over $100,000 per *week* (not counting any bonuses), while some of his new teammates earned less than $20,000 per year. Additional sources of income tilt the balance even more in favor of a select few stars. In sports such as soccer, basketball, and tennis, for instance, the lion's share of the industry's endorsement revenues goes to the small group of players at the very top.

A second characteristic of markets for creative talent is that the level of earnings for superstars is mostly determined by their relative performance—in other words, how they stack up against their peers—as opposed to some absolute yardstick. This feature is perhaps most noticeable in the world of sports. Consider Rafael Nadal, by all accounts an excellent tennis player. If it were not for Roger Federer, who for years stood in the way of Nadal being the top-ranked tennis player in the world, Nadal could have earned millions more in prize money and endorsements. What mattered was not the quality of Nadal's tennis per se, but the quality of his performance relative to that of Federer (and, in more recent years, to that of Novak Djokovic).

The position of quarterback for the New England Patriots

provides another example. When Tom Brady, the team's star, tore his knee ligaments in 2008, Matt Cassel, Brady's backup, saw his earnings increase sharply. Although Cassel should be commended for making the most of the opportunity—in 2009, he landed a six-year, $63 million contract with the Kansas City Chiefs—there is little reason to believe he would have escaped obscurity if it weren't for Brady's temporary absence. Brady himself is well acquainted with the difference between the "haves" and the "have nots": without an injury in the 2001 season to Drew Bledsoe, who was the Patriots' quarterback when Brady was drafted with the 199th pick, Brady may never have gotten his chance to establish himself as the franchise quarterback and reap all the rewards that go along with being on top.

Markets with these characteristics are "winner-take-all markets," a term popularized by the economists Robert Frank and Philip Cook. But as they explain in their book on the topic, a more fitting term might be "those-near-the-top-get-a-disproportionate-share markets." In these markets, the efforts of only a small number of people at the very top—the superstars—largely drive the value of what is produced. Executives like Pérez are intimately aware of the winner-take-all structure—they know they have to pay handsomely to attract stars like Cristiano Ronaldo. But, the question remains, why? Why do these winner-take-all markets for creative talent emerge and persist, despite the seemingly endless supply of people willing to work for next to nothing, hoping for their big break in sports or show business? It is one thing when a single individual is primarily responsible for the product—a solo recording artist, a book author, or a painter—but when entire teams of creative workers come together to produce an entertainment product such as a soccer game or a movie, why would anyone consider paying tens of millions of dollars for an athlete like Ronaldo or an actor like Tom Cruise?

A first (and admittedly obvious) observation is that, even when goods are produced in teams, one creative person can have a profound impact on the success of those goods. Ronaldo can do things with a soccer ball that most amateur—and indeed most professional—players can only dream of. He is faster and more skilled, and he has a greater knack for scoring from impossible positions than all but a handful of people on the planet. His assists and goals make him tremendously valuable to Real Madrid, since his actions often translate into victories that, especially in the European Champions League, can yield substantial prize money. But pure talent is not the only reason why Ronaldo is worth so much. A single creative worker's impact on success is seldom easy to establish, especially outside sports: it is much less clear, for instance, that there are no actors who can match Tom Cruise's, Mark Wahlberg's, or Channing Tatum's acting chops.

This point leads to the second reason why a select few at the top earn such high rewards: they have become what marketers call "product attributes." Many of today's biggest stars are brands in their own right, and they can often be a deciding factor in a consumer's decision-making process. The mere involvement of a certain actor, musician, or sports figure can affect a consumer's choice to buy or pay attention. Ronaldo's actions make people want to watch him—when he is sprinting down the field with the ball, something is bound to happen—which converts to ticket sales for the club or eyeballs for advertisers. Likewise, at the height of Cruise's popularity, hordes of fans would take a gamble on his movies because they had come to expect that the films he starred in would be entertaining. Superstars can also turn a consumer into a fan of the overarching brand. When the LA Galaxy offered David Beckham a very lucrative contract to play for their franchise, the club's executives were hoping that Beckham would not only lift interest in their team, draw new fans, and increase the sale of jerseys and other branded merchandise, but also raise the profile of Major League Soccer as a whole. Creative talent not only makes the product—in many ways, they *are* the product.

Many consumers are perfectly happy to know only a few professional athletes, musicians, movie stars, and other performers by name, just as consumers will typically not care to remember more than a small set of brands of other consumer goods, be they detergents, beverages, or toothpaste. Die-hard fans of a particular form of entertainment may find it difficult to believe, but most consumers simply do not have the energy or time to focus on any but the top performers. And since people are drawn to winners, the best (or even just the most visible) performers enjoy a substantial advantage over their teammates and rivals.

The winner-take-all effect is especially strong in entertainment markets because performances of the most sought-after creative talent can be reproduced at low additional costs. Through media such as books, film, video, television, and recorded music, consumers have easy access to the world's most talented creative workers. The best performers can literally be everywhere at once, especially in the digital age. And since it costs no more to print or stream, say, a record by a superstar like Jay-Z than a record by an unknown rap artist that most people will value less, A-list talent almost inevitably dominates the market. No wonder, then, that the biggest stars in entertainment usually wield a great deal of power at the negotiation table.

To some extent, the pain for entertainment businesses is self-inflicted. Those responsible for casting actors, signing musicians, selecting athletes for endorsements, and recruiting talent for other activities are often tempted to play it safe by hiring an A-list performer even if they do not believe that person is necessary for the task at hand. They hire "a name" for fear of making a mistake. It is difficult to blame them: can we really fault the manager of a world-renowned soccer club for recruiting a proven star player rather than a talented up-and-comer, or a casting director who is staffing a $100 million movie for relying on an A-list actor with a strong track record rather than someone less established? Even if hiring the more obscure actor would involve a much lower fee, the fear of disappointment looms large: after all, if the film stumbles at the box office, it is easy to point fingers at the person who "failed to hire the best." And after a losing season it takes a brave soccer-club president to say, "We'll try again next year with the exact same team," even if losing came down to a last-minute fluke goal. Most executives will feel they need to act—and their reflex often is to bet on established stars and proven winners.

A reliance on popularity also characterizes the industry players involved in marketing a product; they, too, are swayed by the presence of stars. Studios will find it easier, for instance, to sell movie exhibitors on dedicating a large number of screens to the opening of a film that stars Will Smith or Leonardo DiCaprio as opposed to one that has a no-name actor in the lead. And because screen intensity is in turn such a critical driver of revenues, the response from exhibitors helps reinforce the idea that Smith and DiCaprio are bankable actors. Similarly, the attention that advertisers lavish on David Beckham—fashion retailer H&M's 2012 Super Bowl spot featured him in nothing more than his underwear and tattoos— keeps the soccer star in the spotlight, solidifies his brand, and drives up his endorsement fee. Even a performer's personal life can come into play. Beckham's much-buzzed-about relationship with a former Spice Girl first made him a household name among non-soccer fans in Britain, and what initially may have been a subtle advantage for Beckham compared to other top-notch professional soccer players ultimately translated into a highly lucrative career built around the Beckham brand. Often, the more performers are in the public eye, the more they *become* stars.

In most instances, winner-take-all markets emerge because a large number of buyers, be they music aficionados or book consumers, are willing to pay a little more for (or pay more attention to) the services of one performer over another. In some cases, however, the concentration of rewards among top performers is fueled by a small number of wealthy buyers who are intensely interested in a particular winner. Their money can instantly propel talent to the top level of compensation in their profession. Presidents of rich European soccer clubs fit this description: a promise to their fans to sign a certain star player can lead to excessively high transfer sums. When Pérez vowed to bring Figo to Real Madrid if he were elected, he gave Figo's then club, FC Barcelona, every reason to start salivating over the money that would come its way.

Clearly, then, some of the same dynamics that drive blockbuster bets on creative content also foster investments in superstars. For a host of reasons, it is difficult for entertainment executives to forgo relying on A-list talent—and the more it is obvious to everyone that a certain individual is capable of amazing feats or otherwise likely to capture attention, the more those seeking to recruit that person will find themselves in the kinds of bidding wars that also arise for promising manuscripts and other properties. This phenomenon will likely become even more pronounced over time.

Ever wider product releases and growing international markets in film, television, and other media are driving an increased focus on a select few superstars with global appeal. In sports, the expanding role of television and other media as additional sources of revenue (as opposed to ticket sales only) has significantly increased the income earned by the top-performing teams—and sometimes just the most star-studded teams. The growth in endorsement income, which for superstars now often surpasses salaries or winnings, also adds to the greater concentration. Few players beyond those at the very top receive significant revenues from such endorsements. Even legal decisions (such as the introduction of free agency in European soccer) and wider social changes (such as the public's ever-increasing fascination with celebrities) contribute to the winner-take-all effect. And as the revenues generated by the biggest hits rise, so do the payoffs for the top creative workers behind those hits.

For anyone leading an entertainment business, these are challenging conditions. How can executives best invest in and manage creative talent in markets dominated by a small number of superstars? The truth is that few entertainment producers nowadays can build successful, long-lasting businesses without having a strategy that plays to the importance of superstars; there is simply no way to ignore the dominant role that A-list talent plays in every sector of the entertainment economy. Even so, there is a wide spectrum of possible talent strategies.

Real Madrid is a textbook example of a content producer that has chosen to focus on acquiring stars at the peak of their ability—and therefore negotiating power—rather than, say, developing talent from a young age. I call this the "superstar-acquisition" model. "We are buyers more than sellers," is how one Madrid executive described the approach: in each season since 2000, the team has spent significantly more on acquiring players than it has made from selling players to other clubs. For example, in the 2009–2010 season, the club spent a staggering $370 million on player acquisitions and made only $125 million selling players, leading to a loss on player dealings of nearly $250 million.

Pérez pursued the strategy from the moment he arrived: he personally secured a loan of over $70 million to finance Figo's transfer, and Real Madrid used the gains from the sale of the club's former training pitch to acquire other Galácticos in subsequent years. Pérez's hope was that those acquisitions would set in motion a self-reinforcing trend (or, as business consultants say, a "virtuous cycle") in which those stars would not only improve results on the field, but also attract new fans and increase exposure for the club among sponsors and advertisers, thus helping to build the brand as one of the world's greatest clubs. And to Pérez's credit, that is what happened. Real Madrid's greater brand value subsequently drove a variety of revenue streams, including ticket sales, television rights, sponsorship income, and merchandising—which in turn gave the club the resources to recruit more superstars. The central idea behind this approach was that, as one club executive put it, "the best players pay for themselves."

The link with a blockbuster strategy is obvious: the bigger a product's potential audience and the more revenue windows that can be exploited, the more a company can justify large investments in the product—in this case in the players on the field. In the mid-twentieth century, Real Madrid relied on a simpler mechanism to afford the best players: increasing the size of its stadium. President Bernabéu, chosen as the club's president in 1943, built what was then Spain's largest coliseum, capable of seating seventy-five thousand spectators and financed with bonds sold to fans. By building what was essentially the biggest "distribution channel" for the game of soccer—the in-stadium experience, since in those days there were no mass media such as television—Madrid put itself in a position to invest in the most sought-after players. By the early 2000s, the club's strategy had evolved to include a multitude of channels, from the live game inside the stadium to media such as broadcast television, Real Madrid's own television station, online channels, the club's own web site, and a set of club-branded stores. Madrid built an entire marketing infrastructure designed to exploit the club's core content. The club even insisted that star players hand over half of their income from personal image rights.

A breakdown of Real Madrid's revenue figures illustrates just how much the focus on superstars fueled the soccer club's revenues in the past decade. Whereas the club generated around $125 million in revenues in the 2000–2001 season, Pérez's first in office, revenues were up to $355 million at the end of the 2005–2006 season, the last in his first term. Sponsorship, merchandising, and other marketing income was the fastest-growing revenue stream in this period, increasing from $35 million to $140 million—more so than broadcast revenues, match-day revenues, and, a distant fourth, prize money from international competitions. By the 2004–2005 season, Real Madrid had become the world's top-ranked club when measured by revenues, overtaking Manchester United, Juventus, and AC Milan. By the time Cristiano Ronaldo had completed his first season with the club in 2010, total revenues had risen to over $600 million. In 2012, Real Madrid still held on to its number one spot.

Individual stars can drive marketing revenues to a remarkable degree. During the weekend of the Beckham press conference in 2003, for instance, Real Madrid sold some 350,000 jerseys in Britain alone at an average price of $80—that's nearly $30 million in merchandising revenues in a matter of days. A month later, Real Madrid capitalized on Beckham's popularity in Asia with a seventeen-day tour through China, Hong Kong, Thailand, and Japan, netting the club close to $10 million. Almost overnight, Beckham's popularity with fans across Asia became a big asset for the club—even if some of those fans were less interested in his soccer prowess than his looks and celebrity status.

If there is one key lesson Real Madrid's ascendancy to the top of the "football money league" teaches us, it is that a focus on super-stars can help insulate a content producer from losses due to a less-than-stellar performance on the field of play. In theory, recruiting star players should help lift a soccer club's trophy count, which would in turn mean a prize money bonanza; the 2011 winner of the European Champions League, for example, pocketed $70 mil-lion. But even if superstars fail to deliver trophies, revenues do not have to suffer: although Real Madrid has not won a Champi-ons League trophy since 2002 and has not had a particularly good record on the field more generally, the club still rose to the top of the revenue rankings and stayed there.

Having a stable source of income is particularly important when the difference between winning and losing is so slim. In Beckham's last season for the club—when he won his first league title with Real Madrid—the team truly lived on the edge, salvag-ing three of its last four games in the ninetieth (and final) minute, while its main rival FC Barcelona dropped points by conceding final-minute goals. Sometimes luck can make all the difference, and without A-list talent to drive up marketing revenues, the fi-nancial results of a soccer club—or any other type of entertain-ment business—can fluctuate wildly.

Much like Real Madrid, the major Hollywood studios also rely on a superstar-acquisition model. Large studios prefer to bet on estab-lished stars, ideally those who are thought to have broad audience appeal and have a reputation for being "bankable"—meaning that they have played leading roles in films with high box-office grosses. "People really want to see Tom Cruise in *Mission: Impossible*," Alan Horn told me. "If you exchange Tom for his costar Jeremy Renner, and not have Tom, it will have a different appeal." When casting their biggest productions, television network executives take much the same approach. When Charlie Sheen had to bow out of the hit series *Two and a Half Men* after a drug-induced meltdown, the War-ner Bros. executives who produced the show did not spare any ex-pense in hiring his replacement, agreeing to pay Ashton Kutcher a reported $700,000 per episode.

Content producers often serve multiple customers: soccer clubs have fans and sponsors; television networks have viewers and advertisers; symphony orchestras and operas have patrons and donors. Superstar-acquisition models can create compelling benefits for fans, sponsors, and the talent itself. Many fans will delight in being able to see the world's best performers. Advertisers will be gratified to know that their brands are reaching global markets. And for the talent, being a member of a star-studded team can have substantial advantages. "The responsibility here is divided among multiple players," the Brazilian Ronaldo once explained. "Elsewhere it often rested entirely on my shoulders as the star of the team." Basketball superstar LeBron James knows a thing or two about that, too: his desire to play alongside fellow stars Dwyane Wade and Chris Bosh was a big reason why he left the Cleveland Cavaliers for the Miami Heat. Real Madrid's former general manager for sports, Jorge Valdano, once a player himself, made a similar point. "The greatest players aspire to play with Real Madrid, with great talents like them. Players who join us know that they are taking a step forward, in prestige and in satisfaction as a soccer player."

At the same time, though, a strategy of acquiring superstars has important downsides. For one thing, signing a popular performer often forces a content producer to perform a delicate balancing act. For Real Madrid, a new star player might attract global fans that alienate the existing fans. Real Madrid risks upsetting its loyal members if it caters too much to, say, Japanese schoolgirls crazy about Beckham or Ronaldo, or if it "stretches the brand too far" and is perceived as overexposed or overly commercial. Maintaining the support of the core (and mostly local) fans is critical even if they do not represent a growth market—after all, they help create the experience that millions of viewers around the world watch on television or consume through other media. "The fans are part of the show and are part of the brand," one Real Madrid executive pointed out.

A second potential problem is that a star player's brand might come to overshadow the club's brand, leading to a loss of control over the customer base. If Real Madrid attracts new fans by re-cruiting the world's biggest superstars, some of those fans may leave as soon as the stars do. The club's challenge, then, is to turn fans of players into fans of the club, which is far from easy. Third, bets on individual talent are inherently risky. In sports, the threat of a season-ending or even career-ending injury always looms, but injuries of superstars can have especially devastating effects. And fourth, forging a successful team from a set of stars often proves difficult—serious tensions in the locker room are widely thought to have doomed Real Madrid during Pérez's first term. Eager to avoid such problems when he returned as president, in 2010 Pérez recruited another star, coach José Mourinho, not afraid to call himself "The Special One." Mourinho is a lightning rod for attention, but a master at molding star players and big egos into a team.

The biggest problem with the superstar-acquisition model, of course, is the high cost of talent. Especially if the competition for stars increases, bidding wars ensue, thus putting pressure on the model. Real Madrid's executives experienced this firsthand: "Our competitors have seen what makes us so successful on the busi-ness side, and are catching up," one executive in Calderón's cabinet of advisers told me in 2007. "Like any content business, we depend on the availability of talent, and we can't always find or buy the next Zidane, the next Beckham, or another type of player that can become a Galáctico." The problem is exacerbated by wealthy club owners such as Chelsea FC's Roman Abramovich and Manchester City's Sheikh Mansour, who are not always mindful of their club's bottom line when poaching players. Their actions trigger higher player transfer fees and salaries across the board.

In part because of the escalating bidding wars for talent, Real Madrid itself is struggling with a sizable debt. But as long as the growth in revenues—powered by superstars—continues to out-pace the rising expenditures on those stars, as it appears to do for the club under Pérez, the superstar-acquisition model can help improve Real Madrid's balance sheet. One metric that soccer execu-tives watch closely is the percentage of revenues spent on personnel.

For Real Madrid, that figure was as much as 90 percent in Pérez's first years, when the club was pushing hard to find ways to grow. Since 2005, the figure has reportedly hovered under a healthy 50 percent. This doesn't mean the club isn't taking significant risks, but if it were to abandon its strategy of relying on stars now, Real Madrid's financial challenges would likely only increase.

The superstar-acquisition model is hardly the only possible approach to investing in talent. As it happens, the world of international soccer provides another model, one that has significant strengths of its own. In bustling Buenos Aires, we find a legendary club that, like Real Madrid, is owned by its members and among the most decorated sports teams in the world. But its business strategy could not be more different.

When British newspaper the *Observer* asked readers to vote on the "50 sporting things you must do before you die," the top spot was easily decided: watching Club Atlético Boca Juniors play its city rival River Plate at a stadium affectionately nicknamed La Bombonera (which translates to "the candy box" or "the chocolate box"). Gavin Hamilton, editor of *World Soccer* magazine, captured the sentiments of soccer lovers across the world when he wrote:

> The rivalry between Boca and River Plate is the most intense in Argentine football and, perhaps, in the whole of Latin America: the game is a riot of color, noise and energy. Buenos Aires has the highest concentration of football teams of any city in the world. River and Boca are the two leading clubs. Boca are originally from the dockland area so their support is traditionally more working class. River moved away from the area early on in the league's history to a more upmarket district, and they have a slightly more affluent fan base, hence their nickname, Los Millonarios. . . . On the day of the derby [the stadium] is packed with hard-core fans. . . . There is such passion for this match that it is unsurpassed anywhere in the world.

Juan Román Riquelme, one of Boca's former stars, agreed: "The field at La Bombonera literally moves on Sundays. It's an atmosphere you can't get anywhere in the world. . . . It is the only place I know in the world where fans sing the entire game and the stadium moves." Fans were fond of saying that the stadium did not just tremble under the weight of the supporters but that it beat like a heart.

Boca Juniors is the most popular club in soccer-mad Argentina. In a country with more than forty million inhabitants, only two out of ten Argentines consider themselves indifferent toward soccer. Of those who follow the sport, 40 percent call themselves fans of Boca. "We are too big a club for such a small country," then president Mauricio Macri told me in 2006. Its on-the-field record certainly was impressive: in the century since its founding by Italian immigrants in Buenos Aires's La Boca neighborhood in 1905, it had amassed twenty-two Argentine League championships and sixteen international titles—tying it for the record with Italy's AC Milan—including five Copa Libertadores (the South American equivalent of the European Champions League) and three Intercontinental Cups (the world championship for club teams). As a result, Boca was regularly included in worldwide rankings of top clubs. In January 2005, in fact, soccer's governing body, Fédération Internationale de Football Association (FIFA), voted Boca Juniors the world's best club, ahead of Manchester United.

Throughout its record-setting first century, the club developed dozens of star players. Boca's famed youth academy, La Cantera ("the quarry"), was a breeding ground for exceptional players. In each of the ten most recent seasons before 2006, an average of eight former youth players made their debut in Boca's first team. Many of those later moved to the richer European soccer leagues. Widely regarded as one of the world's best soccer players ever, Diego Armando Maradona started his career at Argentino Juniors but came to Boca Juniors in 1981. He later played in Europe for FC Barcelona, Napoli, and Sevilla, returning to Boca in 1995 until his retirement in 1997. Other former-youth-players-turned-superstars, such as Riquelme, Walter Samuel, and Carlos Tévez, began their careers at Boca and later moved to Europe.

Macri was elected president of Boca Juniors in 1996, and then re-elected four and eight years later. In November 2006, he announced that he would not be running for club president again, requested a leave of absence, and made clear his intentions to enter the race for mayor of the city of Buenos Aires. In his eleven years leading the club, Macri had made his presence felt: he increased Boca's net worth tenfold to over $120 million Argentine pesos (around $40 million in US dollars at the time) and almost tripled the club's annual revenues to just under $75 million pesos (about $25 million in US dollars). But despite strong performances on and off the field, Macri faced a constant array of challenges. Not only did he have to keep Boca afloat financially, he also had to satisfy the club's various constituencies, including its more than fifty thousand members, fifty million fans worldwide, players and coaching staff, and governing board.

In his last year at the helm, Macri faced a particularly tricky decision. He had received calls from several leading European clubs, all of which expressed an interest in Fernando Gago and Rodrigo Palacio, two young but prominent players who were considered instrumental to the team's bid for continued success in Argentina and abroad. FC Barcelona's president at the time, Joan Laporta, openly admitted that he was "gaga" over Gago, and he told Macri that he was determined to bring the twenty-year-old midfielder to Spain. But before Laporta could sign Gago, Real Madrid president Calderón swooped in with a $26 million offer. Gago himself jumped into the fray, telling the press that he preferred Madrid: "Between Real Madrid and Barcelona, I choose the white shirt," he said.

Laporta was also interested in Palacio, after seeing him play in the derby against River Plate. He offered $22 million for the twenty-four-year-old striker, but Palacio seemed far from in a hurry to move to Europe—"I'm comfortable here," he stated. Through his agent, however, he indicated that if he did stay at Boca Juniors, he now expected to receive a salary that would be substantially higher than that of his teammates.

Either offer was enough to wipe out the loss the club was expected to incur over the current fiscal year. "If we do not sell any players or generate more revenues in another way, we are bound to lose three million dollars over the year," commented Boca's general manager. With the pressure mounting and supporters demanding "titles, not money," Macri was well aware of the difficulty of the challenge. "Whatever we decide," he said, "there will be very unhappy constituents out there."

Should Boca Juniors sell one or more of its players? The answer, as heartbreaking as it may be to Boca's fans, is "yes." The club has no choice—Boca Juniors operates a "talent-development" model that thrives on player sales. Like Real Madrid, Boca is in the business of producing soccer games and "selling" those to fans and advertisers. But unlike Real Madrid, it is also in the business of developing players and selling those to richer clubs. Even a cursory look at Boca's finances reveals that it can only balance its books if it regularly sells its most talented players, often well before they reach the peak of their ability. Over the decade in which Macri was in charge, when the club was firing on all cylinders on the field and saw solid revenue growth as well, Boca would have reported a net loss of nearly $20 million if it had not sold any players. Instead, it earned a net income on player sales of $60 million, which comprised nearly a third of its total operating revenues. The truth is undeniable: Boca would be a perennial money loser if it did not sell at least one major player every year or two.

The same is true for most other clubs in Argentina, as well as in neighboring Brazil—another country known for having generated many world-class players—and indeed South America as a whole. While the continent's top clubs are a good match for their European counterparts on the field, much less money circulates in competitions in South America. Even though soccer is at least as popular a sport on the continent, its soccer market is worth only $2 billion, whereas Europe's is worth $17 billion.

Economic conditions are much less favorable in South America, and broadcast rights provide a good case in point. In 2006, the Argentine soccer competitions generated revenues of just over $30 million from television rights—"a small fraction of [the income from broadcast rights] in the main European markets," as Macri rightly pointed out—and less than a third of what Argentine clubs make from selling players. Boca Juniors and River Plate, the most popular clubs, each received one-eighth of the total broadcast revenues, but that still puts them at a huge disadvantage compared to top European clubs. Real Madrid alone made $90 million from selling broadcast rights that year—and that was just before the club signed a lucrative new deal that brought the annual revenues from broadcasting up to over $200 million.

Similarly, Brazil's soccer industry would quickly vanish without the sale of players. And this market, like so many others in the sports and entertainment worlds, has a winner-take-all structure: although hundreds of players are sold each year, as much as half of the total amount of transfer fees in 2006 came from one player, star forward Robinho, who moved from Santos to—you guessed it— Real Madrid. South American clubs are also at a significant disadvantage when it comes to international competitions. Prize money in the Copa Libertadores, for instance, is tiny compared to the huge windfall reaped by the top teams in the European Champions League.

No wonder, then, that Real Madrid was rumored to have offered Fernando Gago a salary of $3.5 million per year—fourteen times his salary at Boca. Confronted with such vast differences, Boca can do little to hang on to its players. "Transfers end up being a necessity for the clubs and for the players themselves," Boca's general manager told me. "At Boca, we can only pay one hundred thousand dollars per year to our young players, and five hundred thousand dollars to acclaimed stars. They can make ten times that kind of money at European clubs."

The same inequality profoundly affects other sectors of the entertainment economy. Smaller film and television producers often cannot compete with the larger studios when hiring popular actors, and the same issue torments small "indie" labels when they try to counter the bargaining power of the major record labels. The bigger point, though, is that the factors that cause the inequality are often largely outside the control of any individual company.

This is certainly the case in soccer: because of the wide gap between economic conditions in South America and those in Europe, clubs are inevitably dependent on the income from the "export" of players. It is difficult to envision a situation in which superstar players in their prime play in Argentina or Brazil. (The young Brazilian star Neymar seemed to be one player intent on bucking the trend, but even he could not keep declining offers from European clubs—he agreed to join FC Barcelona in June 2013.) With star players moving to Europe and transfer money flowing back to South America, a talent-development model seems the logical choice for a club like Boca Juniors.

As it often does, context dictates strategy. It is not a coincidence that the biggest media market in the world spawned Hollywood, the biggest magnet for film talent. Operating in a larger home market means that Hollywood studios can shoulder more expensive productions and more effectively compete with rivals in other countries—and get a head start on those rivals in the effort to build an international distribution infrastructure. Likewise, operating in a smaller home market puts Boca Juniors at a substantial disadvantage in the international competition for talent. What is perhaps most remarkable about Boca is that it has managed to compete with European clubs at all.

What is the secret to Boca Juniors' success? First, just like Real Madrid, Boca has found a branding model that, if all goes well, is self-reinforcing. The club identifies and attracts promising young soccer players, and it employs a much-touted system to develop these players into professionals. Ultimately, a select number of superstars are sold to richer clubs, mostly in Europe. The resulting resources are fed back into the club, and the cachet of having its players reach the top of their profession helps Boca build its brand as a world-class developer of talent, which in turn allows the club to repeat the cycle. If Boca continues to execute the model well, its effectiveness and reputation as a talent "factory" will get even stronger over time.

Second, Boca Juniors is extraordinarily well positioned to execute every stage of this talent-development strategy, from unearthing talented youngsters to showcasing them to potential buyers. Argentina's fascination with soccer assures Boca a large base of players to draw from, and the country's culture supports the attempt by gifted athletes to become professional soccer players. Because of Boca's enormous popularity, many young players are fans of the club, increasing the likelihood that, when given the chance, they will choose Boca Juniors over other clubs vying for their attention. As one young player put it to me when I visited La Cantera a few years ago, "We are Boca fans, and always dreamed of playing for Boca. It is what we live for."

Although soccer icon Maradona was not a product of Boca's youth division, he has become a symbol of the club's success. "The best soccer player of all time had to be a Boca man," declared Boca's centennial publication. Even when his active playing days were long behind him, Maradona remained a key figure at the club during Macri's tenure. He could often be seen hanging out of his private box at the stadium to cheer Boca on—and what young player would not be inspired by the idea of one the greatest stars of all time urging him on?

Once at the club, young players have excellent opportunities to succeed precisely because Boca is such a strong exporter of talent. The frequent sale of stars creates openings for new players; at the time Macri was weighing the possible sale of Gago and Palacio, eight of the twenty players on the roster had come up through the youth academy. At home matches, Boca Juniors' players are supported by one of the most enthusiastic fan groups in the world. The club's hard-line fans—known as "La Numero 12" (meaning "the twelfth player")—taunt opponents, creating an intimidating experience that gives the home team an undeniable advantage. Boca is also a mainstay in international competitions, which means that its players gain the experience of participating in highly competitive matches and also get more exposure among potential buying clubs. And Boca's world-famous crosstown rivalry with River Plate helps, too: FC Barcelona officials came to pursue Gago only after they accepted an invitation from River Plate to attend the derby.

Over the years, Boca's managers continued to make every effort to further strengthen the club's position as a talent factory for soccer superstars. Pledging to bring along new players in a more systematic way, Macri invested heavily in La Cantera, beefed up the club's scouting network, and opened a youth clubhouse next to Boca's first team's training ground. By 2006, the club hosted 120 young players between the ages of twelve and sixteen, the large majority of whom lived in its dormitories for free. All the players were initially enrolled in a ten-month program; those that performed up to expectations were invited to re-enroll. Beyond their training on the field, education was a constant focus: players were required to go to school and received supplementary classes in mathematics and English. "Only three out of every thirty players make it all the way to the top," one of La Cantera's coaches said. "Psychological balance is of critical importance for players who aspire to become international stars. We need to prepare them for the pressures they will encounter when they evolve in their careers. Education plays a key role in that character formation."

Talent-development models can be found throughout the entertainment industry. *Saturday Night Live*, NBC's long-running weekly late-night television program, is to aspiring comedians what Boca Juniors is to those seeking a career as professional soccer players. Joining the cast of *SNL* is often a stepping-stone to a career in television and film; on the long list of actors and actresses who got their start on the show are Jimmy Fallon, Will Ferrell, Tina Fey, Eddie Murphy, Bill Murray, Conan O'Brien, Amy Poehler, and Chris Rock. Lorne Michaels, the show's executive producer, is known for having a keen eye for talent. His decisions can make or break careers. "Lorne has had a seismic impact on comedy," Conan O'Brien once told the *Hollywood Reporter*, "but in my opinion his legacy, very simply, is that he has good taste." Michaels elevated O'Brien from *SNL* writer to host of his own late-night venture in 1993. (Michaels's deal with NBC gave him the right to name the host.) Another star who credits Michaels with her big break is

Tina Fey, who after a long stint on *SNL* wrote and produced the NBC sitcom *30 Rock* (a show about the network) and starred in several films. As Fey put it to an interviewer, "He put me on television, and no one else would have done that." The success of *SNL* and its cast members has made Michaels a central figure at NBC Universal.

Disney's cable network the Disney Channel is another striking example of a creative-talent factory. *The Mickey Mouse Club*, the program that kicked off the Disney Channel's first broadcast in 1983, introduced stars such as Christina Aguilera, Ryan Gosling, Shia LaBeouf, Britney Spears, and Justin Timberlake. In more recent years, the channel has given teen stars Miley Cyrus, Zac Efron, Vanessa Hudgens, and Selena Gomez their first shot at fame. Many children hoping for a career in show business now dream of being chosen as a cast member on a Disney Channel show, and the channel holds open auditions every year, attracting thousands of hopefuls. All those contenders, in fact, have spawned a cottage industry that feeds off their dream: casting agents masquerading as talent feeders for Disney, events targeted at kids that promise to increase their chances of getting cast, and acting schools led by actors with "the slimmest of Disney credentials," as a reporter documenting some of the more questionable practices around the casting process put it. Every time a young actor is fashioned into a star by the channel, and every time a former child star makes it big in a subsequent move in the world of television, movies, music, or Broadway, the Disney Channel brand as an originator of such talent becomes stronger, giving it a greater pull with the newest crop of hopefuls.

Smart managers will find ways to capitalize on their companies' talent-development prowess and benefit from whatever next steps their talent chooses to take—indeed, this is the only way to sustain such development efforts over a long period. Disney's executives, for instance, see the Disney Channel as a launching pad for its stars' careers within the wider organization. It is no accident that Walt Disney Pictures produced and released a successful concert movie, *Hannah Montana & Miley Cyrus: Best of Both Worlds Con-*

cert, based on Miley Cyrus and the character she plays on her show. Similarly, Cyrus was for a time one of the biggest stars on the roster of Disney's record label, Hollywood Records. (She left the label in the summer of 2012.) Because Disney's executives have an inside look at which children show star potential and can collect a wealth of information on how their young actors work (whether, say, they can memorize hundreds of lines or deal with an especially challenging dance number), they can move faster and more confidently when signing them up for other projects. And because Disney executives control which shows the young actors are cast in—or even which formats are developed for certain actors—the executives are in a unique position to mold those child stars' brands.

In much the same way, Lorne Michaels and NBC have over the years found ways to benefit from *SNL's* function as a stepping-stone for comedians. First-year cast members are asked to sign strict contracts that effectively allow Michaels and NBC to shape and make money from the next steps in their careers. Precise details regarding these agreements are hard to come by, but the journalist Peter Bogdanovich disclosed some years ago that anyone joining the *SNL* cast for the 1999–2000 season had to sign a contract with NBC that could tie them to the network for as long as twelve years. Many of the terms shocked agents and their clients—as one agent said: "It's like *SNL* puts a gun to your head and says, 'You're auditioning. Sign this!' "

Under the contract described by Bogdanovich, NBC could take *SNL* cast members off the show any time after their second year on the program and put them in an NBC sitcom. A cast member had the option of saying no to the first two shows proposed by NBC but had to accept the third. And NBC dictated the length of the sitcom contract, which could run as long as six years. The contract with *SNL* even gave NBC and Michaels considerable say in the cast members' film careers: SNL Films (a production company co-owned by Paramount Pictures), NBC, and Michaels had a three-movie option that would pay the star a set $75,000 for the first film, $150,000 for the second, and $300,000 for the third. By offering these amounts, NBC could potentially prevent a cast member from earning a multimillion-dollar salary on a film for another studio.

The goal for NBC and Michaels is evident: they wanted to make sure their efforts to turn up-and-coming comedians into household names would not go unrewarded, and to make it difficult for rival media companies to steal them away. "What I was trying to do was to have some ability to keep unknown talent—and they are all unknown before *Saturday Night Live*—on the network after *we* make them stars," Garth Ancier, a former NBC executive who crafted the *SNL* contracts for the 1999–2000 season, told me. "We wanted to prevent a situation in which they would become very well known comedians on our air, but then would leave to do something else." Another executive involved in the contract negotiations described new cast members as "the not-ready-for-primetime players. . . . These are people who are just starting out." He added: "I challenge you to name a network, much less a show, that has created this many stars, ever."

Ancier admitted that the contracts offered that year met a good deal of resistance. "The agents and managers didn't like the new contracts because they limited their ability to use [the show] to make their clients famous and then use that fame to mine other offerings and leave the *Saturday Night Live*/Lorne Michaels family." Even so, Ancier told me, all but one of the hopefuls signed the contract for the 1999–2000 season, and the one holdout was not allowed to audition for the show.

A cursory look at the projects of *Saturday Night Live*'s former cast members suggests that Lorne Michaels's grip on the *SNL* performers continues to this day. His name appears as executive producer on *Late Night with Jimmy Fallon, 30 Rock*, and several other projects. "I think Michaels has a better hold on the talent now than in the past—otherwise you would not see *30 Rock* and all those other shows that are starring *SNL* talent popping up on NBC," Ancier noted.

Contracts that lock new talent into long-term deals are now standard across the television industry. "If we are casting any primetime television show, actors—before they can even audition—have to sign a contract that gives the network the option to secure their services for a total of seven years at a specified rate," said Ancier, who now serves as an adviser to several broadcast and cable networks. "We won't let them read until they have signed onto that deal." When studios or networks want even more control, they push for so-called talent-holding deals. Under these contracts, the studio pays an actor a certain amount of money, in return for which the actor, for a specified number of years, agrees to sign on to projects the studio brings to the actor. The actor can turn down a certain number of projects (usually two), but he or she has to accept the next one. "We would allocate six million dollars a year to a talent-holding-deal fund," said Ancier about his tenure at NBC. "If we thought people were interesting and about to star in television shows, we would offer them a deal—those with leading roles in shows. One of the people we did that with when I was at NBC was [comedian] Steve Carell. It was a very effective way of grooming talent, by making an investment before anyone really knew who they were."

In the music business, record companies have also restructured contracts with artists so that the labels receive a higher return on their talent-development efforts. A "360" or "all-rights" deal gives the record company a share of all of an act's revenue streams, including recorded music, concert-ticket sales, merchandising, commercial licensing, sponsorships, and endorsements. These deals mark quite a departure from a traditional record contract, which grants record labels a share of recorded-music sales only. Lady Gaga, for one, agreed to an all-rights deal with Interscope in 2007—an agreement the label will never regret, given her spectacular success. But Troy Carter also acknowledged the merits of the deal: "Would she be in a position to play in front of 20,000 people a night if the record company had not put up the marketing dollars?" he asked rhetorically. A&M/Octone's executives are fans of the new contract, too, since it fits their artist-development strategy. Diener sees artists not just as sellers of recorded music but also as brands—and he believes labels should get rewarded for building those brands. Boxenbaum agreed: "The all-rights deal is, in reality, a better reflection of what the record industry's business model should have been all along. If a label is doing its job well, it isn't just selling a song or an album, but it's marketing the artist and building the artist's brand."

Boca Juniors and other soccer teams reap the benefit of their talent-development efforts in a more direct fashion: they make money every time they sell a player to another team. Boca has been shrewd about protecting that vital income stream, too: for instance, the team requires youth players and their parents to sign a contract that gives Boca ownership of the player's professional career. The club goes to great lengths to ensure that its contracts are enforced—not easy in a world in which European teams try to lure players away at an early age, and sometimes go so far as to offer their parents a job. Boca has also worked to reduce the influence agents have over the players. It introduced limits on potential earnings for agents by capping both agency commissions (at $1.5 million) and third-party ownership of players (at 20 percent of a player's value).

In the end, Boca Juniors did indeed sell Fernando Gago to Real Madrid in 2006 in a deal that brought $34 million to the club. Palacio, however, remained with the team. Boca's decision not to sell Palacio helps explain the club's push for majority ownership of players: Boca owned Palacio only in part (its share came to 17.5 percent), with the rest remaining in the hands of his former club and a number of private investors, meaning Boca would have missed out on the lion's share of the transfer fee. The complexity of these decisions was perhaps best expressed by Boca's former president, Mauricio Macri. He successfully ran for mayor of Buenos Aires, and when I asked him a few months into his term whether it was more challenging to run a soccer club or a city, he responded: "A soccer club. Without a doubt."

The broader point is that savvy managers will find ways to match their method of investing in talent to their company's overall business model. Real Madrid and Boca Juniors represent two fairly extreme illustrations of the approaches companies can take to investing in talent; most entertainment businesses will fall somewhere between superstar-acquisition and talent-development models. Finding the best balance between developing and acquiring talent is paramount.

A third example from the world of international soccer—FC Barcelona, or "Barça," as its fans call it—provides a good illustration. The club currently occupies second place in the "football money league" revenue rankings, behind Real Madrid. Some soccer enthusiasts like to believe that FC Barcelona has found a way to beat many of the world's best clubs—on and off the field—by virtue of its youth development. But the reality, as often is the case, is a bit more complicated.

FC Barcelona's reputation for developing talent is well-earned. When Barça beat Manchester United in the 2011 Champions League, *Newsweek* magazine—not normally a news outlet that pays much attention to soccer—devoted its cover to the victory, asking "Barça! The Best Football Team Ever?" in giant letters set against a picture of coach Josep "Pep" Guardiola being hoisted in the air by star players such as Lionel Messi, Andrés Iniesta, and Xavi. Inside, the news magazine raved:

> For lovers of the "beautiful game," Barça's onslaught . . . was soccer played at its best, with huge skill and minimum thuggery. The focus of Barcelona's play was on possession of the ball (or on winning it back during the rare moments it was lost), then attacking with an intricate choreography of precise, short passes where players moved on and off the ball in constant, fluid movement.

The performance owed much to FC Barcelona's youth academy, known as La Masia, which produced seven of the eleven players who started in that final. For the first time ever in FIFA's history, three of those players were included in FIFA's list of the world's five best players, with top honors—the coveted Golden Ball award—going to Messi. FC Barcelona's president, Sandro Rosell, described the club's academy as a place "where we work on creating our own players, with the right soccer skills and with our own values—players who put the team first, have respect for others, are humble even in success, and are resilient." Its mission was to bring one or two players into the first team each year. By the summer of 2011, over 560 players had lived at the academy, of which 14 percent had made their FC Barcelona first-team debut, and another 30 percent had played professional soccer elsewhere. Even Guardiola—the most successful coach in the club's history—had been a La Masia youth player.

Lionel Messi is undeniably the academy's biggest star. He left Argentina at age thirteen, hoping to find a soccer club that could pay for the drugs he needed to treat a growth deformity. (Today he is five feet, seven inches, significantly shorter than most of his peers.) Now a three-time winner of FIFA's Golden Ball, in 2012 he broke a four-decades-old record for the most goals scored in a calendar year. Messi has star power, too: when he joined Facebook in April 2011 ("I am so excited! From now on we will be more closely connected through Facebook," Messi wrote), he landed close to seven million fans within seven hours, instantly overtaking tennis star Roger Federer. Many soccer lovers see Messi as the world's most valuable player—not that FC Barcelona is planning to sell him anytime soon.

At first glance, FC Barcelona's focus on talent development indeed seems akin to that of Boca Juniors. The club invests heavily in its youth program: in 2011 the academy moved to a new $12 million facility at the team's training grounds, and it now operates on an annual budget of roughly $25 million and has room for over eighty residents. When I visited the new youth academy shortly after its opening, I found the similarities between La Masia and La Cantera striking. Like Boca, FC Barcelona insists that its most promising youngsters reside in the academy, where they study together, have meals together, play video games and engage in other leisure activities together—and practice their soccer. Each week, youth players play one ninety-minute game and practice close to eight hours. The club teaches players its distinctive style of play, characterized by many short, quick passes and an uncanny sense of positioning. "We want them to really understand our style of play, so all our teams—from the eight-year-olds to the eighteen-year-olds—play the same system," said director Carles Folguera. A network of scouts searches for young talent in Catalonia, in other provinces in Spain, and abroad. In its selection of players, the academy emphasizes both physical and mental strength, based on a belief that "resilience is the best predictor of success," as Folguera put it. And, like Boca, FC Barcelona is very focused on education. "We know that over half of our boys will not become professional soccer players," said Folguera. "That is why giving them an education is so essential."

Make no mistake, however: while FC Barcelona's success is most closely associated with its focus on youth development, the club spends huge sums on superstar acquisitions as well. Executives may like to claim otherwise—"in the choice between buying talent or growing it in-house, we have chosen the latter," the club's chief financial officer said recently—the numbers tell a different story. In the five seasons before the summer of 2011, FC Barcelona made roughly $230 million selling players but spent $540 million acquiring them, an average loss on player transactions of $60 million per season. That number places the club behind Real Madrid and Manchester City—both of which had a deficit that exceeded $700 million during the same period and are among soccer's biggest spenders on superstars—but ahead of Manchester United and Chelsea FC. To those who follow soccer, this may come as a surprise: Chelsea, owned by the billionaire Roman Abramovich and often seen as a poster child for irresponsibly high transfer expenditures, actually showed a *lower* deficit on its player transactions than FC Barcelona over this five-year period. When it chooses to be, Barça is as aggressive about acquiring talent as any club in the world: among the club's biggest splurges were nearly $100 million for Zlatan Ibrahimović and $50 million each for David Villa and Dani Alves. "Even with a good team," explained one of Barça's executives, "we have to feed success by investing in new faces all the time."

The club also rewards its superstars royally. In fact, Barça is estimated to be the world's best-paying sports team: according to

ESPN, in 2011 the club paid each of its players an average of nearly $8 million per year (or just over $150,000 per week), closely followed by Real Madrid with an average of $7.4 million per player per year, the New York Yankees ($6.8 million), and the Los Angeles Lakers ($6.5 million). Several other European soccer teams also appeared on this exclusive list: Chelsea ranked sixth with $6 million, Manchester City tenth with $5.8 million, and Manchester United sixteenth with $5.1 million. With such high talent acquisition and salary costs, no wonder FC Barcelona's chief financial officer worries about repaying the club's debt, which he called "too high for the club to be able to dictate its future."

Because of the economics of the soccer industry and the complex regulations that govern it, Barça may have a harder time locking its young talent into long-term contracts and lower salary brackets than, say, a television network or studio. But that does not change the key takeaway here: for all its success in creating superstars, the club cannot escape the realities of competing for talent in a winner-take-all market. Like so many leading entertainment businesses, it is playing the high-risk, high-reward superstar game. "We won't always win, so our challenge is to make our model sustainable in the ups and downs," remarked the club's chief financial officer.

Barça may be closer to finding the right balance between developing and acquiring talent than most other sports businesses, but the need for investments on both fronts also means that it's tricky for the club to manage its costs. It remains to be seen whether Barça's model can stand up against inevitable downswings in on-field performance. Executives have recently said that they now strive to limit fees spent on player acquisitions, which seems a sensible step. But more than that, the club needs to ramp up its marketing operations so it can compete off the field with clubs like Real Madrid, which rely less on their on-the-field performance to boost revenues and have a head start in exploiting global markets.

Long the undisputed leader in building its business globally is Manchester United, among the biggest franchises not just in soccer, but sports as a whole, with an estimated brand value of well over

$2 billion. FC Barcelona may have gotten the better of them in the 2011 Champions League final, but over the past two and a half decades Manchester United has had a far more consistent record on and off the field. The English club's marketing operation is widely admired; in fact, Real Madrid's executives have explicitly said that they modeled their approach after United's. But much of the credit for the club's achievements goes to one man: Sir Alex Ferguson, the most successful coach in British soccer history, who stepped down at the end of the 2012–2013 season. (As the club's former chief executive officer, David Gill, told me before Ferguson's retirement: "Steve Jobs was Apple. Sir Alex Ferguson is Manchester United.") Covering every aspect of Ferguson's approach to talent management would require another book, but what is perhaps most relevant here is that Ferguson had an especially clever, well-balanced portfolio approach to the club's investments in talent.

First, maybe even more so than FC Barcelona, Manchester United owes its success to its focus on youth development. Upon his arrival in 1986, Ferguson immediately set about revolutionizing United's youth program. He established two new "centers of excellence" and recruited a number of new scouts, urging them to bring him the best young talent. One of the first young players identified and recruited was a willowy thirteen-year-old named Ryan Giggs, who would go on to become one of the greatest British soccer players of all time, playing his entire club career under Ferguson's management. David Beckham is also a product of United's youth program. "The first thought for ninety-nine percent of newly appointed managers is to make sure they win—to survive," Ferguson told me when I visited the team's training facilities. "They bring experienced players in, often from their previous clubs. But I think it is important to build a structure for a football club—not just a football team. You need a foundation," he said, adding, "There is nothing better than seeing a young player make it to the first team."

Second, Ferguson kept a tight focus on the long term. At a moment when other managers might be tempted to reap short-term gains from players who are aging, Ferguson never hesitated to begin the hard work of rebuilding his team. His decisions were driven by a keen sense of players' value over time, and he distinguished three layers of players: "The players from thirty and above, the players from roughly twenty-three to thirty, and the younger ones coming in. The idea is that the younger players are developing and meeting the standards that the older ones have set before." Managing the talent-development process inevitably involves cutting players. "The hardest thing is to let go of a player who has been a great guy," Ferguson said. "But all the evidence is on the football field. If you see the change, the deterioration, you have to start asking yourself what it is going to be like two years ahead."

Third, Ferguson was equally shrewd about how to work the transfer market to his advantage. In the past decade, one in which Manchester United has won the English league five times, he spent less on incoming transfers than the club's main rivals—Chelsea, Manchester City, and Liverpool. He accomplished this by focusing on buying players younger than twenty-five years of age who he believed would become stars; that age group constituted a far higher share of United's total number of transfers than those for its competitors. In addition, partly because of the club's focus on young players, United made more from outgoing transfers than most of its rivals—and put that money to good use. For instance, money from the high-profile sales of Beckham and defender Jaap Stam was invested in two promising but at the time mostly unproven youngsters: Cristiano Ronaldo (the future apple of Florentino Pérez's eye) and England's own Wayne Rooney. It took a few years for their talents to blossom, but the duo ultimately became a dominant force in the English Premier League. And on occasion, Ferguson would shell out top money for a highly regarded superstar—in 2012, for instance, United purchased twenty-eight-year-old Dutch striker Robin van Persie for $35 million.

As Ferguson's strategy suggests, a portfolio approach to investments in talent can help an entertainment business survive and thrive, even in a fiercely competitive marketplace. Thanks in part to Ferguson's relentless focus on finding the right balance between developing and acquiring superstars, he outperformed the typical short life cycle of a coach—and then some. The 2012–2013 season was his twenty-sixth as Manchester United's leader, which made Ferguson the longest tenured coach among all active coaches in professional soccer in Europe. (It wasn't even a close race: the second-longest tenured coach was a decade behind.) Most executives in other entertainment businesses would be thrilled if they held a high-level job for half that long—and no matter what their sector, they would do well to follow Ferguson's example in their own efforts to compete in winner-take-all markets for talent.

Chapter Four

HOW SUPERSTARS
USE THEIR POWERS

n November 2006, movie star Tom Cruise and his longtime business partner, veteran producer Paula Wagner, walked into the offices of Harry Sloan, then the chairman and chief executive officer of film studio Metro-Goldwyn-Mayer (MGM), in Century City, Los Angeles. They were there to finalize a partnership that would catch most Hollywood insiders by surprise: Cruise and Wagner signed an agreement to run United Artists, a dormant studio that was part of MGM's portfolio. Cruise, Wagner, and Sloan made for a unique, powerful trio. Cruise had been one of Hollywood's biggest stars for a quarter of a century, dating back to 1983's *Risky Business*. Veteran producer Wagner had joined Creative Artists Agency, a leading talent agency, in 1980, as one of its first female agents, and she had been carefully guiding Cruise's career ever since. And Sloan was best known for founding a media company in Europe in the 1990s, building it into the second-largest broadcaster on the continent, and selling it for $2.6 billion fifteen years later.

The MGM deal came at a time when Cruise's superstardom was first being questioned, amid heightened media attention for a series of incidents involving the actor that had caught both fans and industry insiders off guard. In the preceding eighteen months, Cruise had jumped on Oprah's couch during a television interview while he effused about his love for then fiancée Katie Holmes, boasted about his plans to eat the placenta of his unborn child, verbally attacked actress Brooke Shields for her use of medicine to help cope with postpartum depression, and lashed out at a German reporter who suggested that Scientology was a pseudoscience. In fact, just two months before Sloan made his unprecedented offer, Viacom's chairman Sumner Redstone, in an unusually abrupt and public way, had ended Cruise and Wagner's fourteen-year relationship with Viacom's studio, Paramount Pictures. The partnership had initially been extremely successful, generating such blockbuster hits as *The Firm*, *Days of Thunder*, and *Mission: Impossible*, and Cruise had long been seen as Hollywood's most reliable and bankable actor. However, Redstone had increasingly come to view the star's controversial behavior as embarrassing and costly.

In a newspaper interview, Redstone directly attributed the disappointing ticket sales for the third installment of *Mission: Impossible* to Cruise's antics. Wagner was quick to counter: "Tom Cruise, in 10 months, for Paramount Pictures, generated just under $1 billion," she said, pointing to the box-office grosses of his last two films with Paramount, *Mission: Impossible III* and *War of the Worlds*. Yet Redstone refused to renew their $10-million-a-year production deal and asked Cruise and Wagner to vacate their offices on the Paramount lot. "It's nothing to do with his acting ability, he's a terrific actor," Redstone told the *Wall Street Journal*. "But we don't think that someone who effectuates creative suicide and costs the company revenue should be on the lot."

Sloan's proposed partnership gave Cruise a chance to strike back and prove his doubters wrong. But the "experiment," as Sloan called it, was notable for other reasons, too. Cruise and Wagner were given a relatively free hand in determining a direction for United Artists—for instance, they could greenlight movie projects costing less than $60 million without MGM's approval—and for a term of at least five years they could develop up to six films a year. All films would be distributed and, at least initially, financed by

MGM, for which the studio would receive a distribution fee of between 7 percent and 15 percent of revenues. In exchange, MGM granted the pair a one-third equity stake in United Artists without asking them to invest a penny of their own money. Wagner, an accomplished producer but new to the role of executive, assumed the role of chief executive officer and was given responsibility for overseeing day-to-day operations. And although he was not given a formal title, Cruise was expected to be actively involved in picking films and working with the talent. Perhaps most remarkably, Cruise was not obligated to appear in any United Artists movies himself, and he remained free to star in and produce movies at other studios.

What could Harry Sloan—a smart, seasoned executive with a strong track record of running global media businesses before he took on the challenge of salvaging the legendary but long-underperforming MGM studio—possibly have been thinking? Did his new partnership with Cruise and Wagner represent a viable approach to playing the high-stakes game for A-list actors and generating blockbuster products for them to star in, or had Sloan lost his mind?

At the time the United Artists deal was made public, many industry observers were as puzzled about Sloan's moves as they were about Cruise's couch jumping. But a closer look at the intense competition for talent in Hollywood, and the evolving role of stars in other entertainment sectors, reveals that Sloan may not have been so crazy after all. Rather, the experiment can be seen as an attempt to solve a fundamental problem—the growing ability of powerful stars to undermine the profits of the studios and other businesses that employ them—that plagues not just the film industry but also a host of other sectors in entertainment. Although the experiment ultimately did not work out as those involved had hoped and in retrospect perhaps should have been set up differently—and although, as we know now, Cruise's troubles were far from over—there is a lot to be learned from studying this unusual arrangement.

To grasp Sloan's motives and understand why his offer would

appeal to Cruise—and to discern what the agreement says about how other executives may try to structure their dealings with superstars in the future—it helps to know a bit about the movie industry's history. When MGM was established in 1924, its head, Louis B. Mayer, and his fellow studio executives held all the power in Hollywood. At that time, in what was known as the "studio system," seven studios, including MGM, owned the movie houses where their pictures were screened and monopolized movie production, working with actors, directors, writers, set designers, film editors, and others as salaried employees.

It may be hard to imagine now, but stars such as Bing Crosby, Bette Davis, Olivia de Havilland, Bob Hope, and John Wayne were required to sign strict and expansive contracts that essentially made them the property of the studios. These contracts typically lasted seven years, and they required the actors to participate in every movie and all publicity the studio desired. The studios created public personas for their stars by typecasting them in familiar roles and generating publicity for their on-screen personalities. The terms of the contract often enabled the studios to control details of the stars' public image, so as to boost their popularity and therefore box-office receipts. The studios scripted stars' interviews, and "morals clauses" dictated their public statements, their photographic poses—and even their significant others. Under orders from a studio, stars sometimes altered their facial appearance, hair color, names, and biographical details.

They did all this in return for salaries that do not come close to those lavished on top actors nowadays: in 1947, for example, the most popular stars were paid less than $100,000 per movie, or approximately $900,000 adjusted for inflation—a hefty sum, but nowhere near the multimillion-dollar fees that today's biggest stars can command. An actor's salary could not be increased until his or her contract expired, so even the biggest stars were locked into a salary bracket for several years. And if actors failed to work, regardless of the reason, studios could invoke a so-called extension clause and automatically extend their contracts.

The studio system was brought to a standstill by legal challenges.

In 1944, a California court ruled against Warner Bros. in a dispute over an extension clause, essentially comparing such contracts to slavery. The decision marked a turning point, and soon power began shifting from the studios to the stars. In the 1950s, studios began to employ actors on a project-by-project basis, and agents and managers helped stars to exploit their newfound power. Over the decades that followed, salaries and perks for the industry's biggest stars skyrocketed. In some cases, studio heads signed "first-look" contracts with production companies founded by stars—Reese Witherspoon's Pacific Standard, Brad Pitt's Plan B Entertainment, and Will Smith's Overbrook Entertainment are just three examples—giving them additional fees and access to office space on the studio lot in exchange for the first option to produce or distribute the movies the stars pursued.

By the mid-2000s, it had become increasingly clear that the tug-of-war between stars and studios was not helping the profitability of movie studios. My own research, most notably a study that examined more than twelve hundred casting decisions made between 2001 and 2005, suggests that whereas movies that starred A-list actors typically had higher box-office revenues, the fees for those actors were so high that they wiped out the extra revenues the stars brought in—leaving studios with the same profits they would have made if they had relied on lesser-known creative talent. In other words, the stars themselves must have captured most of the surplus that resulted from their involvement. If a studio casts, say, Johnny Depp in a movie and so brings in an additional $20 million at the box office, that will do little for the studio's bottom line if Depp demands that same amount in salary. My study is just one in a large stream of research; other academics studying the film industry have also documented evidence for what might be called the "curse of the superstar."

When Harry Sloan took over MGM in 2005, he found himself in this challenging context—a Hollywood in which a handful of stars had become so powerful that studios had to pay ruinous fees to enlist their services. Making matters worse, by the time of Sloan's arrival, the once-mighty MGM—known for *Gone with the Wind, The*

Wizard of Oz, and many other successful and prestigious films—no longer had the resources to compete with bigger studios such as Warner Bros. that had surged ahead. Tellingly, not one of the top movies released by MGM in the years before Sloan reached out to Cruise—*Barbershop 2* in 2004, *The Amityville Horror* in 2005, and *The Pink Panther* in 2006—had exceeded the $100 million domestic-box-office-revenues barrier, and none of the studio's movies had broken into the top 10 during that three-year period. Cruise, by contrast, had been involved in a $100-million-plus movie in each of those years.

Sloan's experiment was essentially an attempt to, as he put it, "align the incentives of the studio and the star." Sloan sought to make it attractive for a star actor of Cruise's caliber to work with a smaller studio such as MGM. But because Sloan could not afford the kinds of budgets that bigger companies spent on films, and by extension on actors' salaries, he had to offer the star something else. Instead of up-front money, Sloan offered Cruise the freedom to pursue the kinds of projects that he and his partner, Paula Wagner, were most excited about, and the promise of a bigger payday in the future, through an ownership stake in the studio.

Sloan's choice of the dormant United Artists as the vehicle for his experiment was appropriate. Founded in 1919 by Charlie Chaplin, Douglas Fairbanks, Mary Pickford, and D. W. Griffith, four of the biggest stars in Hollywood at the time, United Artists was known as "the company built by the stars." The studio was unique in that it gave filmmakers and actors creative freedom and control over their own pictures, while also giving them a share of the film's profits—an arrangement that led one film-industry insider to joke that "the inmates have taken over the asylum."

In the end, Sloan's experiment was widely regarded as a disappointment. Cruise and Wagner produced only two movies under the United Artists banner—*Valkyrie,* which grossed $200 million worldwide, likely yielding not more than a small profit, and *Lions for Lambs,* which failed to make any splash at the box office. Some industry observers suggested that the terms of the contract were to blame: Why didn't Sloan insist on having a say with regard to what films were produced, especially since Cruise hadn't proven his mettle as a studio executive? Others thought the choice of Cruise was wrong, given his troubled public profile at the time. Both are valid points. But Sloan must have sensed that a star of Cruise's stature would be less likely to sign on if the agreement had been more restrictive. Sloan probably hoped that the incentive of owning a stake in the company and the autonomy to greenlight projects would motivate Cruise to focus his attention on United Artists; Sloan had little other means to attract A-list stars and promising projects to his studio. He likely thought Cruise's troubles worked in MGM's favor: the actor might well have been interested in United Artists only because he was now lacking a major studio deal. And Sloan might have felt he had to try something bold to revive his ailing studio's fortunes. Even so, he could have pushed for different terms; for instance, he could have given Cruise better reasons to pursue more mainstream movies—it's no secret that Sloan had hoped Cruise would select the next installment of the popular *Terminator* franchise as his first project.

The experiment was successful in one respect. One of Sloan's primary goals was to attract funds from outside investors and develop better relationships with partners who trusted the value of Cruise's star status. Sloan sought to exploit the actor's power to his studio's advantage, and he did just that: with Cruise's help, he was able to secure $500 million in financing for United Artists, at a time when Sloan was having considerable trouble raising funds for parent company MGM. So although the experiment ultimately yielded no significant upside for MGM, it also exposed Sloan and his studio to very little downside. With a bit more luck, the experiment might have ushered in a new model of collaboration in Hollywood.

For this kind of partnership between entertainment businesses and the talent they depend on to become commonplace, such collaborations will have to help superstars achieve *their* goals as well. They will have to truly "align incentives," in Sloan's words. So in order to understand what the future will look like, it is necessary to consider what an A-list star could get out of engaging in a longer-term partnership with an uncertain payoff—and how such an arrangement could fit his or her efforts to build and profit from a personal brand. In other words, exactly why did Cruise say "yes" to Sloan? And why would A-listers across different sectors of entertainment sign on to other collaborations? Some outsiders may feel there is no rhyme or reason to these decisions, but there is, in fact, a clear logic to how smart stars and their advisers manage their personal brands, and especially to their weighing *what* opportunities to pursue *when*. And the truth is that the preferences of the shrewdest stars create a real problem for entertainment businesses: the more they rely on A-list stars, the more their profitability may be hurt.

The world of celebrity endorsements provides a good backdrop to examine why this might be the case and how it works out in practice. By some estimates, 10 percent to 20 percent of the advertisements that aired in the United States in recent years featured celebrities endorsing products and brands; the percentage is twice as high in some Asian countries. The most sought-after endorsers are richly compensated: in fact, endorsements are a major source of income for many star entertainers.

In July 2004, at the tender age of seventeen, Maria Sharapova became one of the youngest women in history to win Wimbledon, the most prestigious tennis tournament in the world. To say her victory was unexpected is an understatement: when Sharapova went to Wimbledon that year she was ranked number 15 in the world and at best was considered a long-shot contender for the title. But what happened next may be even more remarkable: just two years later, Sharapova was the highest-paid female athlete in the world, making an estimated $25 million a year. The secret behind her off-court success? Her agent, Max Eisenbud, a man perhaps not with the looks of Tom Cruise's character in *Jerry Maguire*, but certainly with his smarts, passion, and hustle—and a wealth of knowledge about what it takes to build a superstar brand.

"That day, Maria's life changed forever, and so did mine," Eisenbud said, reflecting on the tremendous impact of her Wimbledon victory. "I have to admit I cried my eyes out after her win." Only thirty-two at the time, Eisenbud had guided Sharapova's career since she had signed with leading sports agency IMG—Eisenbud's employer—at age eleven. "Max is half family, half agent," Sharapova told me. In the early stages of Sharapova's career, Eisenbud had been focused on helping her achieve success on the court as well as building relationships with corporate sponsors and advising her on business decisions. But even he did not think a Grand Slam win was within reach in July 2004.

"She faced Lindsay Davenport, one of the favorites, in the semifinal," Eisenbud recalled, "and initially Davenport was killing Sharapova. She won the first set 6–2 and was up a break in the second when it started to rain. . . . I thought it was all over, and Davenport's agent actually consoled me. Then, after a two-hour rain delay, she comes back, and—boom! She wins 7–6 in the second set and then beats her 6–1 in the third. Two days later, she played the final against Serena Williams—a skinny little girl against a great champion with enormous physical strength. She won the first set 6–1, and I did not think she could keep it up, but she did. It was just an amazing win."

Sharapova claimed her second Grand Slam, the US Open, in 2006. ("This time I was ready to win," she recalled.) By then, she was not only the world's highest-paid female athlete, she was also the tenth-highest-paid overall, ahead of the men's top-ranked tennis player Roger Federer. Estimates put her income from endorsing such brands as Nike, Motorola, Canon, Tag Heuer, Pepsi, and Land Rover at well over $18 million—despite the fact that she was available for sponsorship commitments for only two and a half weeks per year. "She wants to win titles, so that is all we can afford," Eisenbud told me.

Sharapova brought in these huge sums of money without creating a sense that she was selling out, unlike fellow blond-haired Russian tennis player Anna Kournikova, who had become known more for photographs of her scantily clad body appearing in various men's magazines and an "only the ball should bounce" billboard campaign for a bra brand than for her on-court performance. That is not to say that Sharapova did not bank on her model looks. "Let's not kid ourselves—she is six foot two, blond, and a very attractive woman, and that is one of the reasons why she generates attention," said Eisenbud. But ever since her first Grand Slam win, the members of "team Sharapova" (which included not only the tennis player and Eisenbud but several other IMG representatives) had done an impressive job of both building her brand and reaping the rewards from those efforts through a broad portfolio of endorsements.

One way to think about the careers of creative talent is through the lens of a "talent life cycle," which reflects how a creative worker's brand value changes over time. Marketers in other sectors of the economy often rely on the "product life cycle" to help guide strategic decisions; the underlying idea is that products go through a fairly predictable set of stages, from launch and growth to maturity and decline. Marketers know they will experience a different set of strategic challenges in each of those stages. Because talent goes through its own series of stages, and because in the entertainment industries those who *make* the product often *become* the product (or at least an integral part of it), studying the life cycles of talent is quite useful.

Two characteristics of the talent life cycle readily come to mind: first, the odds of success—any success—are low and, second, careers in entertainment tend to be relatively short. Most people who hope for a career as a professional tennis player, actor, musician, or other type of entertainer don't even come close to achieving that goal. Those who do succeed tend to remain at or near the top of their field for a limited amount of time, especially when compared to professionals in many other domains, such as doctors, lawyers, accountants, or consultants. When we think of careers in entertainment, we tend to think of the big successes—of the few stars with staying power, such as Sharapova, Cruise, or Lady Gaga—but the truth is that most performers come and go, and only a tiny minority manage to remain on top for an extended period. This fact creates significant challenges for creative talent—and for entertainment executives betting on that talent.

When we look more closely at how the value of talent in different sectors varies over time, we find that the result resembles a bell curve. That is, the contribution that creative talent makes to the creative economy generally rises and then falls over time—regardless of whether one defines "value" as the sales generated by a musician's recordings, the size of the audiences willing to pay to see a movie star's performances, or the money generated by a model's photo shoots. As the following charts illustrate, such bell curves are everywhere in the world of entertainment. We find them when we look at the ages of players starting in English Premier League games, for instance, or at the ages of the players behind every goal scored. Or when we consider the ages of tennis players in Grand Slam finals or at the top of the international rankings. Or when we examine the ages of actors and actresses when the Hollywood

Life Cycles of English Premier League Soccer Players

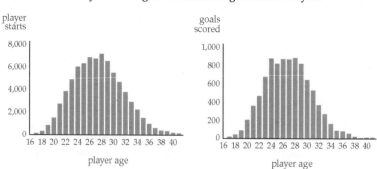

The chart on the left shows the ages of all players starting in the English Premier League games played in the ten seasons from 2001–2002 through 2010–2011; the chart on the right shows the ages of the players who scored goals in those games.

Life Cycles of Professional Tennis Players

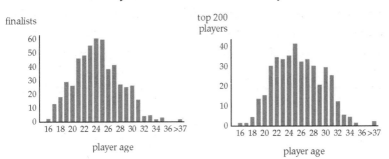

The chart on the left shows the ages of all finalists in the four men's and women's Grand Slams (the Australian Open, the French Open, the US Open, and Wimbledon) from 1980 through 2012. The chart on the right shows the ages of all players in the top 200 on the ATP (men) and the WTA (women) rankings, as of September 2012.

Life Cycles of Hollywood Movie Stars

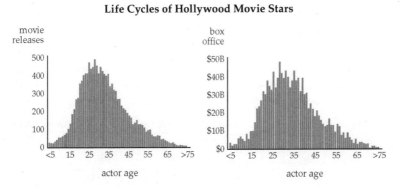

Based on a sample of the 675 movie actors and actresses listed on boxofficemojo.com, a site tracking Hollywood data, the chart on the left shows what age those actors and actresses were when the over thirteen hundred movies they played in were released. The chart on the right shows the total worldwide box-office revenues of the movies they starred in, again by actor age. The data were collected in June 2012.

movies they star in are released and measure how much money those movies generate at the worldwide box office.

But if the broad trends in a given field are predictable, individual careers come in all shapes and sizes. It is far from easy to quantify an athlete or entertainer's current value, let alone predict his or her trajectory over a long period. That's partly because a few individual performers always seem to flaunt the rules of the universe, whether it is Manchester United's Ryan Giggs (who is still going strong even though he is two decades older than some of his teammates), Maria Sharapova (who was so young when she won her first Grand Slam), or Meryl Streep and George Clooney (who both demonstrate enduring star power even as they age). But even aside from those few performers who defy the odds, there are more fundamental reasons why assessing an entertainer's value is so difficult.

One such factor is that early winners often have an inside track on further successes, thus demonstrating what economists call "path dependencies" or "positive feedback effects." Imagine a casting director selecting film actors. She probably has little to go on when trying to distinguish among hundreds of unknown actors auditioning for a small role. But after a particular actor has been chosen once or twice and has met expectations, there is a good reason to favor that actor in the future. As a result, a decision that may have been based on a subtle advantage compared to other actors—if a difference existed at all—could translate into a lucrative career for the lucky winner and a dearth of opportunities for the hundreds of other hopefuls.

Even in sports, seemingly minor initial events sometimes cast a wide shadow on a later career. Sharapova, born in an industrial town in West Siberia, might never have had a chance to reach the top had not the 1986 Chernobyl nuclear disaster forced her parents to move to the Black Sea resort town of Sochi, where the young player found more opportunities to play tennis. And had not she and her father had the good fortune to attend tennis clinics in Moscow just when tennis legend Martina Navratilova was paying a visit, Navratilova, who spotted the then six-year-old hitting balls on the court, would not have been able to encourage Sharapova's father, Yuri Sharapov, to develop her talent further. Sharapov, in turn, would have been much less inclined to seek world-class coaching for his daughter at the famous IMG Bollettieri Academy in Florida.

The same holds true for those who work behind the scenes. When Eisenbud joined IMG in 1999, he was sent to the Bollettieri Academy as part of his training. Had he not encountered a young Maria Sharapova there—"I knew right away that she was special," he said about his first meeting—he might not have developed into the top agent he has become. If he had instead joined IMG a little while later, another agent might have already forged a bond with the girl who would go on to win Wimbledon. Similarly, Tom Cruise was one of Paula Wagner's first clients as an agent, and Wagner would eventually come to advise the careers of actors Demi Moore, Val Kilmer, and Kevin Bacon, as well as film-maker Oliver Stone. It's impossible to say even now whether either Cruise or Wagner would have had the same stellar career had they never met.

This is not to say that superstars and their agents and managers do not earn their success, or that it is always smooth sailing for them after some initial lucky breaks. Eisenbud and Wagner are highly competent agents, and Sharapova and Cruise are both known for their commitment, determination, and remarkably consistent performances. Sharapova has gone on to win a third and fourth Grand Slam—becoming only the tenth woman ever to complete a Career Grand Slam—and is among the top career prize-money earners in women's tennis. And Cruise has starred in more movies that collected at least $100 million at the box office than all of his peers. Rather, the point is that even the biggest superstars need things to fall their way sometimes, especially early in their career. And the point is that an artist or athlete's objective quality—however that quality is assessed—is often not a good predictor of success.

Genuine talent is unquestionably a valuable asset, but for any creative worker there is a very thin line between achieving super-star success and remaining a complete unknown. In soccer, just making the cut for Boca Juniors' youth academy can make a tremendous difference to a player's overall career. The music business is full of stories of stars being dropped by their label or coming very close to it—Alicia Keys, 50 Cent, and Katy Perry are just a few of the many musicians who have gone through that experience. Despite her raw talent, Lady Gaga is another example: she was dropped a mere three months after signing a record deal with top producer L. A. Reid at Def Jam Records, before eventually finding a home with Vincent Herbert's Streamline Records. We can only wonder about the countless potential superstars we have never heard of because they were simply less fortunate and were not given a second chance.

Another complicating factor in assessing an entertainer's value is that when products are made by teams, it is often difficult to isolate a single individual's contribution. This is due to the so-called O-rings principle, named after a key component on the space shuttle *Challenger* whose failure contributed to the shuttle's explosion. This theory, first described in the context of the creative industries by the economist Richard Caves, dictates that an entertainment good's quality depends on all inputs—all workers—performing up to a particular standard. Think of an orchestra: one out-of-tune musician can ruin the ensemble's entire performance. Or think of a movie: as many industry insiders can attest, two actors may be perfectly fine performers by themselves, but when they are put together in one movie sparks sometimes fail to fly. The implication is that one team member's contribution to a product, be it a piece of music or a movie or a soccer game, depends on the strength of the other people involved in producing it.

Establishing the cause of an entertainment product's success or failure is often virtually impossible. A popular actor may star in a movie that sets records at the box office, but that does not mean the actor *caused* the high ticket sales. (It is admittedly tempting to come to just this conclusion, however, when noting that, say, worldwide box-office revenues for *The Bourne Legacy*, the first Bourne movie starring Jeremy Renner, were more than $150 million below the revenues for *The Bourne Ultimatum*, the last Bourne movie featuring the franchise's original star, Matt Damon.) Similarly, the fact that the addition of a certain soccer player to a team's roster happens to coincide with a sudden turnaround of a club's fortunes does not mean that the new player *caused* it. Because entertainment goods such as films and soccer matches are one-off goods that cannot be assembled and reassembled, it is hard to rule out alternative explanations.

A final complicating factor is that entertainers can be superstars for a number of different reasons. Stardom, as Maria Sharapova's career suggests, is not a one-dimensional concept. At the time Sharapova climbed to the top of the "highest-paid" list, several other female tennis players had a better on-court record, so other factors must have played a role in her ascent. Her looks, her determination to win, the careful management of her brand by Eisenbud— all of those played a role, too. Tom Cruise's career illustrates this point in a different way. He has never won an Oscar, and critics may argue he was never among the finest actors in the movie business. And yet for more than two decades he was one of the industry's biggest audience draws. More recently, Jennifer Lawrence garnered acclaim for her acting skills (winning a host of awards, including an Academy Award, for *Silver Linings Playbook*), but she was also widely praised for her endearing acceptance speech at the Oscars (preceded by a spectacular fall on her way to the podium) and her appealing behind-the-scenes interviews, both of which further enhanced her star status.

Despite the difficulty of assessing and predicting a performer's value, most stars do their best to measure how they stack up against their peers so they can better manage their careers. The more accurate their yardstick, the better stars can deal with a recurring trade-off they face—they need to decide, to put it in business school jargon, when to "create value" and when to "capture value." A star's choices with respect to sponsorships illustrate this dilemma: endorsements can build a performer's brand ("create value"), capitalize on that brand ("capture value"), or do a mix of both. Because stars can dedicate only a limited amount of time to sponsorship commitments, choosing between the types of endorsements can be very difficult.

Consider the perspective of a successful movie actor who is trying to choose among a number of movie roles. Some roles may help that actor further develop his craft, establish his brand as a serious actor, or avoid being typecast in one genre ("create value"). Other roles may be less challenging but offer the opportunity to star in mainstream films and so provide a higher income and help position an actor as a bankable star ("capture value"). How this actor approaches this trade-off likely depends on his talent–life cycle stage. If he is at an early stage of his career, he may choose to star in movies that build his brand. If he is at a later, more mature stage in his career, he may want to accept the roles that allow him to capitalize on the brand he has already established. That, at least, corresponds with how a product manager would approach decisions throughout a product's life cycle.

There is a lot to learn from how team Sharapova managed the tennis player's talent life cycle. Early on, Sharapova and her advisers primarily chose endorsements that helped build her brand. Eisenbud was well aware that Sharapova's first commitments after her Wimbledon victory would have a considerable impact on perceptions of her brand and her future opportunities. "I felt it was important to come out with a big global deal with a blue-chip company right out of the gate," he explained to me. So shortly after Wimbledon, Eisenbud and his team made a deal with Motorola. "That set the tone," Eisenbud recalled. "Then Canon and Tag Heuer followed—everything started falling into place."

The Motorola opportunity—which led to a multiyear global deal—seemed like a gift from the gods. Immediately after winning the trophy, watched by millions of television viewers around the world, Sharapova had tried in vain to call her mother on an unbranded cell phone. As it happened, Motorola was just preparing to launch a new phone, the Razr, for which its head of marketing sought an endorser. But if that endorsement deal was irresistible,

Eisenbud turned down dozens of other, even more lucrative opportunities. He preferred to associate his player with companies that stood for the same qualities that team Sharapova wanted to highlight—as Eisenbud put it, that she was "cool, hip, and a champion."

When weighing offers, Eisenbud also considered each deal's timing. In particular, he pursued endorsements that would end at opportune moments during Sharapova's career. "The most important part of these deals is not how much the guarantee is, but when they expire," Eisenbud said. In the months after his star's Wimbledon victory, he sought deals with early expiration dates, because he was already preparing for a time when Sharapova would be in an even better position to command top fees. She ultimately signed lucrative one-year, Japan-only agreements with Pepsi and (remarkably, before she even had her driver's license) Honda. Later, team Sharapova's focus shifted to opportunities that predominantly allowed her to capture value from her carefully crafted brand. Her deals with Colgate-Palmolive, Samantha Thavasa, Land Rover, and other brands positively shaped Sharapova's own brand, but mostly allowed her to cash in on her success.

Creative workers across the spectrum of entertainment businesses need to be thoughtful about which projects are suited to their short- and long-term objectives. The actor Will Smith, for one, is known to be especially shrewd about his choice of movie roles. After making the transition from his television series *The Fresh Prince of Bel-Air* to movies in the mid-1990s (when such transitions were less common than they are today), Smith and his agent carefully analyzed past film performances and chose to be involved in those movies that, they believed, had the characteristics—such as special effects, a love story, and alien creatures—that gave him the highest odds of success in the marketplace. And he surrounded himself with respectable, established movie actors as co-leads, such as Bill Pullman and Jeff Goldblum in *Independence Day*, Tommy Lee Jones in *Men In Black*, and Gene Hackman in *Enemy of the State*, each of whom helped him build his brand as a serious actor while putting together a string of hits.

Of course, managing people as brands can be distinctly different from managing "regular" products. Performers may resist a brand-capitalization opportunity at any stage of their career because they want to "sell" but not "sell out." After all, they will have to live with the personal brand that is created by their choices. Sharapova, for example, has always resisted endorsing a skin cleanser associated with battling acne, even though by doing so she could make millions of dollars for only a couple of days' work.

Agents (and, in sectors such as the music industry, managers) often play a critical role in this process. If performers are "products" or "brands," then agents are "product managers" or "brand custodians." Most superstars enlist the help of agents or other intermediaries to broker deals with the firms that seek their services, and to manage a variety of other business-related matters for them.

IMG, Sharapova's agency, is a major force in the world of entertainment. The firm represents hundreds of athletes, performing artists, writers, and fashion models, as well as television properties, events, and cultural institutions. IMG's agents, in turn, are supported by a global sales team made up of dozens of executives who represent IMG in its contacts with corporate clients. "Our salespeople assist our agents in driving revenue and building their clients' brands through affiliations with multinational companies," one IMG sales executive told me. "We know the decision makers—the CMO, or the head of sponsorship, or the person responsible for buying endorsements—and constantly strive to build better relationships with them. Being a good agency is about who you know . . . and knowing what their 'hot buttons' are." Although compensation plans for agents and salespeople are a closely guarded secret throughout the entertainment industry, agencies like IMG are thought to receive an average of 10 percent of an athlete's prize money and 20 percent of his or her endorsement earnings. Agents, like the stars they represent, will thus want to find the right balance between creating and capturing value from endorsements.

A wealth of evidence suggests that just as movie stars can help studios attract audiences and thus drive higher box-office revenues, celebrity endorsements can boost the financial performance of corporations. My own study of hundreds of endorsements by athletes shows that sales for brands in a variety of consumer-product categories jumped an average of 4 percent in the six months following the start of an endorsement deal, even after controlling for advertising expenditures and other factors that could be expected to drive up sales. (Four percent may not sound like much, but that increase can add up to tens of millions of dollars for even a reasonably successful consumer brand.) Several brands I studied saw sales rise more than 20 percent after teaming up with an endorser. And because spillover effects on other brands in the category were limited, it seems the endorsements helped brands to gain an edge over their competitors. Athlete endorsements, my study shows, can even improve a brand's stock market valuation: on the day an endorsement deal was announced, the endorsed company's stock typically increased nearly a quarter percent. And illustrating the payoff of betting on superstars, athletes with winning records are particularly effective endorsers. In fact, my study showed that each major victory by an athlete could boost both the sales and stock price of a firm he or she has endorsed.

It is only logical, then, that superstars are in a position to capture ever-higher rewards and, spurred on by agents, have a tendency to push for those rewards. That is especially true for stars at more advanced stages in their careers who have accumulated some wealth and thus can afford to take more risks. Those who make investments in talent, be they casting directors, talent scouts, or marketers looking for brand endorsers, should be keenly aware of this dynamic and do their best to make deals that suit their own business objectives. This holds true in all kinds of sectors, but it is imperative in the world of entertainment. Precisely because the odds of success are so low, talent life cycles are so short, and the potential rewards for superstars are so high, those who invest in creative workers are under tremendous pressure to get it right.

Companies hiring creative talent should think deeply about both the value and risk involved in any transactions. Whereas usually the value of talent—and with it the fees that talent can

The Talent Life Cycle

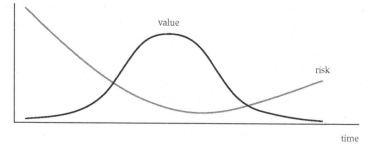

command—first increases and then decreases, the risk involved in any talent transaction tends to move in the opposite way, as illustrated by the chart above. As a creative worker advances through his or her life cycle, the risk inherent in the bets on that worker are likely to first decrease and later increase. Consider the world of soccer: when a player is still young, it's difficult to predict whether he will become a star, but as time goes on, more of his true potential is revealed, thus reducing the risk for a club seeking to acquire that player. When the player ages and the possibility of injury increases, the risk involved in buying the player goes up again.

Whether entertainment businesses can gain the upper hand in negotiations with talent depends in part on the talent's career stage. It was telling that after *Saturday Night Live* executives introduced stricter contracts with new cast members, all but one of the young comedians signed the agreement anyway. They could not resist the lure of the legendary show, despite talent agents and managers advising their clients against the deal. "You are waving their dream in their face," one manager told Peter Bogdanovich. "Once you say to your client, 'You're testing for *SNL*,' they go deaf after that. . . . I kept saying, 'It's a precedent—you cannot let them do this to you.' But they're nothing now. They're not getting paid a dime now."

Later in their careers, successful actors gain more control. The cast of the hit series *Friends* famously waited until the end of their seven-year contract in 2000 to negotiate a new deal, bringing the fees of each of the six lead actors from a low six-figure number to around $750,000 per episode. Their decision to bond together helped them push for what at the time was a tremendously high fee. "They said, 'You have to pay all of us exactly the same and it is all of us or none of us,'" recalled Garth Ancier, who was intimately involved in this negotiation on behalf of NBC.

In the music industry, concert-promotion giant Live Nation tailors the kinds of deals it makes with artists to their career stage. Traditionally, "a promoter [pays] the artist to play in one or more venues, and the artist [enlists] a team that produces the tour—the artist effectively hires the trucks and the buses, the crew, the supporting musicians, and the dancers, and pays for the hotels and the travel," Arthur Fogel, chief executive officer of global touring at Live Nation, once explained to me. This is still the norm: the typical contract places most of the risk with the artist. But for musicians who have proven that they can fill arenas around the world, Live Nation now often negotiates "net deals" in which artists earn a percentage of net income and promoters are responsible for all costs. This is a smart move by Live Nation, since it makes it possible for them to provide a valued service to established artists—who are inherently less risky bets—and simultaneously share in their high rewards. Even Lady Gaga had to demonstrate that the first two dozen stops on her *Monster Ball* tour could sell out before she qualified for a net deal. Because Lady Gaga made well over $200 million more in revenues while signed to that net deal, making her *Monster Ball* tour one of the most lucrative concert series of recent years, no one at Live Nation has any regrets about the agreement.

Anticipating what creative workers will demand and what they will settle for at any given point during their careers is a constant challenge for entertainment-industry executives. The best-laid plans can go awry when a product suddenly becomes a hit and the star involved gains leverage. "Hollywood is notorious for people trying to renegotiate deals in the middle of their contracts," said Ancier. The adult cast members of ABC's *Modern Family* did just that in 2012: they sued producer Twentieth Century Fox in an attempt to increase their fees, even though they all had multiyear contracts in place and had already been offered substantial salary increases that would pay each of them hundreds of thousands of dollars per episode. Sometimes even modestly successful performers will attempt to improve their fees while under contract. As Ancier told me, "A manager of one of the girls in [the 1990s hit television show] *7th Heaven* once called me, saying, 'By only paying her $70,000 an episode, you are breaking a young girl's heart.' It was a seven-year-old. I mean, who writes this stuff?"

Increasingly, superstars in every entertainment sector are fighting for ever more innovative deal structures. The agreements they are pursuing nowadays often include a share of the revenues or an equity stake in the companies they work with. One performer who has been notably creative about pushing the boundaries on these talent compensation models—and the conventions of talent representation in general—is an already legendary basketball star who goes by the nickname King James.

Worth more than $90 million before he even graduated from high school thanks to a sponsorship deal with Nike, LeBron James is one of the biggest stars in the history of the National Basketball Association (NBA). An almost freakishly talented so-called small forward on the court, the Akron, Ohio, native was Rookie of the Year in 2004, won a gold medal with Team USA at the 2008 and 2012 Summer Olympics, and led both his previous team, the Cleveland Cavaliers, and his current team, the Miami Heat, to the NBA Finals, winning the NBA championship with the Heat in 2012 and 2013.

James's contract with Nike—believed to be the richest initial shoe contract ever for an athlete—instantly turned him into one of the country's highest-paid sportspeople, and gave him the freedom to pursue a different model for his business interests. He embraced that freedom as few athletes have. In 2005, toward the end of his second year in the NBA, the then twenty-year-old James fired his agent, Aaron Goodwin, who represented a number of professional basketball players. To the astonishment of many sports-industry insiders, James did not switch to another agent. Instead, he established his own firm to handle all aspects of his business ventures and marketing activities—and he put his childhood friend Maverick Carter, then twenty-three, in charge of the company, along with fellow friends Randy Mims and Richard Paul. They called their firm LRMR, "L" for LeBron, "R" for Randy, "M" for Maverick, and "R" for Richard.

Carter had first met James at his eighth birthday party. He had coached James's summer league team and was working for Nike when James became a bona fide star—when "LeBron turned into LeBron," as Carter put it to me. By 2005, James was keen to run his own business—or, in his words, "be his own business." Carter agreed: "I always felt he should take more control. . . . And LeBron is a true entrepreneur. This is the right fit." Carter saw enormous potential: "David Beckham is bigger than what he actually does on the field. Jay-Z is bigger than Rihanna because of what he does, even though Rihanna's latest album sold many more copies. When Anna Wintour, the editor of [fashion magazine] *Vogue*, called to say that they wanted LeBron on the cover, I knew he had reached that stage, too. He is bigger than what he does."

It took the four friends a year and a half to establish LRMR and assemble a team of experts around them: a publicist, an accountant, an agent for contract negotiations, a PR person, and a lawyer. Taking basketball legend Michael Jordan's billion-dollar brand as inspiration, their vision for LRMR was to pursue a new model of sports marketing—a "new financial model for the 21st-century athlete," as *Fortune* magazine wrote. Instead of pursuing standard endorsements, James sought a revenue or equity share in the companies he worked with. Comparing LRMR with an agency like IMG, Carter explained: "The old model is a salesman's approach. They would sell LeBron like they would sell mattresses! They go like, 'We have six slots for endorsement deals—hurry up before we run out.' Consumers figure this out. They know it isn't real. It should be about the person behind the brand. Selling something is just a transaction. We want partnerships."

One such opportunity emerged in late 2008. By this point, James had signed several lucrative endorsement deals, but he had not made any agreements with a company in the video game market. LRMR received three unsolicited endorsement offers: from

Electronic Arts (EA), a powerhouse in the world of video game development, publishing, and distribution; from 2K Games, a subsidiary of Take-Two Interactive; and from Microsoft, which marketed its Xbox 360 gaming consoles and Xbox Live gaming service.

EA hoped to sign James to be the cover athlete for the new installment of the company's flagship basketball series, NBA Live. EA offered James a two-year contract, proposing to pay him $400,000 in year one and $300,000 in year two. In return, EA expected James to make himself available for two days to shoot commercials and collaborate in the production of other kinds of promotional materials, as well as participate in two media appearances to promote the game.

2K Games, meanwhile, wanted James to become its signature athlete for NBA 2K, the most highly acclaimed basketball video game. It offered a two-year contract that stipulated an up-front payment of $300,000 for year one and $350,000 for year two as well as bonuses tied to various sales targets. (For instance, if the game sold more than 2 million units in year one, James would receive a payment of $500,000; if it sold more than 2.5 million units he would get an additional $250,000; and if it sold more than 3 million units, he would gain an extra $750,000.) 2K Games asked James to participate in three days of production and advertising activities.

The third potential partner, Microsoft, was keen to develop a downloadable Xbox Live game revolving around James. The company offered him a $250,000 advance against a revenue-sharing deal in which James could earn up to a fifth of the game's revenues. Specifically, at less than $1.5 million in revenues, James would earn 10 percent; at between $1.5 million and $3 million in revenues, he would get 12.5 percent, and at more than $3 million in revenues, James would collect 20 percent of sales. Microsoft told James's team that they could be heavily involved in the game's development and decide when it would be released and how it would be promoted.

How should we evaluate James's marketing approach and the opportunities that come his way? It is safe to say that James's business ventures have been better received than his much-hyped decision in 2010 to leave the Cavaliers for the Heat, but his choice to fire his agent and establish his own marketing company has drawn its share of critics. Yet it has also set the tone for more such start-ups. Well before he was relegated to the New York Jets bench and then picked up by the New England Patriots, quarterback Tim Tebow, for instance, jumped on the bandwagon at the height of "Tebowmania" in 2010 by launching his own marketing firm, XV Enterprises, run by his older brother Robby Tebow and family friend Angel Gonzalez. These and other "do-it-yourself" ventures have led some sports-industry insiders to question the traditional agency model.

Striking out on their own allows stars to avoid paying hefty agency fees, thus enabling them to capture more of the value they feel they can create. Robby Tebow described the reason for his brother's entrepreneurial venture as follows: "We interviewed the top 15 marketing agencies in the world and went through their dog and pony show. . . . They were big and smooth and wore three-piece suits and some of them are very good at what they do. But one thing we realized is that they were talking about the things for [Tebow] that we were already thinking about. And when it came to negotiating we could do the job as good as they could and we weren't necessarily worrying about that 20 percent cut." But proponents of the traditional representation model might counter that an agency like IMG helps increase the total pie by lining up opportunities that the star and his family and friends may not realize exist or otherwise cannot turn into reality. Good arguments can be made for both points of view.

Another reason stars may want to establish their own businesses—and arguably one that matters more to James—is the increased control it gives them. They gain the freedom and flexibility to pursue the opportunities they value most. Stars may also use that greater control to drive for innovations in compensation models, which agents and salespeople at traditional, larger-scale agencies may be less inclined to do. In some instances, stars may prefer opportunities that are not driven by profit at all. James, for instance, has spoken of his desire to give his friends a chance to create a professional legacy and give back to the community in which he grew up.

The issue of control brings to mind Tom Cruise's deal with MGM. Cruise may have been motivated by the prospect of a big payday through his ownership stake in United Artists, but it is more probable that the freedom to choose projects was what he was really after when striking his deal. Most actors are essentially selling their talents to studios, and the idea of becoming a "buyer" for once can be very powerful. "Actors are always subject to the vagaries of the marketplace—who is better looking, who is the better actor, who is the hot new person," Alan Horn told me. "Every actor, no matter how big they are, will have heard, 'You know what, we know you are dying to do this, but we think so-and-so is more right for this than you are.' Every movie star can point to the one picture they didn't get." Cruise must have been pleased to be in a position to make casting decisions rather than be subject to them, especially given the number of up-and-coming actors vying for his throne and the uncertainty about his star status at the time. That's not to say, however, that when a star gains greater control over his or her business interests it necessarily leads to the best business outcomes. Although Cruise and Sloan showed admirable nerve when they chose to experiment with new models, they should have realized that major challenges lay ahead.

The same holds true for LeBron James: running a boutique agency like LRMR can create unique advantages, but it is far from easy. For one, LRMR lacks the scale, resources, and experience of an agency such as IMG, so it likely cannot provide the full suite of services that IMG offers its clients. A star like Sharapova, for instance, benefits not only from IMG's team of agents and sales-people, but also from its activities in the world of fashion and modeling (two interests of hers), its representation of Wimbledon and other important sports properties, its influence in the world of broadcasting (which often provides a second career for athletes after their playing days are over), and its wealth management ser-vice. These kinds of offerings may not prove to be important to James, but they can make all the difference to other talented per-formers, limiting LRMR's ability to attract a portfolio of athletes. And LRMR does not have the sales force to be as connected and constantly in tune with the business world as IMG is, so LRMR will probably have to settle for a more reactive and opportunistic role.

James has enormous star power, of course, and that can help limit some of his boutique agency's shortcomings. Capitalizing on James's popularity, Carter and his team have cleverly overcome some of the disadvantages inherent to LRMR's small scale by amassing a strong network of partners. This network includes collaborators such as Nike (where around 150 people work on James's product line on a daily basis), talent agency CAA, Fenway Sports Group (which gave James a tiny share in Liverpool FC, an English soccer club in Fenway's investment portfolio), and even Warren Buffett, who on occasion provides advice. Each year, Carter and his colleagues organize a two-day summit for executives from the various companies that have aligned themselves with James, to share information on their activities for James and discuss the latest trends in sports marketing. James and rapper Jay-Z also cohost an annual party, known as the Two Kings Dinner, during the NBA's All-Star Weekend; numerous celebrity and corporate contacts line up to attend the event each year.

To see what this all implies for how a superstar like James may approach specific partnership decisions, his choice between video game endorsements in 2008 is especially interesting. The deals offered to James reflect the three most common creative-talent compensation models in entertainment markets, illustrated in the chart below: first, a simple fixed-fee payment; second, a bonus or "step-function" fee structure that rewards talent for certain targets

Three Talent Compensation Models

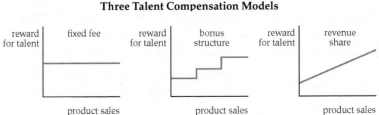

achieved; and third, a "share" model in which the talent receives a certain percentage of sales or profits. Whichever compensation model is selected depends on a large number of factors—including the power of the talent and that of the firms that employ them.

Let's look at the companies' side first. It is not a coincidence that by far the biggest player in the world of video games at the time, EA, offered a fixed-fee payment while the two less powerful studios, 2K Games and Microsoft, proposed that James share in the upside. As the market leader and the studio behind the game with the highest level of exposure and a cover spot that is in high demand among athletes, EA can afford to be less aggressive in recruiting talent to endorse its game. "Being on the cover of an Electronic Arts game is great exposure," said Carter about the opportunity, pointing to the value of, as he put it, "LeBron's face" being "in millions of homes around the country." Microsoft, meanwhile, was trying to grow its Xbox Live platform, so the company may have felt that it needed to sweeten the deal for James in order to compete with producers of better-selling games. If its game with James succeeds, however, Microsoft will end up paying a heavy price for its proposed compensation structure.

Sharing revenues or profits with an endorser is especially problematic for firms in the entertainment industry, where a few hits typically need to make up for the losses on a larger number of failures: a content producer will want to hang on to all the profits of a rare blockbuster hit. This is why most companies enlisting creative talent will generally prefer the fixed-fee structure over both other compensation options. And this is why, in the event they have to choose between those two less-than-ideal options, companies likely prefer the sort of bonus-structure model offered by 2K Games over a revenue-share model. Although this approach to compensation forces the company to increase its spending the more successful its products become, the total potential payment is capped.

Superstars, however, may take an opposing view of these compensation models. As they progress through their career life cycles, popular performers tend to shift their emphasis from creating to capturing value. The more wealth they have already accumulated—or the more confident they are that significant rewards are on the horizon—the more risk they are generally willing to take on when accepting new assignments. Betting on revenue-sharing (or profit-sharing) agreements then becomes quite attractive, because these kinds of contracts allow the talent to capture a significant share of the value that they themselves bring to projects. This is why, all else equal, most established superstars probably prefer a revenue-sharing model.

(If this "save first, take risks later" idea sounds like the opposite of what people in other careers are usually taught about how to manage financial risk, that's because those rules hardly apply to creative workers. It might be fine for newly minted lawyers and doctors to, say, buy stocks rather than deposit their salaries in a savings account, but they are expected to have much longer careers and can therefore afford to take risks early. Athletes, actors, and other performers have more pressure to make their early earnings last, in case their careers are as short as those of most of their peers.)

With such different perspectives on what deal is right, it's no wonder that stars and the companies they work for often find themselves in a tug-of-war. As performers such as LeBron James gain in power and achieve wealth at an ever-younger age, they can accept more risk in subsequent career moves and push for ever-larger rewards. That dynamic, in turn, can seriously erode the profits of the firms that rely on those performers to produce or market content. Yet even if most managers in entertainment businesses worry about their ability to compete for the most sought-after talent, they often find that they can't afford *not* to compete for that talent—at least not in the long run.

Hollywood finds itself in precisely this tug-of-war. In recent years, the major studios have worked hard to curtail spending on star actors. So-called back-end deals with stars have evolved, explained Horn: "It used to be that an A-list star would get, say, $15 million to $20 million against anywhere between eight and ten percent of the first-dollar gross revenues, meaning the revenues after exhibitors take their share. Now, we might still give them their up-front fee, but then we make sure we first get all our costs back and our overhead and interest, and we pay ourselves a modest distribution fee. What's left after those costs are deducted becomes the profit pool of which creatives, including the director and the actors, get a certain share." A shift away from the model that is most advantageous for the superstar, in other words. Hollywood studios' love for franchises involving comic-book characters and other mega-selling properties also helps rein in star power—and thus star salaries. "With *Harry Potter*, the book is the movie star," Horn said. "When you have a film based on a property that everyone knows, you don't need a big star to sell tickets. You need good actors, but they don't have to be stars." There is no need to feel sorry for the A-listers anytime soon, though: for instance, when the dust settled after the box-office run of Marvel's *The Avengers*, Robert Downey Jr. reportedly received $50 million for his role as Tony Stark.

It ought to come as no surprise that LeBron James ultimately chose the offer from Microsoft Xbox over the proposals from EA and 2K Games. Although a multitude of considerations went into that decision, the fee structure played a key role. (In 2013, James subsequently signed with 2K Games, finally making his debut as a cover athlete for the game *NBA 2K14*.) Explaining his client's enthusiasm for the revenue-sharing deal, Carter said: "For LeBron, an up-front payment of a few million dollars does not make a difference. It does not drive his choice. That money just adds to the pile of money he already has—it makes it a slightly bigger pile." He added: "For me, it can determine what kind of floor I can get in my kitchen. But I cannot think about what is best for me—I have to think about what is best for LeBron. And we are trying to build a billion-dollar business."

It sounds a bit like Justin Timberlake playing Sean Parker in *The Social Network*—"A million dollars isn't cool. . . . You know what's cool? A billion dollars." But Carter is on to something here—after all, Michael Jordan's Nike product lines alone reportedly yield revenues of several billion dollars each year. Imagine having even a tiny slice of such a large business—that is increasingly what super-stars like James are aiming for. Among entertainment industry insiders, rapper 50 Cent's endorsement deal with vitaminwater is a much admired example: because he negotiated an equity-sharing agreement before the beverage brand took off and its parent, gla-céau, was sold to Coca-Cola, he is thought to have made well over a hundred million dollars from that deal alone. Spurred on by such successes, IMG and Sharapova have also pursued these sorts of op-portunities. Her most eye-catching deal to date is an eight-year, $70 million agreement with longtime sponsor Nike, in which Sharapova receives a percentage of the sales of a line of dresses she herself helps design.

The high rewards that are up for grabs for stars in the entertain-ment industries create a vibrant, highly competitive market full of supremely talented performers. Businesses that rely on top-ranked talent will experience strong advantages in the market-place. But because true superstars can use their power to secure unprecedented levels of compensation, they are able to capture much of the value they add. The result is that those superstars—and not the firms that pay their wages—often emerge as the big-gest winners.

Chapter Five

WILL DIGITAL TECHNOLOGY END THE DOMINANCE OF BLOCKBUSTERS?

ow do you change the fortunes of a company that went from being called *Time*'s "Invention of the Year" in 2006 to one of the magazine's "10 Biggest Tech Failures of the Last Decade" a mere three years later? Robert Kyncl, YouTube's global head of content, thought he had the answer. It was October 2011, and Kyncl was putting the final touches on a plan that promised to revolutionize the world of online video—and perhaps even of television more generally. Kyncl and his team had come up with an idea to create more than a hundred "channels" with original content on YouTube. Hoping to jolt the creative community into action, they had earmarked a reported $100 million in advances in an attempt to solicit new material from producers, actors, musicians, comedians, and other talent.

The move was a significant departure for the company. Created in 2005, YouTube had built its name by enabling millions of everyday users to freely upload, share, and watch videos. Co-founders Steve Chen, Chad Hurley, and Jawed Karim reportedly came up with the concept for YouTube in early 2005 when the three friends, hanging out at a dinner party, realized they could not easily let others view the short video clips they had recorded that evening.

They began working to create a solution and, in May of that year, a beta version of the site went live with several dozen videos shot by the founders and their friends. The site initially gained little traction, but that all changed when fans posted a *Saturday Night Live* skit, *Lazy Sunday*, in which Chris Parnell and Andy Samberg rapped about going to an afternoon showing of the children's movie *The Chronicles of Narnia* (with masterful prose such as "Yo Samberg, what's crackin'? You thinking what I'm thinkin'? Narnia."). The video quickly went viral, ultimately collecting five million views before it was taken down at NBC's behest—but not before it had given YouTube a huge promotional boost. Within months, the site was streaming more than a hundred million clips a day—amateur recordings of sneezing pandas, Segway-riding chimpanzees, teenagers singing along with pop songs, and snowboarders wiping out, but also music videos, sports highlights, clips and "mash-ups" of movies, television series, and other copyrighted content.

Google acquired YouTube for a jaw-dropping $1.65 billion just over a year after its birth. "We're in the middle of a shift in digital media entertainment," said chief executive officer Hurley at the time. "Users are now in control of what they want to watch and when they want to watch it. They decide what rises to the top, what's entertaining." By 2011, YouTube was the behemoth of the online video space, with eight hundred million unique users a month across the globe, and more than three billion views a day. Living up to the site's motto, "Broadcast Yourself," users uploaded forty-eight hours' worth of new videos to the site every minute.

But despite its wild success in accumulating viewers and views, YouTube struggled mightily. It drew the ire of media companies for, in their eyes, failing to obey copyright laws. Advertisers remained wary of the vast amount of user-generated content on the site: in 2008, for instance, only an estimated 3 percent to 10 percent of YouTube videos were monetized through advertising. And for all its popularity with users, the average YouTuber only spent a paltry fifteen minutes per day on the site, compared with the four to five hours daily the average American spent watching television.

Industry insiders expressed strong doubts about YouTube's

ability to generate profits. "The future seems bleak for the user-generated material players unless they can secure access to sufficient independently produced professional content, . . . or they adapt their model to accommodate a pay-to-download or pay-to-view approach," wrote one analyst in 2010. Another argued: "Google needs to make a decision about YouTube: keep the status-quo and continue to support and grow an ever increasing number of streams via advertising to break even or change the culture slightly to a user-paid model and begin to recognize benefits to the bottom line." Hired away from video rental company Netflix where he negotiated deals with film and television studios, Kyncl initially concentrated on strengthening YouTube's streaming-movie-rental business, the company's first foray into paid content, which had been announced in early 2010. The service, launched with titles from the Sundance Film Festival, never quite managed to compete with rival offerings like the iTunes Store and Netflix.

Now the company's hopes rested on the new "YouTube Original Channels." The concept of channels itself was not new: established media companies such as the Associated Press, CBS, and Warner Bros., as well as homegrown YouTube stars, already offered videos through their own channels on the site under YouTube's "Partners Program," splitting advertising revenues with the site. "This is very much how we see the YouTube platform—with channels helping audiences find the content they love in a really smart way, and make it deeply personal to them," Alex Carloss, YouTube's head of entertainment, told me. However, Kyncl, Carloss, and their colleagues hoped the company's richly funded new initiative would encourage more established writers, directors, and producers to create original content for the site. "What we do is commission channels," declared Kyncl. "We don't tell people how to program the channels. We have certain volume requirements . . . but we are not making show-by-show decisions."

"It feels like a tremendous opportunity to tell the creative community that there is room for an awful lot of players in this space," Carloss said. To help develop their ideas, content creators could apply for up to several million dollars in funding, in the form of advances against their share of future advertising revenues. In return, channel owners were required to supply a minimum number of hours of programming each week. The expectation, Carloss explained, was that content creators would upload "anywhere between twenty and sixty hours of content over the course of a year." He added: "That can be original content—that is what we are funding—but it also can include curated content which speaks to the voice of the channel, or it could be archival library content." The creators would retain ownership, but YouTube would have an exclusive right to the content for a year. "We handle distribution—the creators are responsible for everything else," said Carloss. "YouTube allows them to find their audience wherever it may be. Their job is programming their channel and driving viewership."

Reflecting on the evolution of television, Kyncl commented: "People went from broad to narrow . . . and we think they will continue to go that way—spend more and more time in the niches—because now the distribution landscape allows for more narrowness." He believed people would prefer niche content because "the experience is more immersive," adding: "For example, there's no horseback-riding channel on cable. Plenty of people love horseback riding, and there's plenty of advertisers who would like to market to them, but there's no channel for it [on traditional television], because of the costs. You have to program a 24/7 loop, and you need a transponder to get your signal up on the satellite. With the Internet, everything is on demand, so you don't have to program 24/7—a few hours is all you need." Carloss agreed: "There are many examples of narrower content types that we can focus on. A lot of these channels would never see the light of day in the traditional television infrastructure—they are just too specific—but on YouTube they are a natural fit."

Why would YouTube, long known for its vast assortment of freely acquired amateur videos, switch to making a sizable bet on content development? How likely is it that YouTube will get a solid return on its considerable investment in niche channels? And will television come to look a lot more like YouTube does now—will we see a future in which everyone can be a content producer and tailor their products to thousands if not millions of niches?

These questions go to the heart of a hotly debated issue in entertainment circles—whether digital technology will spell the end of blockbusters, and thus of the effectiveness of blockbuster strategies. Some argue that the rise of online channels, driven by powerhouse sites like YouTube, is a sign that the "old" rules of the entertainment business soon will no longer apply. But the reality isn't quite so simple; indeed, if the lessons emerging from YouTube's evolution about the future of entertainment are anything to go by, the old rules may be more applicable now than ever. It turns out that there are laws of consumer behavior that both explain some of the site's biggest challenges in finding a sustainable business model and accurately predict the struggles experienced by many other businesses in popular culture. Every manager in the entertainment industry should be acutely aware of these laws, for one because they make it apparent that blockbusters will become more—not less—relevant in the future.

To see why, let's start with the basics. What explains the emergence of online video in the first place? The answer is simple: lower costs. The rise of digital technology reduces the cost of doing business in two major ways. First, digitization lowers the cost of *selling* goods. More specifically, new technologies reduce the costs that sellers incur when distributing products and collecting payments. Economists call these "transaction costs"—think of activities such as adding variety, communicating choices and prices to consumers, and managing assortments. Such tasks tend to be much less costly in digital environments than they are in more traditional settings. Online retailers do not face the shelf-space constraints that hamper bricks-and-mortar stores, and Internet businesses can use recommendation engines and other technologies to effectively manage their assortments.

Second, digital technology lowers the costs of *buying* goods. The costs that buyers incur in locating a seller and completing a transaction are often referred to as "search costs." These include activities such as finding products that match one's tastes, obtaining information on prices and other product attributes, and engaging in a transaction. Electronic marketplaces often significantly lower the amount of "effort" that buyers have to exert to accomplish these kinds of tasks. For instance, we can use search engines to quickly find content, rely on one-click options to complete a transaction online (rather than having to provide our credit-card details every time), and easily have products delivered to our homes.

Decreasing transaction and search costs affect almost all industries in one way or another. But the growing ubiquity of digital technology has truly transformed the entertainment sector. That's because in that sector digitization also lowers a third cost of doing business: the cost of *producing* and *reproducing* goods. Advances in cameras, green-screen technology, and editing software now enable professional filmmakers to resort to complex technical effects, shooting scenes that were previously unimaginable or, at the minimum, nearly unaffordable. Similarly, aspiring musicians can now record songs using no more than a laptop and a microphone and achieve a quality that was formerly available only in professional recording studios—and at a fraction of the cost. Many entertainment products can be fully digitized, including television programs, recorded music, books, and sports highlights. That, in turn, makes it possible to create an endless number of inexpensive reproductions and distribute them cheaply via digital channels (rather than having to ship them in physical form). Unfortunately, this feature of entertainment products also triggers *illegal* distribution on a massive scale, since the same forces that make recording and sharing entertainment goods cheaper for everyday consumers make it easier for pirates, too.

But that's not the only reason the effect of digitization is felt more in the entertainment industry. Another contributing factor is that people choose creative goods based on taste more than on a measure of objective quality. When subjective differences among products drive buying behavior, the kinds of tools we often associate with digital businesses—recommendation engines and other collaborative filtering mechanisms—can help people find the products they like. And because consumers of entertainment products are often avid fans who enjoy discovering new products, the lower transaction and search costs that are characteristic of digital channels both enable and encourage people to indulge their passion. Music fans discover new songs through YouTube, sports fans check statistics online, and readers browse stories on the Web—those who shop for more utilitarian products such as toothpaste and lightbulbs often find the buying process much less enjoyable.

Thanks to digital technology, entertainment industries are now rife with amateurs and other industry outsiders seeking to produce and disseminate their own creations—and not necessarily at a profit. Millions of people dream of making it "big" in music, publishing, film, and other creative industries. Since reduced production and distribution costs lower the barriers to entry to these markets, it is now possible for a teenager to self-publish a book and share it with millions of others, for a novice programmer to develop and sell a mobile game, or for a less-than-hip South Korean pop star to conquer the world with a catchy video in which he raps about a rich lifestyle while performing animal-inspired dance moves.

It is easy to see how the decreasing cost of doing business online has spurred the growth of YouTube in online video, just as it has fueled Amazon in books (and a host of other consumer products), and the iTunes Store, Spotify, and Rhapsody in music, to name a few examples. All of these online retailers introduce new possibilities for content creators. In part, that's because unlike traditional bricks-and-mortar or analog aggregators, they have infinite shelf space and allow consumers to search through innumerable options. And in part, that's because online retailers can relatively quickly and cheaply conquer global markets—in 2012, YouTube claimed it had eight hundred million users, of which 70 percent lived outside the United States—and allow content to be consumed across different platforms.

Carloss described YouTube as an example of a "next-generation platform" that "has no geographical borders and no specific devices of access—the screen can be in your pocket, on your office desk, or in your living room." He described a "third wave" of video distribution that he believes will be facilitated by lower costs: "Broadcast was the first wave, with very general content being offered up to a general audience. By the late 1970s and early 1980s, cable came around and more channels were available to consumers. MTV was born for music, CNN was born for news, and ESPN for sports. But launching a cable channel still requires a sufficiently large audience to justify the infrastructure and other expenditures. At YouTube, we now see a third phase—an opportunity to give specific audiences content tailored to them in categories that are underserved by the current media landscape. When you have a global audience at your fingertips, you can develop narrow, niche channels that appeal to specific individuals."

In such a world without limits, betting on a select group of blockbusters and superstars may appear old-fashioned and ill-advised. That, at least, is the central tenet of a best-selling book, *The Long Tail: Why the Future of Business Is Selling Less of More*, published in 2006 and written by Chris Anderson, then editor of *Wired* magazine. When consumers can find and afford products more closely tailored to their individual tastes, Anderson argues, they will migrate away from hit products. The wise company will therefore stop relying on blockbusters and focus on the profits to be made from the "long tail"—niche offerings that cannot be offered profitably through bricks-and-mortar channels. "The companies that will prosper," Anderson declares, "will be those that switch out of lowest-common-denominator mode and figure out how to address niches." The idea caught on with many industry insiders. Google's then chief executive officer, Eric Schmidt, for instance, claimed—on the cover of the book—that Anderson's beliefs "influence Google's strategic thinking in a profound way." And in its communications with analysts and other industry observers, Netflix took pride in calling itself a long-tail company.

No one disputes that online businesses offer much more variety than their analog counterparts. When transaction costs decrease and physical constraints on selection disappear, merchandise assortments can grow exponentially. That's why Apple's iTunes

The Long-Tail Theory

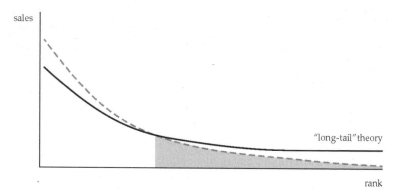

Store lists millions of albums and songs, and why Amazon offers hundreds of thousands of albums, whereas even the largest offline music stores typically stock only ten thousand titles. Similarly, whereas Netflix's DVD title count is in the six figures, bricks-and-mortar retailers usually stock no more than a couple thousand DVDs. And YouTube enables a long tail in online video, by making it possible for users to share videos for which there isn't room on traditional television.

For an illustration of the basic principle, consider the chart above, which ranks all possible offerings in a particular sector (say, all music albums and songs, all books, or all videos) by their sales volume. The shaded part represents the long tail—products that are consumed online but, because they sell only in small quantities, cannot be offered profitably through bricks-and-mortar or other analog channels.

So far, so good. But in his book, Anderson also offers some bold predictions about how demand is evolving. Online channels, he argues, actually change the shape of the demand curve. In his view, consumers value niche products geared to their particular interests more than they value products designed for mass appeal, and as Internet retailing enables consumers to find more of the former, their purchasing will change accordingly. In other words, consumption will shift from the head to the tail of the curve—and the tail will steadily grow not only longer, as more obscure products are made available, but also fatter, as consumers discover products better suited to their tastes. Put differently, with cataloging, search, and recommendation tools keeping a selection's immensity from overwhelming customers, we will experience a democratization of markets. Ultimately, obscure products will erode the huge market share traditionally enjoyed by a relatively small number of hits.

Anderson goes on to predict that "fickle customers" will "scatter to the winds as markets fragment into countless niches." Thanks to the long tail, we will leave "the water cooler era, when most of us listened, watched, and read from the same, relatively small pool of mostly hit content." Now, he says, "we're entering the microculture era, when we're all into different things." Anderson expects the multitude of niches to collectively add up to something big: he forecasts that the many small markets in goods that don't individually sell well enough to justify traditional retail and broadcast distribution will together exceed the size of the existing market in goods that do cross that economic bar. Over time, in other words, the shaded area under the curve in the previous chart will become bigger than the blank area.

While these predictions might be music to any YouTube executive's ears, the changes Anderson describes would spell trouble for a content producer relying on a blockbuster strategy. Fortunately for those betting on hits rather than niches, actual data on how markets are evolving tell a much different story than what Anderson predicted. As demand shifts from offline retailers with limited shelf space to online channels with much larger assortments, the sales distribution is not getting fatter in the tail. On the contrary, as time goes on and consumers buy more goods online, the tail is getting longer but decidedly thinner. And the importance of individual bestsellers is *not* diminishing over time. Instead, it is growing.

Take the music industry. According to Nielsen, which collects recorded-music sales information, of the eight million unique digital tracks sold in 2011 (the large majority for $0.99 or $1.29 through the iTunes Store), 94 percent—7.5 million tracks—sold fewer than one hundred units, and an astonishing 32 percent sold only one copy. Yes, that's right: of all the tracks that sold at least one copy, about a third sold *exactly* one copy. (One has to wonder how many of those songs were purchased by the artists themselves, just to test the technology, or perhaps by their moms out of a sense of loyalty.) And the trend is the opposite of what Anderson predicted: the recorded-music tail is getting thinner and thinner over time. Two years earlier, in 2009, 6.4 million unique tracks were sold; of those, 93 percent sold fewer than one hundred copies and 27 percent sold only one copy. Two years earlier still, of the 3.9 million tracks that were sold, 91 percent sold fewer than one hundred units and 24 percent sold only one copy. The picture is clear: as the market for digital tracks grows, the share of titles that sell far too few copies to be lucrative investments is growing as well. More and more tracks sell next to nothing.

Equally remarkable is what is happening in the head of the industry's demand curve. In 2011, 102 tracks sold more than a million units each, accounting for 15 percent of total sales. That is not a typo: 0.001 percent of the eight million tracks sold that year generated almost a sixth of all sales. It is hard to overstate the importance of those few blockbusters in the head of the curve. And the trend suggests that hits are gaining in relevance. In 2007, 36 tracks each sold more than a million copies; together, these tracks accounted for 7 percent of total market volume. In 2009, 79 tracks reached that milestone; together, they made up 12 percent of the sales volume.

The level of concentration in these markets is so astounding, in fact, that it is nearly impossible to depict the demand curve: it disappears entirely into the axes. Taking a different approach to mapping the sales distribution, the chart that follows shows how much tracks of different levels of popularity contribute to the overall sales in the market. It is staggering to see how few titles at the top contribute to a significant portion of sales, and how many titles at the bottom fail to do the same. Those are the realities of digital markets. Assortments may become more and more expansive, but

Recorded Music Sales in 2011: Digital Tracks

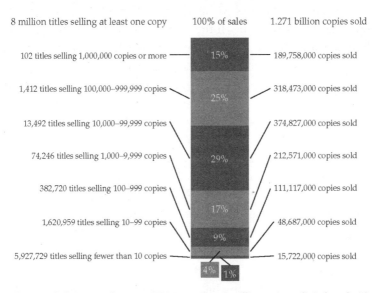

8 million titles selling at least one copy   100% of sales   1.271 billion copies sold

102 titles selling 1,000,000 copies or more — 15% — 189,758,000 copies sold

1,412 titles selling 100,000–999,999 copies — 25% — 318,473,000 copies sold

13,492 titles selling 10,000–99,999 copies — 374,827,000 copies sold

74,246 titles selling 1,000–9,999 copies — 29% — 212,571,000 copies sold

382,720 titles selling 100–999 copies — 111,117,000 copies sold

1,620,959 titles selling 10–99 copies — 17% — 48,687,000 copies sold

5,927,729 titles selling fewer than 10 copies — 9% — 15,722,000 copies sold

4% 1%

In the recorded-music industry in 2011, more than 8 million unique digital-track titles together sold 1.271 billion copies. The figure shows how sales were distributed across groups of titles with different levels of popularity. For instance, nearly 6 million titles—74 percent of all unique titles—each sold fewer than 10 copies, accounting for only 1 percent of sales.

the importance of the few titles at the very top keeps growing, while average sales for the lowest sellers are going down.

The same patterns are visible in album sales. As the next chart shows, out of a total of 880,000 albums that sold at least one copy in 2011, 13 album titles sold more than a million copies each, together accounting for 23 million copies sold. That's 0.001 percent of all titles accounting for 7 percent of sales. The top 1,000 albums generated about half of all the sales, and the top 10,000 albums around 80 percent of sales. Deep in the tail, 513,000 titles, or nearly 60 percent of the assortment, sold fewer than 10 copies each, together making up half a percent of total sales.

The numbers certainly do not come close to the trusted "80/20 rule" that many managers live by, which supposes that 80 percent of the sales tend to come from 20 percent of the products on offer.

Recorded Music Sales in 2011: (Physical and Digital) Albums

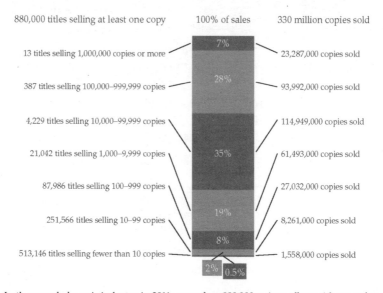

In the recorded-music industry in 2011, more than 880,000 unique album titles together sold more than 330 million copies (including both physical and digital copies). The figure shows how sales were distributed across groups of titles with different levels of popularity. For instance, 513,000 titles—58 percent of all unique titles—each sold fewer than 10 copies, accounting for only 0.5 percent of sales.

For music albums, it is closer to an 80/1 rule—if we can speak about a rule at all. Even if we take a conservative estimate of what would be on offer in a bricks-and-mortar store at any given point in time, Anderson's predictions that long-tail sales will rival those in the head are far off.

Of course the goods in the long tail include not just true niche content but former hits as well. Sales of a blockbuster—even one on the scale of Lady Gaga's *The Fame* or Maroon 5's *Songs About Jane*—will eventually dwindle. Such products can now live forever online, even if they have long been cleared from physical shelves. For old hits, then, digital channels may present a real opportunity. But the large majority of products in the tail were not very successful to begin with. Most of them, in fact, never met the bar for a release through traditional distribution channels. Or, in the case of individual music tracks, they are orphans of unbundling activity: now that online consumers can cherry-pick the most popular tracks on an album, the rest shoot quickly into the long tail.

These statistics for the recorded music industry are no fluke: my research on other sectors, such as video rentals and sales, yields the same patterns. Rather than a shift of demand to the long tail, we are witnessing an increased level of concentration in the market for digital entertainment goods. As illustrated by the chart below, the entertainment industry is moving more and more toward a winner-take-all market.

These trends take on greater meaning when we look at the behavior of individual customers. More than ever, it is vital for managers in the entertainment industry to understand who is responsible for the volume of business in the head and in the tail. Is a small group of fanatics driving the demand for obscure products? Or are large numbers of consumers regularly venturing into the long tail? Entertainment executives who pay close attention to the massive amount of data generated by online businesses can rediscover two old laws of consumer behavior first articulated by the sociologist William McPhee in the early 1960s, in his book

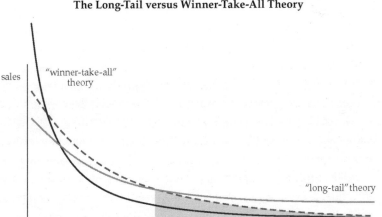

The Long-Tail versus Winner-Take-All Theory

Formal Theories of Mass Behavior. McPhee explored his theories in settings that typically provided fewer than a dozen alternatives. But my research reveals that his findings—which in many respects are directly at odds with Anderson's thinking about the long tail—also hold true for the enormous assortments we now find online.

After reviewing a trove of data, McPhee identified two important principles. First, he found that a disproportionately large share of the audience for popular products consists of relatively light consumers (those who buy a particular type of product infrequently), while a disproportionately large share of the audience for obscure products consists of relatively heavy consumers (those who buy that type of product often). In other words, obscure products are chosen by people who are familiar with many alternatives, whereas popular products are chosen by those who know of few others. Because it seems that hit products "monopolize" light consumers, McPhee called this phenomenon a "natural monopoly." No wonder, then, that when Apple proudly announced it had amassed a hundred thousand iPhone apps in its App Store, over 98 percent of iPhone users had at the time shown no interest in *any* of the ninety-nine thousand least popular apps. In general, most people are perfectly content with the most popular products. (The wide appeal of these top titles is, of course, what makes them popular in the first place.)

Second, McPhee showed that consumers of obscure products generally appreciate those products less than they appreciate popular products. McPhee described this concept as "double jeopardy," because niche products have a double disadvantage: first, they are not well known; second, when they become known, it is by people who "know better" and actually prefer the popular products. Netflix, for instance, should recognize this principle all too well: its niche titles receive significantly lower ratings than its hit titles. It perhaps sounds obvious, but many people intuitively believe the exact opposite—they think that the out-of-the-way movie or book is at least a delight to those who find it. In reality, however, the more obscure a title, the less likely it is to be appreciated.

This is not to deny the joy that a long-tail assortment can bring to consumers. Many YouTube users have felt the thrill that comes from discovering a rare gem of a video, perfectly tailored to their sense of humor or style and theirs to share with like-minded friends. That is also what gives Anderson's and Kyncl's thoughts on catering to the niches such resonance. For Anderson, the strategic implications of the digital environment are clear: companies should learn how to tailor their offerings to niche audiences. But the problem is that for every *Charlie Bit My Finger—Again!*, an immensely popular video of a baby biting its older brother's finger that has amassed over half a billion views, there are millions of other amateur recordings of babies that never appeal to anyone beyond the star's immediate family. And that, in turn, creates significant headaches for content producers and retailers hoping to build lucrative, sustainable businesses online.

With more and more hours of videos uploaded every minute, YouTube's challenge of profitably managing its vast assortment only increases. Even if each title costs a fraction of a cent to store and stream, those small amounts add up quickly given the assortment sizes that online businesses are accustomed to—especially if advertisers are unwilling to help support those long-tail titles. But *not* offering a long-tail assortment isn't a solution: after all, as McPhee's laws underscore, the heaviest consumers have a disproportionately strong interest in the tail, and cutting back on variety may lead them to switch to rivals.

Facing mounting costs for its vast long tail, YouTube and Google's executives have caught on to this reality. Remarkably, Eric Schmidt seems to have had a change of heart about the long tail. Just two years after championing the idea, he said: "I would like to tell you that the Internet has created such a level playing field that the long tail is absolutely the place to be—that there's so much differentiation, there's so much diversity, so many new voices. Unfortunately, that's not the case." Schmidt's revised thinking is more nuanced. "While the tail is very interesting," he said, "the truth is that the vast majority of revenue remains in the head. This is a lesson that businesses have to learn. While you can have a long tail strategy, you better have a head, because that's where all the revenue is." He described it as a "90/10 model," stating, "We love the long tail, but we make most of our revenue in the head." If Google does indeed make 90 percent of its revenues from the top 10 percent of its advertisers, the company is probably doing most of its business with many of the same large advertisers that were active in more traditional markets before Google pioneered online search advertising, and that still account for the biggest share of traditional-media advertising.

Schmidt, once so enthusiastic about Anderson's ideas, now argued for a winner-take-all effect, stating: "In fact, it's probable that the Internet will lead to larger blockbusters and more concentration of brands. . . . [W]hen you get everybody together they still like to have one superstar. It's no longer a US superstar, it's a global superstar. So that means global brands, global businesses, global sports figures, global celebrities."

Insights such as these explain why analysts called for YouTube to find ways to make the tail pay for itself (by charging users to upload content, for instance), why YouTube experimented with video rentals—and even why Kyncl is pushing his "Original Channels" idea. The company's latest strategic shift may have been framed as a desire to cater to niches, but the way YouTube's executives decided to allocate their funds reveals that it is effectively a play for hits.

When Kyncl and his team finished reviewing the flood of proposals he received after making the rounds with his idea, YouTube awarded advances to just over a hundred channels. Among those funded were channels proposed by Madonna and her manager, Guy Oseary, with a dance channel called Dance On; Shaquille O'Neal, with the Comedy Shaq Network; former *Saturday Night Live* comedian Amy Poehler, with Smart Girls at the Party; former professional skateboarder Tony Hawk, with skateboard channel RIDE; and Michael Hirschorn and Larry Aidem, former head of programming at music television network VH1 and former president of the Sundance Channel, respectively, with Life and Times, a channel focusing on Jay-Z's cultural and artistic interests—some of the entertainment world's biggest stars, in other words, and not a

slew of unknowns and amateurs. Although the list of creators receiving advances does include less established names, YouTube's
bet on Original Channels is very much a gamble on the power of
big media stars.

Granted, the artists providing content for YouTube's Original
Channels may not be motivated primarily by fame and fortune.
Creative freedom may be a key reason, just as it was for Tom Cruise
in the United Artists deal. "TV producers are governed by a creative and greenlighting process with a lot of involvement from
the network," said Carloss. "There are notes and strict formats they
have to follow, and a very narrow funnel into a piloting process.
The whole process can take years. Even if their show goes on the
air, it may be canceled two months later. That is very frustrating.
The freedom and flexibility to go from idea to audience within a
matter of days or weeks is very compelling to even the biggest content creators." The ability to test new ideas could be another moti-
vator. As Carloss put it: "They get to see how audiences respond,
and boy, do they respond! These are highly engaged communities,
who comment and like and share. That is very appealing. Content
creators can use YouTube as a farm system to develop new formats
or shows."

True to the principles of how blockbuster hits usually come
about, the company also acknowledges that it has to heavily promote the efforts of those stars. "We are dedicating over $200 mil-
lion to marketing our channels on YouTube," said Carloss. "That is
a big promotional commitment." The marketing comes in the form
of advertising—on, yes, YouTube. "When you have a platform the
scale of YouTube's, your smartest and most efficient venue is the
one that is closest to where the content is viewed, just as television
takes a percentage of its air time and devotes it to promoting its
own shows," Carloss explained. If YouTube is too focused on niche
content, the site will find it difficult to recoup its sizable investment
in content development and marketing. No surprise, then, that
YouTube awarded so many of its advances to established audience
magnets and proven characters.

It is too early to tell how YouTube's Original Channels will fare but so far the results do nothing to dispel the realities of competing in the new media environment. In late 2012, YouTube doubled down on its investment, providing a second round of funding to as many as sixty channel owners. At the same time, though, it pulled the plug on 60 percent of its programming deals. Shortly after YouTube launched its Original Channels, Carloss told me that "the channels are the network chiefs and I think that's very appealing to them." But by terminating so many of its initial deals, YouTube showed that in fact it is ruling the "airwaves" here. Meanwhile, among the ten most popular channels in early 2013 were those run by Jay-Z, auto magazine *Motor Trend*, humor site the *Onion*, Warner Music's video channel *The Warner Sound*, and wrestling giant WWE (World Wrestling Entertainment)—all entrenched, popular brands that could presumably have achieved YouTube fame even without Google's funds. Once again, blockbuster and superstar brands are carrying the day.

Realizing that a few winners still go a long way—and probably farther than ever before—other online businesses are following suit. Netflix has entered the arms race for premium content by spending a rumored $100 million on its own television series *House of Cards*, starring Kevin Spacey. Judging by its pipeline, Netflix is acting more like an old-school television network than the long-tail company it once seemed intent on becoming: both the upcoming Eli Roth horror series *Hemlock Grove* and the Jenji Kohan comedic drama *Orange Is the New Black* are expected to cost up to $4 million an episode. "They're huge budgets shows, they're doing things in a huge way," CAA agent Peter Micelli said about the series. Even Microsoft is joining the fray: the technology giant has hired television veteran Nancy Tellem, formerly in charge of programming at CBS, to produce high-end programming for its Xbox platform.

The premium online video space is quickly becoming crowded. By upending their original models and placing bets on original, professionally produced content, YouTube, Netflix, and Microsoft are moving closer to a fierce competitor in that space—and, in an interesting twist, a site whose very launch was triggered by YouTube's popularity.

Initially scorned as a futile attempt to compete with YouTube, Hulu had by 2009 made great strides toward its goal of, as its then chief executive officer Jason Kilar described it, "helping users find and enjoy the world's premium, professionally produced content when, where and how they want it." ("I'll be the first to say that our mission is extremely ambitious," Kilar admitted.) By 2009, in only its second year of operation, the site had become the premier online aggregator of high-end video content in the United States.

Kilar and his colleagues had faced what many insiders considered an impossible task. In March 2007, Jeff Zucker, then president and chief executive officer of NBC Universal, and Peter Chernin, then president and chief operating officer of News Corp., had announced a deal to launch "the largest Internet video distribution network ever assembled with the most sought-after content from television and film." The idea to join forces and form the venture "started out of frustration that other people were using our video online and creating a business," said Zucker. "YouTube was really built on the back of one of our videos, *Lazy Sunday*. . . . We want to make sure consumers know they don't need to steal our content." The two companies could bring a wide range of programming to the new venture: NBC Universal and News Corp. together had an extensive portfolio of television networks (including NBC, FOX, and several cable networks), television production companies, and motion picture studios.

The announcement met with much skepticism. "Old media guys don't 'get' the Internet," was how one magazine put it. The company's unimaginative temporary name, NewCo., prompted pundits to ridicule it as "NewTube," "Old Co.," or even "Clown Co." Industry insiders openly questioned the idea, pointing to the failure-ridden track record of major media companies working together to battle piracy, such as BMG, EMI, and Sony's MusicNet, which performed dismally. Capturing the prevailing sentiment about Hulu's chances, influential technology blog *TechCrunch* proclaimed: "Name this thing fast, before 'Clown Co.' becomes more than just an inside joke."

In ten weeks, Kilar and a team of around twenty people raced to build a beta version of the service. "We used paper sheets to cover the windows and block the rest of the world out," Kilar told me. "People were sleeping on air mattresses right here in the office." In March 2008, Hulu opened to the public, offering free streams of television shows and movies. The site quickly caught on with users and critics alike: just after the public launch, show business magazine *Entertainment Weekly* called Hulu "the most promising new way for consumers to view television shows and movies online since the almighty iTunes." One year after its beta launch, Hulu counted over forty million unique viewers, offered more than one thousand titles, delivered over one hundred million streams each month, and had served more than a hundred regular advertisers. The Associated Press named Hulu "Website of the Year." Even *TechCrunch* ate its words; in an article entitled "Happy Birthday Hulu. I'm Glad You Guys Didn't Suck," one of its bloggers wrote: "I was wrong. Hulu rocks. Despite ridiculous odds, the company was able to pull off a joint venture between two humongous parent media companies and provide users with a compelling, sexy product."

The founding partners each had an equal minority stake in the company. In return for a 10 percent stake, Providence Equity Partners, a $21 billion private-equity fund, provided a $100 million equity investment. In April 2009, after what Kilar referred to as a "long courting process," Disney joined NBC Universal and News Corp. as the third media conglomerate with an equity stake in Hulu, and agreed to provide Hulu with a set of shows from its popular broadcast network ABC and its cable networks.

Despite the company's early success, Kilar knew that the market for online video was only starting to take shape, and Hulu would have to evolve with it. One of the most pressing issues was the site's business model. Like so many other Web sites, Hulu was completely free to users. But Kilar was convinced that, as he put it, "people want to consume content under reasonable business models," so he and his team began debating whether to move away from that stance. "We could continue our hundred percent advertising-supported model," Kilar explained. "Offering free, ad-supported content was a good first step toward achieving our goal. . . . We are playing in the single biggest pond out there—advertising-supported content is a sixty-billion-dollar industry in the US alone, and the model resonates with the largest group of users. But, we could also consider other revenue models, such as a subscription or pay-per-view model. When we developed our mission, we were very careful to make sure that it did not spell out our business model. Our mission at Hulu is to help users enjoy the world's premium, professionally produced content. A service like HBO has wonderful original programming, and even though HBO's *Entourage* or *Flight of the Conchords* is not explicitly included in that mission statement, we very much mean to include those shows as well."

YouTube and Hulu are different beasts. Unlike YouTube, Hulu from its inception has focused on offering premium content. Driven by the strengths of its parent companies, Hulu emphasizes the head rather than the long tail. But like YouTube, Hulu has enjoyed rapid growth as a direct result of the advent of digital technology and the decreasing transaction and search costs that go along with it.

Hulu deserves the accolades that have come its way. Kilar and his team beat the odds and created an attractive product for consumers seeking high-quality video online. "I needed something new and good in my life, and now I have Hulu," is how one (obviously satisfied) user put it. The team also took the site's popularity beyond anyone's wildest imagination. But to fully appreciate Hulu's business model, it's important to take a step back and understand the pressures that digitization puts on traditional media companies—including Hulu's parents. Two factors stand out.

First, for even the most casual observers of entertainment businesses, the rise of digital distribution is synonymous with the growth of piracy—or, to be more precise, with the consumption of illegal copies of television programs, music, books, films, and other entertainment products undermining the sale of genuine items. Blockbuster bets may be especially vulnerable. "No one pirates copies of albums that nobody wants to hear," A&M/Octone's David Boxenbaum once said about the music industry. Like many other entertainment executives, Boxenbaum has good reason to worry about a downward trend in revenues: "Even when you are succeeding in the marketplace these days, you are still selling millions fewer albums than you used to with a hit record." But while many executives are convinced that piracy is to blame for diminishing sales, academic researchers have not found it easy to prove a causal relationship. True, some studies have shown that illegal downloading erodes recorded-music revenues, albeit to a modest degree. Other researchers, however, have concluded that illegal file sharing has no discernible effect on sales. These studies examined a sector that, by all accounts, has been especially hard hit; evidence that piracy causes revenues to drop in other sectors is even spottier.

The lack of convincing proof is less surprising than it may seem at first glance: after all, not every illegally downloaded file is a lost sale. Not every consumer of an unauthorized copy of a *Lazy Sunday* clip or a *Saturday Night Live* episode would have watched the program on regular television or bought a DVD later. Pirates may be so unwilling to pay that they simply are never going to be in the market for a paid-for version of an entertainment good. It is also possible that some of the most dedicated pirates are also heavy consumers of legal alternatives; they may use illegal downloads when deciding what to pay for later. Worrying about the size of the market for illegally downloaded products—a favorite pastime for industry associations such as the music industry's Recording Industry Association of America (RIAA) and the film sector's Motion Picture Association of America (MPAA)—may therefore be relatively unproductive. But to dismiss any possible negative effects of piracy would be wrong as well.

Second, digitization is hurting the revenues of entertainment companies by making many people less willing to pay for their products—or, more generally, by changing consumers' perceptions of what price is "fair." This could be seen as an indirect effect of piracy: with illegal copies of books, music, films, and video games often only a Google search away, some people may feel that paying a full price for media products is somehow unfair, old-fashioned, or just plain stupid. But piracy is not the only culprit here: new—legal—digital business models may have a similar result. Through digital channels, consumers can access more content than ever before, often at lower prices. With YouTube now effectively serving as a giant jukebox that lets users play whatever song they want for free, and with Spotify, Pandora, and Netflix allowing music, film, and television lovers access to vast libraries of content in exchange for at most a modest subscription fee, consumers may lose interest in paying to own an entertainment product.

Disney's Alan Horn has talked about "new technologies decreasing the pie, at least in the short term" in the film industry; as just one example, new movie streaming and rental options may be crowding out more lucrative DVD sales. That most consumers have a limited understanding of the peculiar cost structure of entertainment goods makes it harder to manage their perceptions of what prices are fair. In my experience, the public often overestimates how much it costs to manufacture, package, and ship hardcover books, CDs, DVDs, or other physical products, causing many people to expect greater savings on digital products (which eliminate many of those costs) than media businesses can realistically offer.

The challenging combination of illegal downloads on the one hand and the pressure on consumers' willingness to pay for content on the other hand means that producers who venture online may encounter unfavorable economics. Consider the perspective of free, over-the-air broadcast networks such as ABC, CBS, FOX, and NBC. They obtain programs from the television arms of their own parent companies, from competing media conglomerates, or from independent production companies, and generate revenues by selling advertising around those programs. Networks live and die by so-called CPM rates, which express the cost for advertisers to reach one thousand viewers. When Kilar and his team were re-thinking Hulu's business model in 2009, CPM rates for thirty-second advertisements during prime-time slots on the major broadcast networks varied between roughly $20 and $40. With at least sixteen minutes' worth of such commercials in every hour of television, the networks made around $1,000 per thousand viewers per hour.

Hulu's CPM rates have been much higher from the start, in some instances more than twice the going rates on broadcast tele-vision. That's because Hulu took "advantage of the unique attri-butes of online media that can make for a more targeted, interactive, and effective advertising experience," as the company's senior vice president of advertising, Jean-Paul Colaco, put it. Hulu gave adver-tisers new advertising formats and targeting capabilities. But it also showed far less advertising: relying on what Kilar described as a "less is more" approach, Hulu carried only a quarter of the advertising load of a broadcast network in 2009. As a result, even with its higher rates, advertising revenues per thousand viewers per hour of programming tended to be lower on Hulu than they were on broadcast television.

Granted, the picture is a bit more complicated than any back-of-the-envelope calculation can capture. And several parties partici-pate in these revenues: the networks share some of their revenues with the broadcast stations that help them reach viewers, and Hulu pays fees to content owners and distribution partners. But the mes-sage is clear: even if Hulu were to increase its advertising to 50 percent of the load carried by the broadcast networks—which Hulu's executives have said they consider the upper limit—it is difficult to match the economics of broadcast networks. And these calculations do not even include subsequent revenue windows that could be cannibalized by online video distribution. For in-stance, syndication revenues that stem from selling series to other networks can run into the hundreds of millions of dollars for top-performing shows, and income from DVD sales can amount to tens of millions of dollars for hit series. The growth of Hulu and other online video sites may well undermine these revenue streams.

Hulu's advertising model is even less lucrative when compared to cable networks such as The Disney Channel, NBC Universal's Bravo, and News Corp.'s FX. "On average," Kilar explained, "about half of [their] revenues comes from advertising, while the other half comes from fees paid by cable operators" such as Comcast and Cablevision. Prime-time CPM rates for original dramatic content on cable networks may be lower than those for broadcast television, but with such a large share of revenues coming from license fees, an hour of cable television yields total revenues per thousand viewers per hour that are significantly higher. And the more popular the cable network, the higher the income from license fees. "In deciding whether to put their programs online, cable networks will consider the per-subscriber fee that they receive from cable operators," noted Hulu's Andy Forssell, who was senior vice president of content acquisition and distribution until he was appointed interim chief executive officer when Kilar departed in 2013.

If the economics look so unfavorable, why did Hulu's parents concoct the plan to launch Hulu in the first place? Well, because losing a customer to piracy and collecting no revenues whatsoever is clearly worse. Helping to prevent these scenarios from happening was the original idea behind Hulu. Kilar's less-is-more approach must be viewed in that light: minimal advertising helps Hulu compete effectively with online rivals and with pirated content. Hulu is focused on creating a compelling offering for its users, explained Colaco: "We want a fair balance between the amount of advertising viewed and premium content consumed."

At the same time, even though Hulu is a hit, it is tough to blame television executives who tread carefully into the world of online video. As long as viewership on regular television is more lucrative than viewership on Hulu, and as long as the time spent viewing television still far outstrips that of watching online video, network and cable executives will have decidedly mixed feelings about fostering online video viewership—and in particular about tempting audiences to switch from watching, say, their favorite comedy series on NBC to watching that same program on Hulu.

Powerful cable operators, which control about 70 percent of the paid-for television market in the United States, will feel much the same. Their cautious stance may seem shortsighted and lacking in an innovative spirit—indeed, such accusations are often hurled at television executives—but it is simply the result of economic realities. It is not surprising, therefore, that Jeff Gaspin, then president of the Universal Television Group and the man responsible for NBC Universal's cable channels, was keen to find a model that, as he put it, "gets our content out there when and where people want it, but that also preserves [the] dual revenue stream and [the] relationship we have with our distributors."

The dilemma faced by television content producers is a classic one in the world of entertainment: should an established company risk cannibalizing its revenues in a traditional channel by pursuing a strong competitive position in a new channel? Managers in the television industry are hardly the first to struggle with this question. In the music industry, major record labels were initially hesitant to embrace online channels. In the face of growing piracy concerns, the labels focused instead on protecting traditional distribution methods. And with Amazon pioneering the online sale and now digital distribution of books, publishers have had to strike the right balance between exploiting new channels and working with existing bricks-and-mortar partners such as Barnes & Noble.

Conclusive answers to questions about which approach is best for content producers in these situations are hard to come by. Is the smart move to go on offense and embrace the new digital channels? Or is it more sensible to play defense and protect the existing business? Good arguments can be made for each stance. And if market conditions or other circumstances change (a shift in corporate ownership, for instance, or a greater willingness of advertisers to spend money online), the optimal strategy may change.

What has *not* changed—regardless of the way in which media producers choose to approach digital channels—is the relevance of blockbuster content. With their bet on Hulu, and thus on premium film and television content, NBC, FOX, and ABC were better positioned for success online than YouTube, with its stronger focus on long-tail content. Before YouTube began to make forays into higher-end original programming, Hulu accounted for less than one in every twenty video streams, but it collected a whopping quarter of the total online-video advertising revenues. YouTube's CPM rates were only a fifth of Hulu's in 2009—even though YouTube only sold advertising for a small percentage of the videos in its vast long-tail assortment. Advertisers, like regular consumers, are drawn to popular programming. And thus far, even in online channels, premium video content appears to have the highest odds of becoming popular.

Although Hulu has assembled a solid lineup of partners who bring their hit content to the site, signing up broadcast and cable television series (as well as A-list Hollywood movies) is an ongoing challenge. In 2009, FX asked Hulu to pull three seasons of *It's Always Sunny in Philadelphia* over fears that offering the show online would undercut its ratings and DVD sales. Turner Broadcasting System has refused to license Hulu popular shows such as *The Closer* that air on its cable network TNT. And in March 2010, Viacom's Comedy Central pulled *The Daily Show with Jon Stewart* and *The Colbert Report*, both of which consistently ranked among the most popular shows on Hulu, only to reverse its decision several months later. Even popular broadcast shows from equity partners are not always available on Hulu: FOX's juggernaut *American Idol*, for example, has been noticeably absent from Hulu's free service. "There can be friction between serving content owners and users," remarked Kilar.

Having demonstrated that the economics for premium content are more favorable than those for long-tail assortments, Hulu—much like YouTube, with the launch of its Original Channels—began to think about ways of tightening its hold on the head of the demand curve. A subscription service fits this goal: it provides a steady source of revenues and establishes an economic model that suits cable television, thus allowing Hulu to better compete for hit broadcast and cable shows. And so, after Kilar and his team investigated various options, the company wasted little time: in June

2010, Hulu Plus saw the light. For $9.99 a month, consumers could gain access to more shows and view them on more platforms, from Apple's iPhone and iPad to video game consoles. By late 2012, Hulu had amassed more than three million paying Hulu Plus subscribers, more than double the total for the year before. Hulu's estimated revenues rose to nearly $700 million in 2012. These amounts still pale in comparison to the rewards up for grabs in the traditional television industry, and it remains to be seen whether Hulu's parent companies will continue to support the young company and its business model. But Hulu's good results have already proved a critical point: a significant number of consumers are willing to pay for popular content online.

Developments in online video show us that digital technology is unquestionably a disruptive force that poses significant challenges for established content producers. That is not the whole story, however. Some existing entertainment businesses have switched to digitally distributing their products without being pressured into it by pirates or competitors and are reaping the benefits. A prime example can be found in the world of opera—not necessarily the first sector one thinks of when searching for clues about the evolving media landscape beyond, well, the nineteenth century, but actually an intriguing context for anyone hoping to understand the enduring relevance of bets on blockbusters and superstars.

In the 2006–2007 season, the Metropolitan Opera ("the Met") went where no opera house had gone before: to the movies. Or, to be more precise, general manager Peter Gelb started broadcasting (or "simulcasting") the Met's performances live in high-definition (HD) to movie theaters across the United States and Canada. The Live in HD program was a revolutionary move for a performing arts organization: never before had live productions been instantly accessible to mass audiences beyond the confines of auditoriums.

Concerned about its future, the Met conceived of the program as a way to attract new audiences to the opera. This was a critical goal for the Met, which had seen the average age of its audience base increase from sixty to sixty-five within just five years. (You know you have a problem when your audience is literally dying off.) Although opera attendance had risen in the 1980s and 1990s, it had waned since then. By 2007, Gelb's third year at the helm of the 124-year-old opera house, less than 5 percent of adults in the United States attended opera at least once a year, about a third of the number of Americans attending a Broadway show or symphony orchestra performance. "My aim is to strip away the veil of elitism," Gelb declared about the Live in HD program. "This is opera for the widest possible audience."

The largest independent performing arts company in the world and one of the oldest in the United States, the Met in 2007 had an annual attendance of 780,000 and an operating budget of over $220 million. As a nonprofit institution, it defined its purpose as "sustaining, encouraging, and promoting musical art, and educating the general public about music, particularly opera." As Gelb explained, the Met combined "every aspect of the performing arts into one," with a 120-member symphonic orchestra, a full-time chorus, a full-time dance company, and hundreds of stagehands. The Met staged twenty-five to twenty-eight different productions per season, and up to 240 performances annually, in its thirty-eight-hundred-seat opera house. Around two-fifths of its budget came from ticket sales, another two-fifths from private donors, and the remainder from government grants. Gelb—who had worked as an agent for Columbia Artists Management and served as a president of Sony Classical Music prior to his appointment at the Met—was determined to broaden the organization's revenue base by pursuing a multimedia strategy for the Met akin to the windowing strategy of Hollywood movies.

The inaugural season of the Live in HD program involved six Saturday matinee performances. Mimicking the release of a new movie, the shows were transmitted live and simultaneously across the country to nearly 250 movie theaters equipped with high-definition projectors. From the start, Gelb said, he wanted to "conceive of it as an event." But that didn't come cheap: the simulcasts required substantial investments in technology. They also involved a production team of about sixty people and some fifteen cameras to film the action onstage and backstage. The cost for each simulcast was about $1.1 million, or a total of $6.6 million for the season. To enable distribution of the performances, Gelb partnered with National CineMedia (NCM), the leading supplier of alternative programming to large movie theater chains such as Regal Cinemas, AMC Theatres, and National Amusements Theatres. As part of their agreement with the Met, the theaters agreed to share equally the revenues from ticket sales, with each ticket selling for around $22.

The first opera to feature in the Live in HD program was *The Magic Flute*, on December 30, 2006. Audiences across the United States experienced the opera at the same time as their counterparts in the Met itself, but at a much lower price—and with popcorn within reach. They saw a richly detailed performance that revealed performers' facial expressions and other subtleties normally not visible from even the best seats in the opera house. And if the opera they were watching had breaks, audiences followed the camera backstage and saw interviews with performers and exclusive footage about such things as costumes and set design. In total, three hundred thousand people turned out for the Met's first season of simulcast performances, yielding $3.3 million in revenues for the company.

In April 2007, as audiences settled into their seats for the last performance of the season, a new production of *Il Trittico*, Gelb watched from behind the stage where singers and musicians were getting ready for yet another performance. He faced an important decision. The Live in HD program had received mostly positive reviews in arts communities. But it had lost over $3 million—a significant sum that could make it impossible for the Met to break even, which in turn could upset donors. There were other lingering concerns. Some opera lovers feared that the simulcasts would cause a deterioration of the artistic quality of opera. Others speculated that the broadcasts would adversely affect ticket sales for live performances, including those staged by rival opera companies. As the Opéra de Paris, the Royal Opera House at Covent Garden, and other opera companies around the world announced plans to produce their own simulcasts, some feared that the intensified competition would hurt the long-term viability of the Met's costly initiative. After considering all these issues, Gelb had to answer a straightforward question: would the benefits of the simulcasts outweigh the necessary investments?

I'll cut to the chase: thus far, the answer for the Met is a resounding "yes." Gelb decided to continue to fund his Live in HD program, and it has had a major positive impact on the Met's bottom line. Accomplishing a rare feat for any new venture, the program was profitable in only its second year, when eight operas were broadcast to six hundred cinemas in twenty-three countries, selling 920,000 tickets. By the 2010–2011 season, a total of twelve operas were simulcast to fifteen hundred theaters in forty-six countries, selling nearly 3 million tickets and generating $11 million in profits. Within a few short years, the Met's Live in HD program became a powerful illustration of how digital technology can make a positive difference, even in a rather sleepy sector like opera. But that's not the only insight emerging from the Met's initiative. In fact, a close analysis of the Live in HD program's impact on the market for opera reveals other important lessons that apply to the entertainment industry more generally.

A first observation is that when thinking through the effect of new distribution channels, it helps to consider the "bundle of benefits" delivered to the customer in each context. The benefits of going to the Metropolitan Opera House are evident: a live opera at the Met is a special event taking place at a world-class venue with superior acoustics, where patrons are a part of an exclusive experience, dress up for the occasion, and mix with others of their ilk. But the simulcasts also have advantages: the $22 ticket prices are a far cry from the $400 that live operagoers have to shell out for orchestra-level seating; going to a local movie theater tends to be more convenient; there are fewer restrictions on what audiences can and cannot do (walking out in the middle of a performance, for instance, or munching on popcorn); simulcast-goers can see elements of the performance that are visible only on the screen; and they are able to view interviews and other bonus content. One form of consuming opera isn't necessarily better than the other—they are simply different. And the more these bundles of benefits are different, the more likely it is that new and existing channels are complements rather than substitutes. Gelb rightly compared the simulcasts to the popular *Monday Night Football* broadcasts that have significantly increased the popularity of the NFL: "Just as sports teams have discovered that fans still want to come in and experience the live thing, this will only enhance our live performances in New York City."

Customer benefits often change when products are distributed through different channels, even if the only apparent change is the "pipe" through which offerings reach the customer. Consuming television programs through Hulu, for instance, is different from consuming those same programs via regular television. Traditional television is linear: it takes place at a scheduled time, is limited by "what is on," contains mass-media advertising, and is more of a collective, "lean back" experience. Viewing videos through Hulu, by contrast, can take place whenever users want, gives viewers access to a vast assortment, shows them tailored advertisements, and is more of an individual, interactive, "lean forward" experience. Delivering these different benefits places new demands on content producers and their creative talent. The more the Met relies on simulcasts, for example, the more it may want to recruit opera singers who are trained in on-camera work, who have voices that translate well to the movie theater—and who look great up close. In this way and others, Gelb's Live in HD program is bound to change the market for opera.

The new technology is also likely to create bigger blockbusters. Opera has seen remarkably little innovation: at the time Gelb was mulling over his decision about whether to continue the Live in HD program, most major opera companies focused on nineteenth-century repertoire—works by composers such as Verdi, Puccini, and Mozart. Over the past twenty years, only twenty-six different operas had appeared in Opera America's list of the top ten productions, including just one American opera, *Porgy and Bess*; no modern operas appeared in the list at all. With the simulcasts attracting a different and (as Gelb hopes) younger audience, the opera house may be tempted to offer new content. So far, however, the same operas that are popular with live audiences—the few blockbusters that have stood the test of time, such as *Carmen*, *La Bohème*, and *La Traviata*—seem to appeal to simulcast-goers. Early evidence emerging from surveys offers an explanation: many of those who watch the productions in a movie theater tend to be relatively light opera consumers who are looking for a convenient way to supplement their occasional trips to see live opera. McPhee's natural monopoly concept teaches us that light consumers usually converge on the most popular products. Over time, therefore, the Met's already very popular interpretation of the love story of Carmen and Don José will probably become an even bigger hit around the world.

But even more dramatic changes to the market for opera are afoot. In the early 2000s, there were close to 180 American opera companies with total gross receipts of $720 million. Attendance figures and revenues were quite concentrated: the top four companies accounted for nearly 50 percent of the industry's revenues, and the Met had a budget nearly four times as large as the second-ranked player, the San Francisco Opera. The Met's Live in HD revolution will, in all likelihood, increase the level of concentration even further and so amplify the winner-take-all structure of the market as a whole. To see why, we have to consider the competitive position of both larger and smaller opera houses.

The top echelon of the market stands to gain the most from the new distribution technology for several reasons. First, only a few world-class opera houses can afford the necessary investments in technology. The costs associated with simulcasting may come down dramatically over time—advances in digital technology tend to have that effect, after all—but for the time being, at over $1 million in expenses per simulcast (a sum that is largely made up of recording-equipment rental and labor costs), a Live in HD program is out of reach for the lion's share of opera houses.

Second, only a few opera houses can acquire and retain A-list

talent. The Met employs dozens of opera singers and musicians—
their compensation accounts for over 30 percent of the Met's
total expenses. The market for opera talent is highly concentrated:
although becoming a professional opera singer requires years of
training in vocal technique as well as a mastery of languages and
acting skills, few men and women actually enjoy a long-term career as a professional singer. According to Irene Dalis, a former
Metropolitan Opera principal singer, only "one in 15,000 opera
singers makes it." But those reaching stardom, be it a Renée Fleming or Joyce DiDonato, can command $15,000 or more for a single
operatic performance, and the biggest stars may appear in nearly
fifty performances per year. The best-known and highest-paid opera singer in recent history, Luciano Pavarotti, reportedly earned
$100,000 for a recital by the late 1980s; as a member of the Three
Tenors, alongside Plácido Domingo and José Carreras, he earned a
rumored $10 million. An elite group of musical directors and con-
ductors also enjoy high-profile roles within opera companies.
Many, like the Met's James Levine, spend the majority of their professional careers associated with the same organization. The entertainers that come to dominate their professions and appeal to
audiences and donors alike find themselves in a powerful position, forcing opera houses to compete for their services. Inevitably,
the richest houses are in the best position to win the battle for
A-list talent.

Third, because middling productions and mediocre talent are
no substitute for superior production values and premium talent,
only a few top opera houses can compete for global audiences. Imagine that several opera companies took a gamble on simulcast technology, and audiences in a movie theater somewhere on the planet
had a choice between *Carmen* by the Met, *La Bohème* by London's
Royal Opera House, and *La Traviata* by the Lyric Opera of Kansas
City. The Lyric Opera's production would undoubtedly be excellent, but who would bet on that show to sell the highest number of
tickets? Audiences expect to find the best operas and opera singers
at the major opera houses, and these houses are global brands.
Since the market for simulcast opera can only bear so much vari-

ety, Kansas City and other second-tier opera companies would find it difficult to compete. Consequently, it's likely that only a few internationally renowned opera houses will be able to participate in the technological arms race. They will reap most of the rewards associated with any new distribution channels.

That's not to say that smaller, local opera houses will not see any benefits from the new technology. The simulcasts may well stimulate a broader interest in opera, which could in turn be a boon to smaller opera companies. A Boston Lyric Opera representative who acknowledged that her opera house does not have the best talent but rather "the next level down," believes that the simulcasts in the Boston area stimulated an interest in opera and brought new audiences to their opera house. But managers of other smaller operas are more concerned. Reed Smith, the general manager of Tri-Cities Opera in Binghamton, New York, said about the Met, "they are invading our space, to put it bluntly." It may take years to properly assess the impact of simulcasts on smaller operas, but unless these houses find ways to differentiate themselves, it is likely that at least some of them will struggle to compete with the richer, bigger opera companies, which will further fuel a winner-take-all market.

In opera as in other entertainment businesses, content producers that have scale are best equipped to win the race for new technology and for the best talent, and therefore ultimately for audiences. David Gockley, general manager of the San Francisco Opera, has called the Met's innovations "a bombshell." He has sought to emulate the strategy, albeit with limited success. Other top-tier opera companies across the world have also stepped up their efforts to distribute operas through new channels. The Washington National Opera simulcast its productions to schools and universities, the Royal Opera House in London tried staging opera and ballet performances inside and outside Europe, and the Teatro Alla Scala in Milan distributed a live worldwide simulcast of its gala opening night. Meanwhile, the Metropolitan Opera has gone from strength to strength: in the 2010–2011 season, the Met collected a record-high $182 million in private donations and—evidence of its battle for the best content and biggest stars—ran on a whopping $325 million operating budget. The Met spent more putting on operas during that season than any other company in the world, and its budget was bigger than the next eight largest companies in the United States combined.

All in all, although advances in digital technologies may at first blush seem to have a "democratizing" influence, in reality they tend to have the opposite effect: they foster concentration and a winner-take-all dynamic. By making reproducing, distributing, and consuming media content easier and cheaper, new technologies increasingly give people around the world access to the most sought-after television programs, movies, books, and opera performances. In this rapidly evolving marketplace, blockbusters and superstars gain in relevance—and blockbuster strategies thrive.

Chapter Six

WILL DIGITAL TECHNOLOGY THREATEN POWERFUL PRODUCERS?

"I like the people at our record company, but the time is at hand when you have to ask why anyone needs one," said Thom Yorke, singer and guitarist of British band Radiohead. It was 2007, shortly before the band would take the media world by storm by announcing a highly unconventional release plan for its new album *In Rainbows*. Radiohead would release its music as a digital download on the band's web site only—and would allow each fan to decide how much to pay for it.

Formed in 1985 by five friends attending an elite private boarding school in England, Radiohead was one of the most popular and artistically significant bands of the late twentieth and early twenty-first centuries. Known for its brooding style, Radiohead made a splash in the US market with its single *Creep* in April 1993, which introduced music buyers to the band's debut album *Pablo Honey*. The band released five more albums between 1995 and 2003, with *OK Computer* garnering the highest sales and most acclaim. It won the band its first Grammy Award, for Best Alternative Music Album. By 2007, Radiohead's six albums collectively had sold over eight million copies in the United States alone, and the band had accumulated a huge following—"large enough to make albums zoom to number one and devoted enough to plaster the Internet with Radiohead fan sites, blogs, song discussions, and bootleg recordings," as one reporter from the *New York Times* described it.

In 2003, with the release of its sixth album, *Hail to the Thief*, the band fulfilled its contractual obligations to its longtime record label, EMI, and chose not to renew its contract. By early 2005 Radiohead had begun to record *In Rainbows*, with no plans to sign a new contract with any record label. A two-year recording effort, the self-produced album's music was shaped by feedback from fans who attended a tour in 2006. Many of the songs played on that tour ultimately found their way onto the album, and live versions were posted on the Internet by fans who had recorded them at concerts. "The first time we did *All I Need*, boom! it was up on YouTube," Yorke said about one of the songs. "I think it's fantastic."

By the time Radiohead was ready to release its new album, the music industry was nothing like what it had been when the band started its ascent to the top. Bricks-and-mortar record stores accounted for just over 30 percent of all album sales—an all-time low—compared with over half of all album sales a decade earlier, having consistently lost share to mass retailers such as Walmart and Best Buy, digital retailers such as Apple's iTunes Store, and online subscription services such as Rhapsody. Music piracy, meanwhile, had proliferated, too: files were traded at an estimated ratio of twenty illegal downloads for every track sold.

Amid those difficult market conditions, Radiohead now planned to release its album in a fashion unprecedented for a musical group of its magnitude: not only would the full album be available exclusively through Radiohead's web site for digital download, but consumers would have the option of setting their own price for it. When visitors to the site clicked on a question mark next to a blank price box, a message saying "It's up to you" would display, and a subsequent screen would confirm, "No really, it's up to you." Only a service charge of £0.45 (or about $0.90) would be assessed for any download. Radiohead retained all rights to the album, and worked out an arrangement with its longtime music publisher, Warner/Chappell, to allow for proper payment of publishing royalties.

Some industry insiders dismissed the plan—conceived by the band and its managers Chris Hufford and Bryce Edge at UK-based Courtyard Management, and a significant break from the industry standard of fixed prices for music—as another nail in the coffin of the dying music industry. But Yorke was undaunted. Describing traditional strategies as a "decaying business model," he declared: "You can say we've earned the privilege to do things our way."

Radiohead's front man may be right about the band having earned the privilege to do what it wants, but it is debatable whether self-releasing an album in this manner is a smart move. And even now, more than five years after *In Rainbows* was released, industry insiders wonder whether Radiohead's actions foreshadow the future of the music industry, or whether the unusual album launch will remain a one-off experiment among superstar acts. What is clear is that there is a lot to be learned from how *In Rainbows* was received.

From the moment Radiohead announced its plans, the name-your-own-price gimmick was all that journalists covering the music business could write about. It suited Radiohead's eccentric style, and the band had already established a reputation for experimenting with unconventional album release tactics. For instance, *OK Computer* was introduced with a single, *Paranoid Android*, which had no chorus, several tempo changes, and lasted six and a half minutes—much longer than the average radio-friendly pop song. The label also sent one thousand media-industry insiders a Walkman with the album permabonded inside. For *Kid A*, the band's fourth album, Radiohead eschewed a traditional promotional approach, forgoing a single, a music video, and an accompanying US tour. Instead, the band released a collection of 10- to 40-second music "blips," combining images of nature, animations, and photographs of the band's members with audio clips, on music television channel MTV and on the band's web site. Tony Wadsworth, president and chief executive officer of EMI, remarked that Radiohead "want[ed] to find other ways of doing what has to be done to get their records into as many hands as possible."

Radiohead may not have been motivated by profits but, helped by the free publicity, the *In Rainbows* release was quite successful. To the surprise of many music-industry insiders, a significant number of consumers showed they were willing to pay even when it was not required—or, in true "stick-it-to-the-man" fashion, perhaps *because* it was not required. According to market research company comScore (which tracks hundreds of thousands of computer users), nearly two out of every five downloaders (38 percent, to be precise) paid for the album. Those who paid gave an average of $6, leading to an average amount spent per paid or free download of $2.26. A small group of fans pushed the average price up: one-sixth of all downloaders accounted for nearly 80 percent of total revenues, and close to one in every twenty downloaders accounted for nearly 30 percent of total revenues. Although Radiohead itself has not given out any sales figures, insiders estimate that the band sold between $6 million and $10 million's worth of albums. At the same time, illustrating the pull of illegal downloading even in the face of such an appealing pricing scheme, the album was a big hit on peer-to-peer networks, too. *Forbes* and BigChampagne found that on the day of *In Rainbows'* release, 240,000 people downloaded the album for free over BitTorrent, with another 100,000 people per day doing the same over the following days.

Another aspect of Radiohead's innovative release should have attracted more attention than the pricing plan, however, since it is possibly of far greater strategic importance. Radiohead released its album through its own web site, without the support of a label or retailer. That tactic spoke to a second high-stakes debate about the effect of digital technologies on the future of the entertainment business. If one key question is whether these new technologies will create a profitable long tail of millions of niches at the expense of blockbusters, another is whether technological advances undercut the traditional role of content producers and distributors. Will digitization "disintermediate" them? That is, will established producers and distributors become superfluous when it is easy for artists and other talent to market their creations directly to consumers, as Radiohead did? If this were to happen, the end would be near for content producers and retailers—and thus their block-buster strategies.

Fortunately for those established players, a close look at Radiohead and other examples suggests that wide-scale disintermediation is very unlikely. But that is not to say that this debate does not raise critical issues. Indeed, the possibility of disintermediation is a much greater threat to the business models of existing entertainment companies than the supposed rise of the long tail, and it is paramount for media producers to respond swiftly and adequately.

Exactly what is happening, and why? When questioning whether a type of business may be disappearing, we have to consider what marketers call the "marketing channel"—essentially all parties that are involved in producing, selling, and consuming a good. In its simplest form, the conventional channel for entertainment products consists of four "channel partners": one or more creative workers, a producer, a retailer, and a consumer. In the recorded-music industry, the marketing channel can consist of a band such as Radiohead, a record label, an offline retailer such as Walmart or an online retailer such as iTunes, and a music fan.

People most often associate the growing importance of digital technology, and the lower transaction and search costs that it causes, with the distribution of products via digital stores—iTunes and Spotify in music, Hulu and YouTube in video, and Amazon in books. But digital technology can alter channels much more fundamentally and in many more ways, as illustrated by the chart that follows. Some of these effects—the threat of piracy, for instance, or the desire of amateurs to become producers—lie at the core of YouTube, Hulu, and many other new businesses. Most central to the question of disintermediation are two observations: first, that online media enable talent to skip its traditional channel partners and "go direct" to the consumer, as Radiohead did; and second, that producers can pass over retailers and market entertainment goods directly to consumers, as happened when EMI co-launched the web site MusicNet on which it sold its music.

Being able to go direct is one thing, but will creative talent

How Digital Technology Impacts Channels for Entertainment Goods

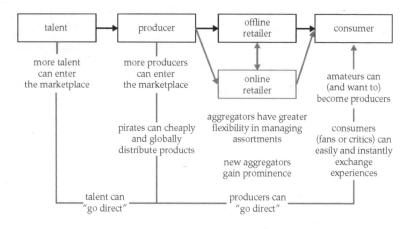

make use of that ability, to the detriment of producers and retailers, their existing channel partners? Answering this question involves thinking through the functions that producers and retailers currently perform, which marketers call (rather unimaginatively) "channel functions." The central idea is that it is possible to eliminate a channel partner only if someone else steps up and takes over the essential functions performed by this partner. This is the "iron law of distribution," which dictates that while you may be able to work around a channel partner, you cannot simply eliminate the channel functions that the partner performs.

Take the example of record labels in the music industry. Labels traditionally perform a wide range of channel functions: among other activities, they discover artists and help them develop their sound; advance artists money to cover their living and other expenses; provide career guidance; enlist the help of collaborators such as producers or music-video directors; fund recording sessions; enable the physical production of albums and songs; distribute the music to retail accounts; market the music (by getting music played on radio stations, for instance, or by connecting with retail partners to arrange in-store promotions); and handle royalty payments and other accounting issues. Granted, digital technology makes some of these tasks a lot easier or cheaper. Recording studio-quality music has become less expensive, and so has manufacturing albums—when all music is consumed digitally, there is no longer a need to produce physical copies. And distributing digital music is much simpler and cheaper than having to send out physical copies. For instance, Radiohead's manager told me that the band shipped the digital version of *In Rainbows* around the world for a few pennies per album, taking all costs into account.

But many other tasks remain as expensive, cumbersome, or labor-intensive as before, even in a fully digital world. It is unlikely that anyone else in the marketing channel would be able to—or would even want to—take over all the roles performed by the labels. Consider just one of these functions, that of giving advances to aspiring artists. If no retailers or other music-industry businesses advance money to a promising artist, having a record label shell out, say, a $100,000 advance against future earnings can make all the difference. That money can allow the artist to stop moonlighting as a Starbucks barista to earn a living while trying to find time to finesse her tunes, and instead devote all her time to her craft. How many aspiring musicians, when given the opportunity to sign a record deal that involves a significant advance, would pass up that opportunity? Most artists take the record deal—and that is unlikely to change anytime soon.

Or consider the marketing function: if a label no longer funds an artist's promotional expenses, uses its industry relationships to secure prominent placements, and otherwise organizes effective marketing campaigns, the artist will be left to fend for herself in marketing her music—certainly not an option for the faint of heart. And few artists will look forward to learning the intricate accounting rules and royalty-payment procedures that a label will normally take out of their hands.

The long list of channel functions performed by record labels makes it quite clear that the large majority of artists will continue to want and need those functions to be performed by others. In fact, the lower the barriers of entry into the music industry, the stronger the need for labels. That's because the more artists compete for attention, the more standing out in a cluttered media world becomes paramount, which in turn means that the development and marketing budgets as well as the expertise of major labels will become increasingly important. The International Federation of the Phonographic Industry (IFPI), an international music trade body, estimates that it typically costs $750,000 to $1.4 million to "break" a new act in a major market, including up to half a million dollars in marketing alone; even then, only one in five acts ends up with a successful career. Globally, the IFPI estimates, record companies invested $2.7 billion in A&R and another $1.8 billion in marketing in 2011. It is unclear which player besides the labels is willing and able to absorb the significant risks associated with launching new acts.

Wide-scale disintermediation of record labels and other entrenched entertainment businesses therefore seems an improbable scenario. Even for new creative talent that has gained prominence in online channels, the benefits of signing with a record label, publisher, or other kind of established content producer are often too tempting to ignore.

Canadian pop sensation Justin Bieber's successful career offers a vivid illustration of the continued relevance of record labels. Bieber first made his name among teenage fans through his YouTube videos and social-network presence. His manager, Scooter Braun, discovered him in 2008 through those same videos after (or so the legend goes) clicking on one of them by accident while searching for a different artist. But when it came time to conquer the mass market, Bieber and Braun smartly relied on a partnership with R&B star Usher and a recording contract with L.A. Reid's Island Records, which belongs to Universal Music Group. "I chose a major label because I knew Justin had it in him to be a worldwide act, and I needed to have foot soldiers on the ground," Braun explained to me. "To build a worldwide act, I needed offices in Australia, and in Japan, and in Malaysia. . . . I needed people who know the culture in each region. And Universal Records is the best company in worldwide music. They can get us on the radio, and they can get us good retailing opportunities around the world. They have the right relationships, and have nurtured those relationships. I did not want to struggle through the creation of a worldwide infrastructure by myself—that would have taken years and years and years."

Braun sees no reason for Bieber to spurn a major label like Universal and venture out on his own, even though his main client has now become a global phenomenon. "I still don't have an office in Japan, the second-largest music market in the world," Braun said. "But do I have people working there every single day thanks to my business partnership with Universal? Absolutely." He added: "It is possible to become a worldwide act without a major label. But why dedicate all that manpower to selling records when you can spend your time on other things instead? Universal Music Group has an amazing roster of talent that they can leverage to help put artists into better situations in the music industry worldwide."

In the book-publishing industry, Amanda Hocking made a similar choice. Described as "the darling of the self-publishing industry," the Minnesota native started writing when she was seventeen. Eight years later, in 2010, while working full-time in an $18,000-a-year job, she began selling her young-adult paranormal and dystopian novels online. She undertook this effort without the help of a traditional publisher; instead, she worked directly with retailers such as Amazon and Barnes & Noble's BN.com. By 2011, she had seven books on *USA Today*'s bestsellers list and had sold over a million copies of her books, priced between $0.99 and $2.99. Held up as an example of an author who had shrewdly circumvented the established publishing industry and promoted her novels via social media and blogs, she became only the second self-published author to sell more than a million e-books through Amazon's Kindle Store. And yet, that same year, she shopped a new four-book paranormal series, *Watersong*, to major publishers, eventually signing with St. Martin's Press, an imprint of major publisher Macmillan.

Why? Hocking's explanation boils down to a desire to have St.

Martin's carry out the kinds of channel functions that publishers traditionally perform, thus allowing her to focus on what she enjoys doing. "I want to be a writer," she wrote in her blog not long after the deal was announced. "I do not want to spend 40 hours a week handling e-mails, formatting covers, finding editors, etc. Right now, being me is a full-time corporation." She added: "I don't think people really grasp how much work I do. I think there is this very big misconception that I was like, 'Hey, paranormal is pretty hot right now,' and then I spent a weekend smashing out some words, threw it up online, and woke up the next day with a million dollars in my bank account. . . . This is literally years of work you're seeing. And hours and hours of work each day. The amount of time and energy I put into marketing is exhausting. I am continuously overwhelmed by the amount of work I have to do that isn't writing a book. I hardly have time to write anymore, which sucks and terrifies me." Self-publishing is "easier to get into but harder to maintain," she wrote. "It may be easier to self-publish than it is to traditionally publish, but in all honesty, it's harder to be a best seller self-publishing than it is with a house."

Even though digital technology makes it possible for authors, musicians, and other entertainers to "go direct," it is unlikely that many artists who find themselves in Justin Bieber's and Amanda Hocking's shoes will take a different path than they did. In the recorded-music business, major record labels still reign supreme: of the top one hundred albums on the *Billboard* chart in 2012, eighty-seven were released by one of the "big four," Universal, Sony, Warner Music, and EMI. And if wide-scale disintermediation of content producers is unlikely to occur in the recorded-music and book-publishing businesses, it is even less probable to disrupt the movie and television industries, where complex entertainment goods such as films and television programs bring together large teams of creative workers and require huge up-front costs. For most creative talent, no matter what kind of entertainment business they work in, established producers provide valuable services that they would prefer not to perform, or simply cannot perform as effectively, by themselves.

Even so, it would be a mistake to dismiss disintermediation as a myth and simply get on with business as usual. The fact that entertainers can use online channels to interact directly with consumers has real consequences for media producers and the profitability of their businesses.

First, digital channels give a small group of successful entertainers the opportunity to build up sizable fan bases by themselves. This gives them power in negotiations with media producers, which, in turn, enables those stars to secure higher compensation. St. Martin's had to overcome several other major publishers' bids in a hotly contested auction for Amanda Hocking's new series of novels, eventually paying a staggering $2 million for the global English-language rights. Because she keeps 70 percent of all revenues generated with her self-published e-books, Hocking could afford to push hard for a top-dollar deal when making the move to a traditional publisher—if the advance had been less than spectacular, she certainly could have walked away. After all, self-publishing had provided her with a viable and lucrative alternative, and at the rate she was selling e-books, she could have afforded to hire her own editor, publicist, marketing manager, and assistant to ease the non-writing workload. Likewise, if Justin Bieber had not been a YouTube phenomenon when he signed with Island Records, he surely would have received a lower advance. For media producers, the upside is that Hocking and Bieber are safer investments because of their track records, but those better odds of success come at a price.

Second, even if only a few superstar acts disintermediate producers and sell directly to consumers, as Radiohead did, that could have severe implications for the portfolios of major publishers, record labels, and other content providers. Losing the superstars that major content producers have so carefully developed and marketed can wreak havoc with their finely tuned blockbuster strategies, not least because top artists tend to bring in the highest revenues and profits. Adding fuel to this fire is a problem of timing: it is the superstar entertainers that may feel most motivated to leave, as they often are at a stage in their life cycle when they would prefer to take on more risk in return for a larger share of the revenues generated with their brands.

The release of *In Rainbows* came at just this career stage for Radiohead. After deciding to release the album themselves, the band got to keep nearly all the revenues, whereas it would have had to settle for around 15 percent of album and song sales under a conventional record deal. Provided they can drum up sufficient demand, stars who choose to sell their products directly to consumers can reap huge rewards. Yorke acknowledged as much: "In terms of digital income, we've made more money out of this record than out of all the other Radiohead albums put together, forever—in terms of anything on the Net. And that's nuts." We should not read too much into Radiohead's motivations in this single instance (as Yorke once said: "It was simply a response to a situation. We're out of contract. We have our own studio. We have this new server. What else would we do?"), but the financial result of the experiment was striking.

Another instructive example of talent selling direct to consumers comes from the world of television. In 2011, the entertainer Louis C.K., known for his stand-up comedy shows that aired on HBO and Showtime, among other networks, sold his self-produced and self-directed comedy special, *Live at the Beacon Theater*, through his own web site. Addressing his fans (or, rather, the "People of Earth," as he put it) four days after the launch, C.K. wrote: "The experiment was: if I put out a brand new standup special at a drastically low price ($5) and make it as easy as possible to buy, download and enjoy, free of any restrictions, will everyone just go and steal it? Will they pay for it? And how much money can be made by an individual in this manner?" Quite a bit, it seems: C.K. sold 50,000 copies within twelve hours, and 110,000 copies in those first four days, yielding a profit of $200,000 ("after taxes $75.58," he quipped). "We can safely say that the experiment really worked," C.K. concluded. Total sales of the special are now reportedly well above $1 million. Fellow comedians Aziz Ansari (helped by C.K.)

and Jim Gaffigan promptly followed suit, also self-releasing their specials. C.K. took his adventure one step further in 2012 when he decided to forgo Ticketmaster and instead sell tickets to his stand-up tour directly from his site.

Not every established superstar with a large following will take this route—for one thing, it requires an entrepreneurial spirit that not every artist possesses—but those who do can use online channels to command a bigger cut of the income streams involving their brands. The odds are decidedly stacked against niche acts, however. As Thom Yorke said about Radiohead's success with *In Rainbows*: "It only works for us because of where we are." Less established artists without a strong fan base and without any marketing clout generally have little monetary value to gain from going direct.

Digitization, then, has given rise to two intriguing phenomena. First, a number of creative workers have used the new technologies to sell their products directly to consumers, risen to the top in online channels, and subsequently landed big contracts with established media producers. Second, a few superstars who have come up in the traditional way have used online channels to venture out on their own under more lucrative revenue models. Rather than undermine the role of blockbusters and superstars, digitization therefore only further fuels a winner-take-all trend. Over time, an even higher share of the total income is likely to go to the top talent, and we will probably see more—not less—concentration in markets for entertainment goods.

Anxious about the possibility that advances in technology may prompt their best talent to leave, content producers are fighting back. In the music industry, labels are turning to longer-term contracts with newly signed talent. Locking acts in when they do not yet have any bargaining power ensures that the labels can benefit longer from their investments in talent development. Record labels are also diversifying their activities to give artists more reasons to stay. This trend is reflected in the "360" deals that virtually all labels now ask new artists to sign; such deals allow labels to benefit in multiple ways from their efforts to build an artist's brand.

The same factors that make it difficult for talent to take over a content producer's functions also prevent wide-scale disintermediation of retailers. That is not to say that online retailers won't replace bricks-and-mortar retailers—in fact, such a trend is very much under way, as the closings of Tower Records in music, Borders in books, and Blockbuster in movie rentals illustrate. Online retailers offer a compelling set of benefits to consumers. For instance, they usually offer a wider assortment and therefore more choice, enable easy browsing using recommendation engines (as opposed to requiring consumers to sort through shelves of physical products), and provide the convenience of placing orders from home. But even as retailing moves online, creative talent will find it difficult to take over the core functions these retailers perform. It is one thing for Radiohead to generate publicity and attract audiences to their web site; it is another thing entirely for a little-known artist to do so.

Retailers also help consumers by effectively acting as a filter and aiding them in making choices. In a market without retailers, consumers would somehow have to make themselves aware of all the product offerings in a favorite category—albums by hip-hop artists, for instance, or books by up-and-coming fiction writers—and then find a way to choose among them. While some consumers may enjoy the endless searches that doing so would entail, most people are perfectly happy to pay a little extra for the luxury of having someone else do this work for them.

In fact, rather than weakening the position of retailers in the marketing channel, the shift to online selling is actually creating ever more powerful retailers and other aggregators. The iTunes Store has a larger share of the online music market than any single retailer ever had of the bricks-and-mortar market for recorded music. iTunes has already overtaken Walmart in market share in music retailing in general. Similarly, in advertising-supported online video there are really only two players that matter, YouTube and Hulu, while Amazon dominates online book sales. Here, too, the rise of digital technology has fueled concentration—and not fragmentation—in the marketplace. And because these retailers are responsible for such a large percentage of the sales generated in certain entertainment sectors, creative workers in those sectors bypass them at their peril. Aside from a few superstars with massive followings, most artists will find it very difficult to generate significant levels of demand for their products without the help of these retailers.

Just as creative workers have been experimenting with selling their products directly to consumers, many established content producers have begun rethinking their role in the marketing channel, and specifically their position vis-à-vis established aggregators. Indeed, one of the keys to the future of entertainment markets lies in the evolving relationship between producers and retailers. The world of sports—which seems ahead of many other entertainment sectors in the search for ways to use digital channels to generate revenues—offers important clues.

When a special request comes in from Apple's highest echelons to send two of your best people to the technology giant on a three-week assignment during the most hectic months of the year, without any other information to go on, is it wise to agree without blinking an eye? Bob Bowman, chief executive officer of Major League Baseball Advanced Media (commonly referred to as BAM), was about to find out. It was late January 2010, and Bowman made his way to a fifth-floor conference room in BAM's offices, where a team of executives, product managers, and engineers had gathered for their weekly mobile meeting. Among those present were the two team members who had just returned from their stay at Apple's headquarters in Cupertino, California—a visit that culminated in their appearance onstage with Steve Jobs, then Apple's chief executive officer, as part of the much anticipated unveiling of Apple's new mobile device, the iPad. Now, Bowman would learn how much BAM still needed to do to turn the demo shown to the audience in Cupertino—which had garnered rave reviews from tech industry insiders—into a fully workable app, and devise a marketing strategy for it.

It was fitting that Apple had selected BAM to showcase the only sports-related app for the iPad. BAM was known for having the best league web site in professional sports—and, in fact, was widely regarded as one of the most remarkable success stories in the emerging digital media industry as a whole. Started in 2000 with what amounted to a $2.6 million investment from each of the thirty Major League Baseball (MLB) teams, the idea behind BAM was to establish a separate company for MLB's digital operations, in an attempt to improve the league's competitive balance. MLB's thirty team owners had unanimously voted to give BAM the responsibility for all digital activities, including the teams' own web sites, and had agreed that all revenues would be divided equally across the teams. MLB found office space for BAM above Manhattan's trendy Chelsea Market in a building filled with dot-com start-ups, a short cab ride but seemingly a world away from MLB's headquarters at 245 Park Avenue.

The first year was far from easy. MLB had virtually no digital media expertise—tellingly, just months before Bowman was hired, the URL MLB.com directed visitors to a Philadelphia law firm. "It was tough," Bowman said. "We encountered many technological and editorial glitches. We made our way through 2001 as best as we could, fixing problems as they came up, and rebuilt the site in the off-season." Initially, skeptics doubted that MLB.com would serve as anything more than a marketing vehicle and a venue for selling licensed merchandise. And not every new idea worked. For example, BAM supplied Japanese-language play-by-play calls for every game played by superstar outfielder Ichiro Suzuki in his debut year with the Seattle Mariners. The project cost $50,000 but drew fewer than one thousand Japanese fans. (Ever since, whenever someone at BAM made what was deemed an idiotic suggestion, co-workers would respond with "Japanese audio!") Before long, however, many of BAM's products and features began clicking with users, and traffic and revenue numbers improved dramatically.

By early 2010, its tenth year, BAM had grown considerably. Now operating with a staff of 475 employees, the company expected to generate $475 million in revenues that year from ticketing, paid content, advertising, and merchandising. Paid content, which brought in nearly a third of the revenues, comprised two distinct streams: income generated from licensing content to partners, and income derived from selling content directly to end consumers. With respect to licensing content, for example, BAM had a five-year digital-rights deal with ESPN that ran through 2013 and was thought to be worth close to $20 million a year. This agreement gave ESPN the right to live stream all Sunday, Monday, and Wednesday night baseball telecasts on its online television network (ESPN360 .com, later renamed WatchESPN.com) and ESPN Mobile TV, as well as show some video highlights.

But BAM became best known for its direct-to-consumer products. Bowman advocated the idea of developing products for an array of different platforms. "Heaven is the ability for people to touch baseball every day in the most convenient way possible," he told me. One of his colleagues confirmed that Bowman's strategy was working: "Business-to-consumer content is the fastest-growing source of revenue." While most content producers had failed to find viable business models for their digital operations, in 2009 BAM had amassed well over fifty million unique visitors per month on the MLB.com web site and 1.5 million paying subscribers for multimedia content delivered via the web. That included half a million customers who subscribed to BAM's flagship video product *MLB.TV*; priced at $100 or more a season, it allowed subscribers to watch live baseball games via their personal computers. In 2009, the company's *At Bat* Apple iPhone application was the nation's second-highest-selling app. Named "Best Multimedia App" by *Macworld*, two million downloads and sixty million videos had been streamed since its July 2008 debut. Summarizing the prevailing sentiment, *Newsweek* called BAM "the grand-slam online leader among major sports."

Now, BAM's iPad app would have to live up to the high standards Bowman and his team had established. In late December 2009, after months of intense speculation from technology enthusiasts about Apple's intention to launch a tablet device (but no news from Apple itself), the company approached Bowman and asked him whether he would be willing to send two employees to Cupertino to work with Apple on an unspecified assignment. "When Steve Jobs calls with such a request, you say 'yes,' even if he gives no other details," Bowman recalled a few weeks before the iPad's launch. The BAM employees jumped at the chance: "I'm always excited by top-secret opportunities I know nothing about," quipped one, a director of product development. "We have a philosophy here that we want to be the first on any new device. We like to be leaders." Bowman agreed: "You just don't know in this technology world what is going to take hold."

During the meeting in January 2010, Bowman talked with his team about the unusually short development time for the new app—only sixty days remained until baseball season's opening day—and the decisions that still needed to be made. How should they price the app? And should BAM offer free live games, as it did with the iPhone app? One team member pointed to a major challenge: "Video is going to look a lot better on the iPad than on the iPhone, which ironically creates some issues for us." Bowman knew how high the stakes were. "The iPhone has been a great success, which led to strong sales for our *At Bat* app, and the iPad could become equally important," he told his team. "We have got to get this right."

MLB is a powerful content producer—it effectively has a monopoly on professional baseball content in the United States, which means it can count on a loyal audience of sports enthusiasts. Often called "America's national pastime," baseball is one of the country's most popular sports: in the 2009 season, seventy-three million tickets to live games were sold. (The NBA was a distant second that year with twenty-two million.) And MLB's efforts to develop direct-to-consumer paid content have, by many measures, been extraordinarily successful. In fact, BAM was one of the first companies to demonstrate that consumers are willing to pay for content online.

But BAM's success also raises some key questions. Do the company's bold initiatives predict a future in which major media producers sell their content directly to consumers using a plethora of new channels, thus bypassing traditional partners such as the broadcasters that now televise baseball games? It is tempting to jump to such a conclusion, but that would be premature, and most likely flat-out wrong.

Admittedly, online channels create enormous opportunities for media producers to connect with audiences. The sport of baseball seems especially well positioned to take advantage of digital media: major-league teams play almost twenty-five hundred games each year, roughly twice that of the NBA and ten times that of the NFL. "We play every day," is how one executive put it. No television network can broadcast all those games. Online media allow MLB to tap into "displaced" demand—enabling, say, Boston Red Sox fans to watch a Sox game they cannot watch on television because they live outside New England, or because they are at work when the game airs and only have access to a computer. Online sports media thrive because of such demand. Baseball also has a strong community of avid fans addicted to baseball news, rumors, and statistics. Digital media are ideally suited to provide such die-hard fans with a barrage of information before, during, and after games—to "super-serve" the biggest fans. And, like all sports content, baseball is best consumed live. That makes consumers more willing to pay for live content, and makes illegal downloading of content much less of a problem than in other entertainment sectors such as music and film.

When the Internet, smartphones, and other new channels emerged, content producers faced a simple choice: let others develop products for those channels and hope they ask for your content, or take a hands-on approach to building those channels yourself. BAM chose the latter. Bowman openly speaks about his desire to be "a technology leader." When BAM launched, no industry player had the capability to do what baseball executives wanted to do— ESPN, for instance, was lagging in developing streaming technology. If BAM wanted to exploit new distribution platforms and ensure that products met their high quality standards, Bowman and his team needed to take responsibility for developing those platforms and products themselves.

And so BAM developed—from scratch—video-editing software that enabled employees to produce highlights in a matter of minutes. It also built a full-fledged studio filled with dozens of computers on which editors watched games in real time; as soon as something significant happened, editors could rewind the game, mark the highlight, save it, and then pass it on to another editor who could send the highlight out over the Internet. During the season, BAM would routinely send out hundreds of highlights a day.

"We bet big on broadband in 2002 and were willing to stream games when that was nothing more than showing a series of photographs, like in the old-fashioned flipbook," Bowman said. "We bet on wireless in 2005 when only Sprint was capable of handling multimedia content. We got lucky because the iPhone came along and triggered exponential growth." In the long run it may make little sense for one content producer to be pioneering new technologies, but in the short run doing so helps a producer grow a new business in a manner that suits its fans, its content, and its market position. Or, as Bowman put it, "if we are not willing to take risks and make mistakes, then we are never going to figure out what tomorrow looks like."

In the pursuit of that tomorrow, MLB seemingly jeopardizes what makes it so strong today. For professional baseball, as for all other major sports leagues, lucrative contracts for television rights remain critical to the bottom line. In 2010, MLB had ongoing television rights deals with the broadcast networks ESPN, FOX, and TBS. The contract with ESPN, owned by Disney, was worth $2.4 billion over eight years, or $300 million per year. The agreement allowed ESPN to televise up to eighty games per season, to feature a single team on its exclusive Sunday night games up to five times per season, and to start a series of Monday night baseball broadcasts. MLB also had a seven-year deal with FOX worth around $250 million per year (giving the network the rights to selected Saturday afternoon games and making it the exclusive home for the World Series and the All-Star Game), as well as a seven-year contract with TBS for around $150 million per year, bringing the total to roughly $700 million a year.

Those numbers dwarf the approximately $70 million in revenues that BAM made in 2009 from its online paid-content products, including *MLB.TV* and its iPhone *At Bat* app. When the company was pondering how to respond to the iPad launch, selling content directly to consumers accounted for only one-tenth of the revenues generated by its television rights deals—despite BAM's leading position in the paid-content market. Bowman and his team knew that digital revenues were likely to grow rapidly, but the league was (and is) a long way away from making as much money from paid content as it does from traditional media. Moreover, even online, licensing content to media partners is just as important as selling content directly to consumers: in 2009, for instance, $70 million of BAM's revenues came from licensing deals with ESPN and other media companies—many of the same partners the league works with in negotiating television-rights contracts.

While BAM's moves are great news for fans—"the fan is much better served now than in the past," Bowman said—MLB risks upsetting its television partners if it moves too aggressively into distributing digital content directly to consumers. As fans are given more options to watch live games and other baseball-related content online, broadcasters will inevitably worry that their viewership may decline. Even if other factors drive ratings down—the lack of a compelling matchup in the divisional play-offs or the World Series games, for example—those broadcasters may be quick to blame BAM and threaten to lower their bids for MLB television deals upon the next negotiation. And in a television landscape where sports leagues compete intensely for a share of the rich contracts offered by a small group of networks, getting on the wrong side of a broadcaster may be the last thing a sports-content producer wants to risk.

Why, then, would MLB allow Bowman's BAM to make such a forceful push into the digital age? As counterintuitive as it may sound, BAM's pursuit of direct-to-consumer, paid-content products actually *strengthens* MLB's existing revenue model. BAM increases the league's leverage over its existing distribution partners. MLB's aim is to gain the upper hand in negotiations with television networks—not to eventually displace those networks as channel partners. This is a common theme in markets for entertainment: when content producers pursue new channels, they typically do so not to disintermediate their current distribution partners, but rather to increase competition and drive up fees for their content. In MLB's case, the more it has a significant online presence and a direct route to the consumer, the more the league can credibly threaten to walk away from a deal it deems insufficiently lucrative. After all, when trying to profit from its content, MLB is no longer completely at the mercy of its distribution partners.

The same strategy of gaining leverage over distributors also goes a long way toward explaining why MLB launched its own television network, MLB Network. Introduced in 2009 to fifty million homes that subscribed to a digital cable subscription package, MLB Network airs live games as well as original programming (including *MLB Tonight*, a live, nightly studio show), highlights, classic games, and coverage of baseball-related events. The league's network may seem like an attempt to bypass existing broadcast partners. But here, too, MLB has little interest in jeopardizing its relationships with, say, ESPN and FOX by locking them out of many more live games. One reason is that MLB's high television-rights fees, paid up front each year, provide a solid financial foundation for its operations, so the league has a powerful incentive to keep the likes of ESPN satisfied. Another reason is that broadcast networks, by virtue of their mainstream programming, make it easy for MLB to reach more casual baseball fans and attract those new to the sport—and thus expand their customer base. Just as with BAM, MLB Network offers a way for MLB to strengthen its existing licensing model. The league's challenge is finding the right balance between going it alone and relying on the rights fees that its partners pay.

The television networks themselves are on the opposite side of a similar tug-of-war between media producers and retailers. Consider the role that Hulu plays: television production companies and networks use Hulu to offer their programs directly to consumers—without cable operators such as Comcast and Cablevision that stand between them and the consumer. As Hulu's Andy Forssell put it, "Hulu is about the content owners taking matters into their own hands—about participating in the value created through the distribution of their content." Especially for cable networks which rely strongly on fees from cable operators, distributing programs directly is a bold step. That is why powerful cable operators, fearful that Hulu may undermine their position as the exclusive source of certain programming, are fighting back. They have taken a hard line against cable networks whose shows were streamed on Hulu, with some cable companies going so far as to stipulate that the networks limit the number of episodes they make available online, or even imposing an outright ban.

The tensions are also prompting new alliances between content producers and aggregators. In a more comprehensive effort to protect its business model and role in the marketing channel, leading cable operator Comcast teamed up with media conglomerate Time Warner in June 2009 to pioneer an industry initiative called "TV Everywhere," which gives consumers who pay for cable channels access to the same content online. A month later, major broadcaster CBS—at the time the only top-four broadcaster that was not a Hulu owner—joined a TV Everywhere trial to test the authentication system necessary to distinguish paying from non-paying customers.

As the online video market continues to evolve, television networks have shown a greater inclination to play by the rules of the existing industry structures, which includes a strong role for the cable operators. The networks have good reason to do so, since they continue to depend heavily on the considerable income stream those cable operators provide. And although critics may dismiss initiatives such as TV Everywhere as futile attempts by the old guard to hang on to a dying business model, the truth is that none of the major players in the television industry have a strong economic incentive to cause upheaval. They benefit from protecting current revenue models and safeguarding their place in the marketing channel. True threats to existing structures are much more likely to come from outside the industry.

As these examples from the worlds of baseball and television suggest, it makes little sense to believe that advances in digital technology will cause powerful content producers to simply push out existing distributors. What is actually happening is both more complicated and more interesting. Even as digitization is creating a multitude of ways through which consumers can get media content, some of the biggest media producers are actively contributing to this trend by launching their own channels to gain leverage over existing distributors.

Taking this clever approach to the use of new distribution technologies to an even higher level is another sports league, the NFL. Much can be learned from the way in which the nation's most-watched sport—and arguably one of the most successful entertainment properties in the world—has managed its content strategy, for it says a great deal about how markets for entertainment goods are evolving.

In late 2009, the NFL was wrapping up its biggest season in twenty years, with each of the league's games averaging well over sixteen million US television viewers. Yet Brian Rolapp, then the NFL's senior vice president of media strategy and digital media, had little time to celebrate the league's latest milestone. As fans across the country eagerly anticipated a round of play-off_games that would culminate in the forty-fourth Super Bowl, Rolapp and his digital media team faced a decision regarding the league's strategy for the mobile space. Various potential allies were vying to replace Sprint as the NFL's official wireless partner. With the fate of valuable rights for the mobile platform hanging in the balance—such as video highlights, access to live games, and even live streaming of the NFL's flagship cable channels NFL Network and NFL Red-Zone—a lot was riding on the choice.

"We are a media company as much as we are a sports company," the Harvard-educated Rolapp, who had been with the NFL since 2003 and in charge of the league's digital media group since 2005, told me. "We are focused on monetizing the game of football as best as we can, and media rights are a critical source of revenues." He had a point: the NFL collected $8 billion in revenues in 2009, about half of which came from media licensing—primarily from contracts with television networks—and a quarter from ticket sales. Cable channel ESPN annually paid the league well over $1 billion, while the broadcasters CBS, FOX, and NBC paid $600 million to $700 million each and satellite provider DirecTV another $700 million. Broadcast partners also played a key role in building the league's brand. "The NFL only has a small marketing budget," said the NFL's vice president of fan strategy and marketing. "We buy very little media. But we receive over $200 million in media from our broadcast partners as part of the deals with them, in the form of spots we can run during the games."

For the distribution of content on mobile phones—or, to be more precise, smartphones—the NFL had partnered with Sprint since 2005. The carrier paid the league $100 million per year to be the NFL's exclusive wireless partner, with about half that amount earmarked for NFL-related advertising and promotion. Because the partnership was set to expire in April 2010, however, the NFL had begun discussions with other parties. Determining the right approach was far from easy. "We want to be where the fans are and have a partner that can deliver the best quality experience for our fans," said Rolapp, "but at the same time we do not want to lose sight of the fees we can collect in the fierce competitive landscape of the wireless space."

Rolapp's team had identified three strategic options. First, the NFL could pursue an exclusive partnership with one wireless carrier, much as it did with Sprint. "This may be the last exclusive deal cycle for us in this sector," said Rolapp, pointing out that the wireless industry was changing fast. "The avidity of our fans is amazing, which enables us to be more selective," added Hans

Schroeder, vice president of digital media. Second, the league could push for a set of non-exclusive deals with wireless carriers such as AT&T, Sprint, and Verizon, giving each the right to carry NFL content on mobile phones, but no one party the exclusive right to do so. "An exclusive deal can severely limit the number of fans reached, as even the biggest carrier can only deliver twenty to twenty-five percent of the total audience," noted Schroeder about the market conditions in late 2009. "Non-exclusive deals could help the NFL reach a bigger audience on mobile devices, much like the current deal structure allows us to do on television." A third option was to work with current or new broadcasting partners on a joint television and wireless deal. The league had excluded mobile phone distribution rights in the latest round of negotiations with broadcasters, so the NFL could go back to the networks and offer the rights to show live full-game video or in-progress highlights, as well as the rights to live video from NFL Network and NFL RedZone. Rolapp knew that the broadcasters, which he called "strategic partners," would consider the mobile rights highly valuable. ESPN, for instance, had its own product for mobile phones, ESPN Mobile, and the network was keen to add NFL content to its line-up.

Significantly upping the ante and underscoring how much the NFL was seeking to expand its business, NFL commissioner Roger Goodell had recently set a goal of $25 billion in revenue by 2027. Rolapp's task was to develop a strategy for the mobile space and do his part to help the league achieve that ambitious number.

The NFL is not known for leaving money on the table when negotiating business deals—and that is putting it mildly. The country's richest sports league achieved its leading position by being smart about getting the best possible contracts when licensing its content to media companies. The NFL's approach to mobile phone rights is no exception: spurred on by Goodell's bold targets, Rolapp ultimately chose to pursue a partnership with only one wireless carrier, and that decision led to what sports industry insiders regard as a landmark licensing deal. When the agreement was announced in March 2010, the sports world learned that Verizon would pay the NFL $720 million over four years—the most valuable wireless agreement for the league ever. (The deal was renewed in 2013 for a fee of $1 billion, nearly a forty percent increase.) To some, the outcome was surprising: why, they wondered, would the NFL choose to form an exclusive partnership, and how did that fit the league's overall distribution strategy? The answers to these questions go to the heart of why the NFL has become so powerful, and how it uses advances in digital technology to its advantage.

Media producers often face difficult trade-offs when they, like Rolapp, have to decide which distributors to partner with. Those trade-offs can be captured by what I call the "three Cs" of media licensing deals: compensation, coverage, and cooperation (also because alliteration makes everything sound more interesting). Companies can maximize compensation by pursuing the deal that yields the highest fee; maximize coverage by choosing the set of partners that collectively provide the broadest audience reach; or maximize cooperation by avoiding actions that upset their partners—what marketers call avoiding "channel conflict." But content producers can rarely do all three at the same time. In fact, in most situations they can only maximize one C: focusing on one C almost unavoidably comes at the expense of the other two Cs.

Rolapp found himself in precisely that position when choosing among potential wireless partners. The third option, partnering with one or more television networks, would have helped solidify the relationship between the NFL and its existing media partners, thus maximizing cooperation. Because television rights are so critical to the NFL's bottom line—Rolapp labeled television networks "strategic partners" for a reason—and because wireless rights are still only a fraction of the value of television rights, selling wireless rights to a television partner such as ESPN would have been the path of least resistance.

Pursuing the second option—a series of non-exclusive deals with several wireless carriers—would have helped the NFL increase the number of fans they were reaching. It would have maximized coverage. This would have been a significant benefit since at the time, as Schroeder pointed out, no single carrier could deliver more than a quarter of the total potential audience. The financial opportunity would have been appealing, too: if the NFL had been shrewd in its approach to the negotiations with multiple partners, it could have ended up securing a very high total rights fee.

But in the end Rolapp and the NFL pursued neither option because they knew that the first option—making an exclusive deal with one carrier—came with the highest potential rewards. Choosing this option maximized compensation, as suggested by the large sum that Verizon paid for the right to carry NFL content on smartphones. The league's rich deal stems from the fiercely competitive nature of the wireless market, where growth has stalled and each rival carrier appears to take a now-or-never approach to striking deals in order to survive. And it follows from the unavoidable fact that only an exclusive deal will allow Verizon to fully benefit from its association with the NFL's brand in the form of a sponsorship commitment: as the lone rights holder, the carrier can claim to be the "official wireless partner of the NFL," and for that it gladly pays a premium. Fittingly, influential trade magazine *SportsBusiness Journal* described the deal as marking "the biggest overlap between a sponsorship and media deal in American sports league history."

The NFL's strategy is the polar opposite of MLBAM's in a number of ways. For instance, while the NFL focuses on licensing partnerships with media companies, BAM puts more emphasis on its paid-content offerings to consumers. The NFL has integrated its digital operations and its traditional media activities—Rolapp and his group are based at the league's headquarters in New York City—whereas MLB has set up BAM as a relatively separate arm. And while the NFL takes a less proactive, more deliberate approach to the development of digital media—as Rolapp put it: "We don't have to be first, we have to be good. We are fine with not being the most aggressive of the sports leagues"—BAM's Bowman emphasizes the need to be first on a given platform, focuses on experimentation, and spearheads the development of technology.

In one respect the two sports leagues' strategies are a match, however: like MLB, the NFL also uses new distribution channels, made possible by the development of digital technology, to gain leverage over its media partners. For the NFL, snubbing existing television partners when selling wireless rights is not a sign of a diminishing role for television or other substantial shifts in the media landscape—it is a way to achieve a more powerful negotiating position. When explaining his strategy, Rolapp talks about "three pillars" of his team's activities: "First, we want to reach fans through new platforms. Second, by developing rights and products for those new platforms, we can pursue new partners who are interested in buying those rights and in reaching our fans. Third, new platforms force our existing partners to compete, which should make our packages more valuable." Rolapp's last point is crucial: the NFL wants to foster a rivalry between its partners, because with more partners vying for rights, prices for its content will go up.

Having a way to distribute content directly to consumers supports that philosophy. The NFL has two of its own cable networks: NFL Network and NFL RedZone. NFL Network airs pre-season games, past NFL Super Bowls, and other NFL "Classics," as well as shows about coaches, players, and fans, and the annual NFL Draft during which teams select new players. NFL RedZone, launched in 2009, allows viewers to follow multiple Sunday games at the same time: whenever a team is inside the twenty-yard line (the "red zone") and about to score, the channel cuts to that game. Thanks to these channels, the NFL is no longer at the mercy of its television partners' distribution infrastructure, enabling league executives to more forcefully negotiate contracts with current or potential licensing partners. "Television is important to our business, so it's good to have our own beachhead in television for the distribution of our games," Schroeder told me. "NFL Network gives us that." Direct-to-the-customer channels are great tools for content experimentation, too: the more the NFL knows about how consumers are interacting with its content, the better the decisions it can make.

One look at the list of distribution partners reveals just how far the NFL has taken the concept of encouraging competition among its licensing partners. After the NFL closed its new wireless deal, football content was available through the broadcasters CBS, NBC, and FOX; the cable network ESPN; the satellite television provider DirecTV; satellite radio network Sirius; wireless carrier Verizon; and the NFL Network, NFL RedZone, and NFL.com. The NFL is a master at "slicing and dicing" its content, giving each of its distribution partners an exclusive piece—such as American Football Conference (AFC) or National Football Conference (NFC) divisional games for CBS and FOX, Sunday night games for NBC, Monday night games for ESPN, or the rights to mobile phone content for Verizon. Meanwhile, the league has consistently put what Rolapp called "a premium on control." Citing just one example, he said: "When renewing broadcast rights in 2005, we held back many of the digital rights. We figured if partners want those rights, they should tell us what they are going to do with them and what they are worth."

This strategy—and the resulting proliferation of the ways in which fans can consume NFL content—creates some tensions. Shortly after the Verizon deal was announced, *SportsBusiness Journal* reported that "companies that spend nearly a combined $4 billion a year on TV and satellite rights" were "closely watching how the league's recent moves" would affect their business. One executive whose network owned the rights to some NFL content was quoted as saying: "We are keeping our eyes on this. It's starting to nibble at the edges."

So far, television executives' worries seem to center on NFL Network and NFL RedZone. There was an outcry among those executives when, in 2006, NFL Network made a move into live game programming and began to exclusively produce and air eight regular-season NFL games as part of a new Thursday/Saturday package. Soon the league found itself battling with cable providers such as Time Warner Cable and Comcast, who balked at NFL Network's high fees per subscriber and its insistence that the network had to be included in those cable providers' basic packages (as opposed to being bundled only with other sports content). And RedZone, by giving viewers access to all games, competes with DirecTV's *NFL Sunday Ticket*. It also may draw viewers away from regular games airing on Sundays on CBS and FOX, especially those fans who are more passionate about following the league as a whole than about following one particular team. That the league often reminds users they see all touchdowns and no advertisements could be a sore point for television executives who have coughed up billion-dollar rights fees—and so could the league's slogan: "If you want the NFL, go to the NFL."

Why do the NFL's distribution partners allow the league to get away with these practices? The answer is familiar: because the NFL gives them the blockbuster content they desperately need. It is hard to overstate the mass appeal of NFL games: over 70 percent of all Americans proclaim themselves football fans, and half of the people in that group consider themselves avid (as opposed to casual) fans. More US fans cite football as their favorite sport than any other sport. The league's fans spend an average of well over nine hours per week engaged with the NFL, including almost four hours watching live games—both numbers that dwarf those for other sports. Seven of America's top ten favorite professional sports teams are NFL teams. Viewership for major NFL games regularly beats that for events such as the *Academy Awards* and the *American Idol* finale. And the annual Super Bowl, the game that determines which team can call itself champion, has become an unofficial American holiday. Over a hundred million people tune in to the Super Bowl broadcast nowadays. In fact, as of early 2013, four Super Bowls belong to the top five most-watched American shows of all time. The Super Bowls in 2010, 2011, and 2012 each set ratings records; 111 million viewers watched the broadcast in February 2012.

Although ratings for the big five broadcast networks have

declined in recent years, the NFL seems immune to this trend. No surprise, then, that television executives seem willing to run through a formation of 250-pound linebackers to get their hands on a slice of the ever more popular NFL content. Longtime NBC Sports chairman Dick Ebersol called the NFL "the surest bet in the television universe" for programmers. "The dominance has been mind-numbing," he said. "The NFL is more of a guarantee of success than if you've got Brad Pitt, George Clooney and Angelina Jolie doing a drama series for the network." The numbers prove him right. Advertisers like their odds, too: in 2013, they reportedly paid as much as $3.8 million for a thirty-second advertising spot during the Super Bowl, a sum that far exceeds any other placement on television. CBS, FOX, and NBC, among which the game rotates annually, directly see those benefits. ESPN, which pays more for NFL content than any other form of programming, receives about $5 per cable subscriber per month from cable providers—more than any other cable network—so it, too, will do whatever it can to maintain its winning formula. And just as DirecTV relies heavily on NFL content to acquire and retain satellite customers, Verizon expects the league to help it improve its market position in wireless.

NFL executives are acutely aware of the value of their blockbuster content. "When the NFL puts content behind a platform, we can drive growth for it," Rolapp pointed out. Schroeder agreed: "The NFL has a pretty good track record of people building businesses around our content." And so the NFL will continue to push its distribution partners for top-dollar payments. But competing head-to-head with its partners or locking them out of its marketing channel entirely is not an aim. The NFL relies too much on the lucrative licensing income—paid up front—that it receives every year from its existing media partners, and on the marketing power that those partners provide.

The NFL's goal is clear: the league wants to increase control and leverage for the benefit of its existing business model—not to replace it with a riskier proposition that relies less on channel partners. The league thrives as a result of the proliferation of ways in which its games can be delivered to fans. Like MLB and other smart producers, the NFL takes full advantage of an unrelenting demand from distributors for content that can command an audience. And like those other producers, the NFL understands that those who offer blockbuster content will only gain in power.

Chapter Seven

THE FUTURE OF
BLOCKBUSTER STRATEGIES

When Shawn Carter—better known as hip-hop megastar Jay-Z, and one of the world's best-selling musicians of all time—in 2010 insisted that his publisher launch his memoir, *Decoded*, in a way that was different from every other book release in history, he got his wish—and some of the strangest of bedfellows any product launch has ever seen.

Carter's desire to push the envelope had fueled the idea to write a book in the first place. Far from a traditional autobiography, the forty-year-old rap mogul's publishing debut was what he called a "lyrical memoir" that explained the hidden meanings behind some of his most provocative songs and provided a personal narrative of his life and art. In a collage-like manner, the book pieced together an assortment of autobiographical fragments, lyrics, and images—effectively "decoding" the metaphors and veiled messages captured in his many hit songs—and took the reader on a tour of Carter's life, thereby providing a unique perspective on the history of hip-hop music and culture. John Meneilly, Carter's manager and a partner in Roc Nation—a joint venture between Carter and Live Nation that serves as an umbrella company for Carter's artist management, music recording and publishing, touring, merchandising, and other new business ventures—saw the book as a profound statement. "For us, the book is a way to communicate that rap music is a real art form, that it is serious, and not a set of nursery rhymes," he told me. "Every single word in a song is there for a reason."

Spiegel & Grau, an imprint of the world's largest trade publisher, Random House, purchased the rights to *Decoded* in 2009 and planned to publish it in November 2010. "We see a lot of celebrity projects and most do not interest us, but we felt that Jay had something very interesting to say," remarked Julie Grau, senior vice president and publisher at Random House. She was one of a select group of publishers invited to meet with Meneilly to discuss the book. Meneilly knew that the format Carter had chosen might come as a surprise to potential publishers. "When Random House walked into the room, I am sure they thought it would either be a biography or business book," Meneilly commented. "But when we said it was a lyrical memoir, they embraced it."

Carter and Meneilly soon told Grau they did not want the publisher to pursue a traditional book launch. Grau distinctly recalled their conversation: "[Carter] said, 'Don't tell me to do something because that is the way it is done. That is a reason for me not to do it.'" Meneilly added: "We told Random House, 'Take everything you normally do when you launch a book, and throw it out the window. We don't want to just check boxes. Of course we have to do the nuts and bolts—we'll do a book signing—but we want to be innovative.' That is Jay-Z's mantra: do something different every time."

And so, not long after acquiring the book, Spiegel & Grau reached out to David Droga and Andrew Essex, co-founders of the young advertising agency Droga5, for help in developing a groundbreaking campaign. Essex, a New York City native, served as Droga5's chief executive officer, while Australian-born Droga served as the agency's creative chairman. (He also supplied the agency's name: when he was a child, his mother stitched "Droga5" into his underwear to distinguish them from his four other brothers' undergarments.) As it happened, Droga5 was just then wrestling with another challenge: how to drive higher usage of Bing, Microsoft's new search engine. Droga5's solution was to kill two birds with one idea: a massive, interactive scavenger hunt. In the months leading up to the *Decoded* release, each of the memoir's three hundred pages would be unveiled in various media (from billboards and bus shelters to more unconventional advertising surfaces such as cars, jackets, and even the bottom of a hotel pool). Players around the world would search for clues distributed via Bing to find the locations of those pages, "unlock" them, and gradually piece together the book in both the physical and digital world, winning prizes along the way. "Jay-Z's book is unique in its design and its concept," said Essex of the memoir. "We feel it deserves a unique campaign, too."

Droga5 expected its bold idea for Jay-Z's campaign to cost approximately $2 million in labor and materials alone. But Spiegel & Grau lacked the funds to market Carter's memoir at a scale fit for a superstar; the publisher's advertising budget, Grau admitted, "won't even buy us a billboard." This is where Bing came in: Droga and Essex hoped that Microsoft would see the innovative campaign—when powered by Bing—as a unique opportunity to help Web users "break the Google habit."

Droga5's co-founders faced a difficult task as they worked to broker an unprecedented partnership among Roc Nation, Random House, and a team overseen by Yusuf Mehdi, senior vice president of Microsoft's online services division. For Carter, Roc Nation, and Random House, two factors were critical: selling books (rather than giving them away for free) and maintaining a high degree of control over the campaign. "Jay-Z has to sign off on everything," said Meneilly. For Microsoft, having the final say was key, too: "If we pay for the campaign, we want to be the approver," said Mehdi, whose primary objective was to grow awareness and usage of Bing. While Droga5's co-founders worried about "whether the center of the partnership would hold," as Essex put it, they had to weigh the possible benefits and costs for Droga5 itself. If Jay-Z's memoir was going to succeed in the marketplace, the unlikely group of partners would have to find a way to share their playbook.

What should we make of the deal among Roc Nation, Random House, Microsoft, and Droga5? Although undertaking this alliance may sound like a formula for disaster, if we analyze the situation we learn that it in fact makes good sense for each of the players. More importantly, the story of the *Decoded* campaign tells us a lot about the future of blockbuster strategies. The highly innovative book launch—which in the end won Droga5 several of the advertising industry's most prestigious awards—has everything to do with how digital technology is changing the entertainment landscape. And don't get me wrong: even if fears about the long tail overtaking blockbusters or content producers being disintermediated are almost certainly overstated, technological advances *are* having a dramatic impact on entertainment businesses. The *Decoded* campaign illustrates that point in multiple ways.

Let's start with the good news. For those who spend their days (and nights and weekends) launching and promoting entertainment products, digital technologies open up a world of exciting possibilities. The campaign that Droga5 envisioned for *Decoded* is a prime example: the book's innovative release simply would not have been possible without advances in technology and the remarkable innovations they have triggered, including social networks, interactive maps, mobile phones equipped with cameras, and photo-sharing applications. These new tools enabled Droga5 to integrate an outdoor and online campaign, blending on-the-street and Internet experiences and ultimately fostering a sense of real contact between Jay-Z and his fans. Such a product launch was unimaginable in a fully analog world.

Here is how the campaign unfolded. The agency released the book in the form of two hundred placements through various media across the globe in the month leading up to the launch. Each release of a new page—every day of the campaign saw about ten of them—provided an opportunity for people to discover a location that was important to Jay-Z's life and music. The campaign used traditional outdoor media—including billboards, subway stations, and bus shelters—in such high-profile places as New York City's Times Square, the Strip in Las Vegas, and London's Covent Garden. But it also employed more adventurous advertising surfaces, such as the inner lining of a Gucci jacket featured in the window of Gucci's flagship Fifth Avenue store, the bottom of the pool at Miami Beach's high-end Delano Hotel, the rooftop of a New Orleans building, and the stage curtain of the Apollo Theater. Some of these placements were true works of art.

The book's pages were not just randomly placed, either: the location of every page was inspired by the story on that page, which helped fans put Carter's memoir in context. For example, if page 24 of *Decoded* referred to a particular street corner in Brooklyn where Carter used to sell drugs, that page was displayed on a billboard on that corner. Or if page 156 discussed Carter's co-ownership of the restaurant The Spotted Pig, that page was printed on the restaurant's plates or place mats. Each page was branded with a "Decode Jay-Z" watermark and a description of how someone could participate in the game. By texting a simple code to a designated number to "decode" a page, players could win a variety of rewards, including autographed copies of *Decoded*.

Meanwhile, in the game's online component, Jay-Z released a pair of clues for each page on his Facebook and Twitter accounts and on the game's web site, bing.com/jay-z. The first clue narrowed down the geographic region in which the page could be found, while the second clue pinpointed the page's exact location. The first players to decipher both clues and enter the correct location on a digital map were then able to "unlock" a page and gain the chance to win a second set of prizes, including a personal Facebook message from Jay-Z. In addition, on-the-street players could submit a photo they had taken of the page to the game's web site. As more and more pages were discovered on the street, the web site gradually revealed the entire book. Those players who digitally assembled the entire book were automatically entered into a drawing for the grand prize that was the dream of every Jay-Z fan: two lifetime passes to each of the star's concerts, anywhere in the world.

The campaign delivered the result Random House and Carter

hoped for. Millions of people interacted with the game, and an active community of players exchanged information about the book's pages online. Jay-Z's Facebook followers grew by a million during the campaign. Even more important to the book's event-style launch, major news outlets and cultural influencers across the globe covered the campaign: in one month, the launch earned over a billion media impressions. Even other celebrities weighed in: "Jay-Z killed it with the Bing promo for his book," tweeted Trey Songz, and Ryan Seacrest wrote: "This is crazy. . . . Jay-Z is hiding 300 pages of his new book around the world . . . fans get to find them." Many tweets included links to the "Decode Jay-Z" web site, fueling even more excitement for the memoir. Helped by the free publicity, *Decoded* hit the bestsellers list and stayed there for nineteen straight weeks. Priced at $35, the book sold three hundred thousand copies—ten times as many as fellow rapper Eminem's 2008 book, *The Way I Am*, and more than enough to ensure that Spiegel & Grau earned back its advance to the author.

The *Decoded* launch was unique, but many other entertainment products have also benefitted from eye-catching digital campaigns. For instance, a so-called alternate reality game (or ARG), which relies on digital media to create immersive entertainment experiences, powered the marketing of *Year Zero*, an album released by the band Nine Inch Nails in 2007. To promote the record, digital agency 42 Entertainment orchestrated an elaborate quest that began with secret messages and phone numbers hidden on T-shirts sold by the band, and later involved an intricate network of web sites, an unmarked USB stick (found by a fan at a concert venue restroom) that contained a never-before-heard track and other clues, and voice messages distributed through cell phones. The quest culminated in a gathering of hundreds of fans at an abandoned warehouse, where they were treated to a surprise Nine Inch Nails performance. The album received a great deal of free online and offline publicity as a result.

Similar tactics have been used to promote movies, too. Warner Bros. teamed up with 42 Entertainment to develop an ARG (known as *Why So Serious?*) for its blockbuster movie *The Dark Knight*. In

May 2007, more than a year in advance of the film's release, fans uncovered the first photograph of actor Heath Ledger as Batman's nemesis the Joker, who through various clues made it known that his goal was to build an army of henchmen. At the comic-book convention Comic-Con, "Jokerized" $1 bills were handed out to attendees, a plane wrote messages in the sky, and scores of fans ran through the streets of San Diego dressed as the Joker. In a yearlong game that involved hundreds of Web pages, interactive games, e-mails, videos, and collectibles, fans were given the opportunity to explore the characters and themes of the movie through events that prompted them to do everything from searching for ringing cakes with baked-in cell phones to organizing real-world protests in support of the fictional character Harvey Dent.

More recently, movie studio Lionsgate won accolades for its digital-marketing campaign for *The Hunger Games*, which used Twitter, Facebook, and other social networks to connect with fans of the book on which the film was based. Well ahead of the movie's March 2012 launch date, the studio's digital team launched a site, TheCapitol.pn, that allowed fans to register for a fictional "district," giving them an identity and making it possible for them to interact with other fans inside and outside their district. Tumblr pages and YouTube videos showcased the movie's costumes and makeup. The release of each central character's poster and trailer became huge events online—one trailer accumulated eight million views within twenty-four hours—that were then integrated with offline events such as media appearances by cast members.

It is virtually impossible to say to what extent these digital-media efforts helped drive sales, even though *Year Zero* peaked at number two on the Billboard Top 200 album chart and both *The Dark Knight* and *The Hunger Games* were smash hits at the box office. But digital media definitely provide novel ways for writers, musicians, filmmakers, and other media producers to forge connections with their fans. Another advantage of digital-media campaigns is that they can make marketing dollars go a long way. That's because the most successful examples engage audiences and motivate them to help: when celebrities spread the word on Jay-Z's book release, or when regular consumers participate in scavenger hunts, share videos and other campaign materials, or buzz about product launches to their Facebook friends, they can substantially increase the reach of a campaign.

In my own research, I have examined how movie and video game trailers get passed around online. The raw data for well over a hundred trailers show that sharing happens on a massive scale: videos that the studios upload on video-sharing sites such as YouTube are frequently redistributed by users, either in their original form or as altered "derivative" works in the form of spoofs, remixes, and mash-ups. Such user-generated placements, my research shows, can significantly—and cheaply—enhance the spread of advertising campaigns. For many trailers in my study, in fact, the number of views generated by users' videos was several times greater than the number of views for the original videos planted by advertisers. For instance, of the six million views that the trailer for Sony Pictures' movie *Angels and Demons* (starring Tom Hanks) amassed on YouTube, more than 70 percent came from videos placed by users, not the studio itself. And that film is an *under*performer: across the sample of trailers, 89 percent of the three hundred million advertising views came from videos placed voluntarily by users. With the right strategy, the study shows, producers can benefit from the work done by fans and inexpensively reach many more potential customers.

No one who understands the entertainment industry would take this to mean that content producers can forgo traditional advertising spending, however. Producers who rely on digital media when launching their creations should not expect any miracles. In fact, many of the same factors that drive success offline also drive success online. Consumers may actively participate in promoting new entertainment products online, but they turn out in force primarily for the biggest brands—titles such as *Call of Duty* and *The Hunger Games*—that spend heavily on traditional advertising. Here, too, blockbuster strategies pay off handsomely.

It is a boon to entertainment businesses that new digital tools can enable more innovative—and sometimes less expensive—product launches, but that is not nearly the full story. The *Decoded* launch also illustrates another aspect of the likely future of blockbuster strategies: the growing importance of partnerships between content producers on the one hand and corporations that often have distinctly different goals on the other. Although the pairing of Roc Nation and Microsoft may have been odd, such connections will become more commonplace. With the campaign for his memoir, Jay-Z is pointing the way to a new model that is born out of both opportunity and necessity. In today's world, publishers and other content producers often can't afford the kind of blockbuster campaign that a superstar of Jay-Z's caliber expects and deserves.

Random House, a division of the private German media company Bertelsmann, is one of the "big six" publishing companies and generates well over $2 billion in revenues across hundreds of titles each year. But its Spiegel & Grau imprint releases only about twenty new hardcover titles each year, and *Decoded*—which Grau acquired for what she described to me as a "seven-figure" advance—instantly became one of the imprint's biggest investments. Grau was well aware of the risks, especially given the difficult business climate: "The book-publishing industry is under fire, and we've been left with Barnes & Noble and Amazon as the two major national accounts. With a book by Jay-Z, you will have content that is unsuitable for accounts such as Walmart, so we are staking everything on a small number of retailers," she said. Some of Grau's fears were eased when she attended Carter's *The Blueprint 3* tour at Madison Square Garden. "I realized that everybody in the audience—this whole carpet of twenty thousand people—knew the lyrics to every Jay-Z song. I was like 'Okay, we are good here.'" But with only a small team (which besides Grau consisted of executive editor Chris Jackson, a marketing director, a publicist, and two digital-content experts) working on the book, options for a huge campaign were limited.

The publisher's budget was not quite what Jay-Z's team had anticipated. "When we first got around to discussing the marketing plans, we asked Random House what kind of budget they had," Meneilly recalled. "Grau nervously wrote down a figure on a piece a paper and slid it over to me. It said $50,000. I was shocked. You have to realize—this barely covers Jay-Z's costs when he travels to an event. I thought she was missing a couple of zeros." Grau assured him that she had written down the right amount and later explained: "There are a lot of costs that we incur that are not included in that number—the galleys that you create for a book, for instance, or the promotional co-op costs that keep the book on a front table at Barnes & Noble throughout the holiday season. But even then, I knew what we could do would amount to a tiny fraction of what gets spent to promote an album for a superstar like Jay-Z."

A sizable gap often exists between a content producer's available budget for a product launch and the cost of adequately reaching that product's potential audience. In today's hypercompetitive media landscape, much of which is now dominated by global brands and global superstars, it is getting increasingly difficult to make product launches work. Because consumers are bombarded with marketing messages and have an abundance of media outlets to choose from, standing out from the crowd often requires big budgets.

That's why Random House approached Droga5—the publisher wanted to draw attention to the book with a relatively small budget. That's also why the parties in turn reached out to Microsoft. Recalling the moment when the Droga5 team first presented the "Decode Jay-Z" campaign idea to Roc Nation, Meneilly said, "[Carter] got it immediately, and loved it. . . . But then I asked, 'Now who is going to pay for it?' Random House doesn't have the budget, and we do not want to pay for this out of our own pockets. So I asked that question repeatedly—'Who is going to pay for it?'" David Droga recognized what happened: "Jay-Z is a pragmatist, and he immediately recognized that we had a big and ambitious idea. 'Big and ambitious' often translates into 'expensive.'"

Campaigns like the one Droga5 developed for Random House and Roc Nation certainly are a vast undertaking. For the "Decode Jay-Z" project, the agency assembled a fifty-person team of content strategists, art directors and writers, game designers, media negotiators, community managers, graphic designers, mobile developers, programmers, print and digital producers, photographers, clue writers, interaction architects, and user experience designers.

Droga5 also worked to identify the right technical product team within Microsoft and suitable team members within Roc Nation. (Even Jay-Z himself was part of the creative ensemble; he helped write many of the six hundred different clues.) And to ensure that the agency could quickly react to actions by participants in the campaign—a key feature of well-executed digital marketing efforts—Droga5 designed what it called a "nerve center" and set up a team to constantly monitor the campaign's progress.

Many content producers don't yet have the expertise to imagine and execute the kinds of campaigns that push the boundaries of what digital technology can do, and they find it almost impossible to keep up with the rapidly evolving possibilities. But agencies like Droga5 specialize in such innovative campaigns. In fact, even though Droga5 has been in existence for only seven years, it has already proven its ability to break the mold. In a 2006 campaign for fashion company Marc Ecko Enterprises, for example, Droga5 created and leaked a grainy online video of what appeared to be hooded graffiti artists climbing barbed-wire fences and sneaking past guards with dogs to spray the words "still free" on Air Force One. The video became a viral phenomenon. And during Barack Obama's 2008 presidential campaign, Droga5 launched "The Great Schlep," an initiative aimed at generating votes for Obama from Jewish constituents. The agency created a web site and online video that featured comedian Sarah Silverman urging young Jewish voters to fly to Florida to talk their grandparents out of casting their ballots for Obama's opponent, John McCain. Not your average marketing tactics, in other words.

Couldn't Carter have paid for Droga5's campaign for *Decoded* himself? Yes and no. By 2010, *Forbes* estimated that the star had amassed a net worth of over $450 million, and his contract with Live Nation was worth $150 million alone, so a $2 million campaign would have been a drop in the bucket. But Carter is not only a highly successful musician—his 2009 record *The Blueprint 3* became his eleventh album to reach number one on the Billboard charts, one more than the record previously held by Elvis Presley—he is also an extremely capable businessman. In 2007 Carter sold his

Rocawear clothing line for over $200 million, and he remains active in several other businesses, including as an investor in the beauty brand Carol's Daughter, as a co-owner of the 40/40 nightclubs in New York and Atlantic City, and even as a founder of a sports agency, Roc Nation Sports. When Carter was presented with Droga5's idea, he did not consider paying for the campaign himself. As Droga put it, "like many smart entrepreneurs would in that situation, his impulse was to try to find a partner."

What Carter ultimately got from working with Droga5 and Microsoft was worth much more than $2 million. Although Droga5 sent Microsoft a bill for that amount, the labor, the media, and the production of materials were all billed at cost. "Normally we would expect a profit margin of at least twenty percent," Droga5's chief financial officer said. "And on a short-term, labor-intensive project like this, additional fees of $1 million to $1.5 million for our services would have been common practice." Moreover, the partnership enabled Carter to gain access to Microsoft's team of engineers, its technological expertise, and the tools the $63 billion tech giant had developed over the years, including its search and maps technology. These enormously valuable tools—worth billions of dollars— would have been virtually impossible to enlist on a short-term basis otherwise. And Carter did not pay a dime for them.

The same challenges that drove Jay-Z and Random House to find a partner for the *Decoded* launch also plague many other content producers. It is therefore only logical to predict that the search for partners will become more commonplace in the world of entertainment. Grau's observation that the book publishing industry is "under fire" is important here—and publishing is far from the only sector of the entertainment industry to be in that fateful position. The advent of new technologies does not just bring opportunities—it often brings decidedly bad news, too. New distribution methods and other advances in digital technology tend to put considerable pressure on the revenues that media producers can generate. One painful effect is piracy; another is the erosion of what consumers believe to be a fair price for an entertainment product.

A third disruptive force is what economists call "unbundling." Although this phenomenon has not received nearly as much attention as the threat of piracy, unbundling may in fact be a far bigger menace. Take the music industry as an example: thanks to digital technology, consumers can purchase recorded music in three ways. They can buy a physical copy of an album, they can download that album in a digital format from a store such as iTunes, or they can select whatever subset of downloadable songs on the album they like most. That's a significant shift from the old analog days when (with the exception of one or two singles that were deemed to have the highest hit potential) it wasn't economically feasible for record labels to sell songs individually. Or think of the television industry: without significantly adding to the costs of production and distribution, each of the episodes that make up a season-long television series can now be sold individually through digital channels. In both examples, producers are moving from a strategy of "pure bundling" in which they sell just the bundle (only the music album or the series' season) to one of "mixed bundling" in which they sell both the bundle and all or most of its components (the songs or the episodes) separately.

The impact of unbundling on revenues can be positive or negative. In the music industry, for instance, record companies could *lose* revenue if some consumers switch from buying albums to buying only the individual tracks that they like most on those albums. But the labels could also *gain* revenue if the losses in album revenues are offset by a higher total amount received from the sale of individual tracks. Because unbundled tracks are available at a low price, it is not inconceivable that the total demand for an artist's music may be larger than when only more expensive, bundled products can be purchased. Which outcome is more likely depends on how groups of consumers differ in their willingness to pay for the products.

A hypothetical situation can perhaps best illustrate this point. Imagine that a group of Jay-Z fans heavily favors the hit track *Otis* on his 2011 album *Watch the Throne* (a collaboration with fellow rapper Kanye West), and that they are willing to pay up to $6 to buy that track but do not want to shell out more than $0.50 for each of the eleven other songs. At sale prices of, say, $1 for a song and $10 for an album, selling albums exclusively—a pure bundling strategy—leads to higher revenues than selling both albums and songs. (Here is the math: when unbundled songs are available, the fans will only buy *Otis*, yielding revenues of $1 from each fan, whereas when only albums are sold, consumers will "add up" their willingness to pay for each song and easily clear the hurdle of the $10 album price—they are willing to pay $6 for the *Otis* track plus $0.50 for each of the eleven other tracks, or $11.50 in total—and thus buy the bundle.) However, if there is a second group of fans that is willing to pay up to $1.50 per song for three songs—say, *Otis*, *Made in America*, and *Welcome to the Jungle*—and $0.50 for each of the other nine songs, a mixed-bundling strategy will yield more revenues from this group. This hypothetical group of fans will purchase the three songs for a total of $3 but will not want to purchase a full album. When both groups exist in the marketplace, the relative size of each will determine whether a pure or mixed-bundling strategy yields higher sales.

That's the theory, anyway. In practice, unbundling is usually detrimental to the business models of traditional media producers. My own research shows that unbundling has had a strong negative impact on music revenues. After closely examining trends in sales for more than two hundred artists for a period of nearly two and a half years in the mid-2000s, I found that music revenues decreased significantly when digital downloading gained ground, even after controlling for a rise in illegal downloading. The dollar amounts gained through new song sales were far below the level needed to offset the losses resulting from lower album sales. Although albums by the biggest stars with the strongest track records were hurt less—yet another indicator of their power—even they felt the effects.

During this period, revenues declined substantially across the board: according to my estimations, weekly sales dropped by

one-third as a direct result of consumers switching to digital channels where they could forgo buying music in bundles. As my study
suggests, rather than buying albums, music consumers have increasingly turned to cherry-picking one or only a few tracks from
those albums, without buying enough songs from other albums to
make up for the difference. Not at the current price levels, that is,
where the price of an individual track is often less than 10 percent
of that of an album. (The record labels accepted such low prices for
individual songs when they signed on to Apple's iTunes Store a
few years after Napster first appeared on the scene—without ram-
pant piracy, the labels likely would have never agreed to unbundle
in the first place.)

Fearing a similar effect on revenues, established players in television are fighting to hang on to their bundling models. Existing
television networks have little to gain from opening the door to a
world in which consumers no longer have to buy a package of cable channels if they are only interested in, say, AMC or ESPN.
Likewise, those networks will resist the idea that the "TV Everywhere" bundle that connects television and online consumption
should be broken up. This point was powerfully illustrated in 2012,
when tens of thousands of fans begged premium cable network
HBO to make its HBO GO service available for purchase. United
under the Twitter hashtag #takemymoneyHBO, fans demanded
that HBO change its policy of limiting access to those who receive
HBO programs as part of their cable subscription. The highly vocal
fans hoped that "cord-cutters"—television viewers without a
subscription—could be in on the action, too. Asked to explain why
HBO had so far refused to stray from its current model, HBO
president Richard Plepler used just one word: "math." Plepler will
know that its strong online service puts HBO in the driver's seat
if changes in the media landscape were to demand a shift in strategy, but for now the reality is that unbundling provides no clear
economic benefit.

A final factor causing pressure on content producers' existing revenue models, and again one that perhaps has not received the con-

sideration it deserves, is the rise of massive online retailers and other content aggregators with sometimes razor-thin margins on entertainment goods. Because companies like Amazon, Apple, and Google dominate the sectors in which they operate, they have amassed the power to influence—and sometimes dictate—how and at what price entertainment goods are sold. This, in turn, is putting tremendous pressure on the business models of established producers.

Here, too, the music industry led the way. After launching its iTunes Store in 2003, Apple has quickly become the leading online music retailer in the United States. By mid-2012, it was responsible for well over 60 percent of legal digital music downloading, and nearly 30 percent of all music sold at retail. And because Apple makes the large majority of its profits from its computers, phones, and other hardware, it can afford to slash prices on the entertainment content it sells in the iTunes Store, now used by some 425 million people. The company insisted on its $1-a-song price upon the store's launch and, indicative of Apple's power, it took the record labels years to convince Apple to agree to a price increase. (The iTunes Store now has a three-tier pricing structure in which songs sell for $0.69, $0.99, or $1.29, but record labels price virtually all of the top-selling songs at the highest level.)

Book publishing is another sector that has experienced increased retailer concentration. The shift to online channels may help publishers better manage the return of unsold books—traditionally a significant problem, since often at least a third (and sometimes much more) of all books that publishers ship to stores are sent back after spending some time on the shelf. The emergence of e-books eliminates the costly problem altogether. But the rise of online channels has made Amazon an undeniable force in book retailing, and the company is now responsible for nearly 30 percent of total book sales and about 60 percent of e-book sales in the United States (with the e-book category as a whole now accounting for more than a fifth of book sales). The company's vast range of products generated $48 billion in revenues in 2011, and although its net income of $630 million was sizable, that figure is a paltry 1 percent of revenues.

Chief executive officer Jeff Bezos's strategy appears to be to sacrifice short-term earnings in order to reap higher profits at some unknown point in the future.

Offline retailers of books—Borders went out of business in 2011, leaving Barnes & Noble as the only major bricks-and-mortar chain—and smaller online retailers find it difficult to compete with Amazon. Meanwhile, Apple is under investigation for alleged cartel-like behavior in its dealings with several of the biggest publishers in the e-book market. These trends are of great concern to many publishers, who worry about their loss of bargaining power over Amazon when it comes to setting prices and terms. It is hardly surprising, then, that Grau and other publishers are fretting over the limited number of major national accounts in today's retail environment.

In the film industry, online retailer Netflix comes closest to playing the role of a disruptor. The company undoubtedly helped topple offline retailers such as Blockbuster, thereby putting pressure on the windowing strategy of Hollywood studios, which formerly could count on DVD sales and rentals being more lucrative sources of income. Netflix has seen its power wane more recently, but the low-cost subscription service continues to rely on its large customer base to gain leverage over content producers when bidding for the rental and streaming rights to films and television programs.

The result of all these forces—each driven by advances in digital technology—is that the blockbuster strategy is becoming more necessary than ever, but also harder to pull off. The threat of piracy, the lower perceptions among consumers of what price is reasonable, the unbundling of content packages, and the increased concentration in retailing put tremendous pressures on existing revenue models. The bets made by content producers are becoming riskier—only those titles in greatest demand have a shot at earning back their production and marketing costs, with the remaining products more likely to fall by the wayside. What we end up with is a world still dominated by blockbusters, but one that is possibly even more lopsided.

One way content producers can react to this new reality is by doubling down on blockbuster investments and focusing even less on smaller bets. Such a trend is already under way in several markets. The film industry, for instance, has cut back on the quantity of films it produces—but it has not reduced the number of tent-pole bets. "Because technology is shrinking the pie, at least in the foreseeable future, we'll have to make fewer smaller movies, or make those smaller movies for less money," Disney's Alan Horn commented.

Another way to react is by seeking help in making blockbuster investments and their wide launches possible—that is where brand partnerships are so critical. Little wonder, then, that entertainment producers and personalities increasingly rely on alliances with firms of some scale. Shawn "Jay-Z" Carter is far from the only superstar to do so. A familiar pop star managed by another Carter also reaps rich rewards from her ties with corporations.

How many brand partners does it take to launch one hit album? In March 2011, Lady Gaga's manager hoped the answer was one less than the number he had tried to line up. That's because Troy Carter, still on the road with the *Monster Ball* tour, knew that a planned deal with mass retailer Target to benefit the launch of his client's third album, *Born This Way*—an agreement that would have given Target exclusive retail rights to a special version of Lady Gaga's album in return for distribution and marketing support—had just fallen through.

Reflecting her influence on popular culture, Lady Gaga had already established partnerships with several leading consumer-goods companies. One of these was with Beats by Dr. Dre, a line of high-end music headphones. Itself a partnership between Interscope chairman Jimmy Iovine and legendary hip-hop producer Dr. Dre, Beats was introduced in 2008. A year later the brand launched an extension, Heartbeats, that was co-designed by Lady Gaga. The headphones were well received: an influential technology web site described the $100 in-ear headphones as "undeniably unique" and likely to "attract fashionistas far and wide." Virgin Mobile was another marketing partner. The same day that Lady Gaga's second album, *The Fame Monster*, hit the shelves, the mobile telephone network operator announced its sponsorship of the US dates of the *Monster Ball* tour, promising to reward fans with free tickets if they agreed to help homeless-youth organizations.

Polaroid joined Lady Gaga's lineup in January 2010, when the company used the spotlight of the Consumer Electronics Show to announce that Lady Gaga had been appointed as creative director for a special line of forthcoming products. Lady Gaga and her creative team planned to take an active part in the relationship, she said at the time: "Lifestyle, music, art, fashion! I am so excited to extend myself behind the scenes as a designer and to—as my father puts it—finally have a real job." And a month later, MAC Cosmetics partnered with Lady Gaga, featuring the pop star in the MAC Cosmetics' Viva Glam advertising campaign that supported the MAC AIDS fund, and releasing products bearing her name.

For the *Born This Way* launch, Lady Gaga would be partnering with brands such as Amazon, Belvedere Vodka, Best Buy, Gilt Groupe, Starbucks, and Zynga. Amazon offered the album for 99 cents to promote its new cloud-based service. Belvedere sought to promote its vodka by holding a contest in which participants could compete for tickets to a special live performance by Lady Gaga in London. Best Buy bundled *Born This Way* with the purchase of a phone. Gilt Groupe offered a lineup of Lady Gaga–inspired merchandise and other special items, including a one-of-a-kind dress worn by Lady Gaga herself and VIP access to special events. Starbucks added the album to the lineup of albums featured in its stores and planned several online initiatives. And Zynga, the social gaming giant, added the Lady Gaga brand to its popular game *FarmVille*, launching a neighboring Lady Gaga–inspired farm called *GagaVille* and giving exclusive access to the album prior to its release.

Lady Gaga's plans with Target, however, had to be scrapped. The proposed partnership broke down over the retailer's support for political candidates who opposed gay rights. While Target maintained it was committed to supporting the gay community, the retailer had recently drawn considerable criticism from gay groups. Describing Lady Gaga as an "activist," Carter said: "We simply had to pull the plug on the deal." Interscope's vice chairman Steve Berman agreed: "It was a partnership to drive big business, but when you step back, you are still dealing with an artist, and you can never forget that. We have to stay credible and authentic."

"Brand relationships are very important to Lady Gaga, but she has never done a true endorsement, in the sense of her holding up a certain product, telling people, 'Hey, I'm Lady Gaga, go buy this,'" observed Bobby Campbell, chief marketing officer at Carter's management firm Atom Factory. "These products are right in line with who she is." But now, with the launch of Lady Gaga's new album just a couple of months away, it was up to her marketing team to finalize their plans for leveraging the many partnerships.

Troy Carter and Lady Gaga's approach to forming alliances with companies is quite similar to that of John Meneilly and Jay-Z. In fact, Meneilly has spoken about the partnerships involving Jay-Z in almost exactly the same terms, pointing out that "Jay-Z doesn't do straightforward endorsement deals." It is no coincidence that two of today's biggest superstars are leading the way when it comes to such arrangements: even though the planned launch of *Born This Way* was not as innovative as the *Decoded* campaign, corporate partnerships once again played an essential role. But given that Carter had already put together a dazzling array of partners for the album's release, why did he feel that Gaga could benefit from a partnership with a corporation like Target?

The answer lies in what Carter called the "enormous scale" of the album's launch. The fact that team Gaga pursued as wide a rollout as possible, with an intensive marketing effort to support it, is critical. As Carter put it, "A launch of such scale can't be done with just a record label—they don't have the resources. In order for the album to be everywhere, we would need nontraditional retail relationships." Berman agreed: "A big movie launch costs tens of millions of dollars in advertising alone—we don't have those kinds of budgets. And if we want to go beyond the record stores and other traditional music retailers like Walmart and Best Buy, we have to pursue marketing alliances and work with super fans, bloggers, and the press—and do so around the world." Especially after the dramatic changes in the music landscape, including the loss of the record labels' traditional retail partners (which in turn requires new, and often more expensive, approaches to wide launches), music-industry players simply don't have the means to fund a massive launch of a new product by a superstar. Partnerships with corporations help music companies overcome their shortcomings—and better execute their blockbuster strategies.

In some ways, today's alliances hark back to the early days of radio and television entertainment, when consumer-goods manufacturers such as Procter & Gamble served not just as sponsors but also as producers of entertainment goods—that's how soap operas got their name. Procter & Gamble started funding programs as early as in 1949 through a separate division of the company, then known as P&G Productions and now as P&G Entertainment. The practice continues to this day, whether it is NBC broadcasting two family films funded by P&G and Walmart in 2011, or Lexus paying a share of the production costs for a special episode of the Food Network's *Restaurant Impossible* in 2012.

But the new partnerships with corporations are different in their design and scale. Jay-Z's partnership with Bing was designed to solve a *marketing* problem for the entertainer—to build awareness for and interest in the artist's upcoming book, using Microsoft's vast resources. Lady Gaga's multitude of partnerships was created to solve both a *marketing* and *distribution* problem. Not only is it team Gaga's goal to ensure that the public knows of her album's release; they also want to make sure that *Born This Way* is within reach when consumers are ready to buy it—or, better yet, ensure that consumers run into the album during their daily routine, whether they are buying coffee, shopping, or playing games online, so they are reminded to buy.

The genius behind these tactics boils down to the reasons why blockbuster strategies work in the first place. Consider the Target deal. In Berman's view, "It was a great opportunity to be affiliated with Target. They were going to give us an incredible amount of 'real estate' in the store, were going to spend millions of dollars advertising the Gaga brand upon the album release, and would help us sell licensed merchandise and apparel." Because entertainment products are often bought on a whim, securing a large distribution footprint for an album can be a major advantage. If consumers see a product displayed everywhere, the chances that they will actually buy the product increase. Target would have helped Gaga execute a "pile 'em high, watch 'em fly" strategy in a way that traditional music retailers never could have.

In markets that are increasingly global and competitive, and in a time when fashions seem to come and go faster than ever, breaking through the vast media clutter and reaching mass audiences requires enormous budgets. In the film industry, a tent-pole launch now involves thousands of screens in the United States alone, and thousands more across the world. Most blockbuster movies open in different territories within a short time frame—partly to give pirated copies less of a chance to flood the market before the legal alternative arrives—and each major market receives a glitzy premiere and a big publicity push, driving distribution and marketing costs up. In the music industry, the pattern is the same; labels are becoming ever more inventive about pushing their products onto the market with great intensity, which inevitably triggers higher distribution and marketing expenses. With digital technologies putting pressure on revenues and profits, it is only natural that content producers warmly welcome—and actively court—partners willing to help shoulder those rising costs.

Taylor Swift is another superstar who has embraced this trend. In late 2012, when she released her album *Red*, Swift did so with "a little help from her brands," as music-industry magazine *Billboard* quipped. Target sold a deluxe version of *Red* and gave it a promotional push via a television campaign. More than sixteen hundred twenty-four-hour Walgreens stores prominently displayed Swift's new album and put it on sale at midnight the day of the launch. Even Papa John's sold *Red*: the pizza chain's customers could get a large one-topping pizza and the CD of *Red* for $22, or add it to any order for $13, $2 below the retail price. Meanwhile, pizza boxes featured the album cover and Papa John's web site included a page dedicated to Swift that streamed audio clips of the new album.

Swift's other brand partners, including Keds, Elizabeth Arden, American Greetings, CoverGirl, and Macy's, also helped drive awareness. "We're always looking at, 'How can we create more doors? How can we make it as easy as possible to get this?,'" remarked Scott Borchetta, the chief executive officer of Swift's label Big Machine Records. The focus wasn't just on distribution. The partnerships gave a boost to marketing and publicity, too: *Billboard* estimated that the combined *Red*-related advertising spent by the star's brand partners easily surpassed $15 million, and that did not even count a Macy's television campaign that also featured Swift. The massive launch worked as it was designed to: *Red* debuted at the top of the *Billboard* album chart—and in fact became the first album since Lady Gaga's *Born This Way* to break the one-million-copies-sold mark in its first week. Underscoring the importance of the wide distribution strategy, more than four hundred thousand units were sold at Target.

A third pop-music diva, Beyoncé, is getting in on the action, too. In late 2012, she closed a $50 million brand partnership with Pepsi that, as representatives for the company put it, set out to develop "a new way for brands to engage with musical artists, moving from sponsor to partner." The deal involves the kind of terms often found in standard endorsements—the pop star will appear on a limited-edition Pepsi can, for example, and be featured in commercials and other advertising—but it also covers support for the singer's chosen creative projects. Don't be surprised if much of the promotion blitz will coincide with the launch of Beyoncé's new album. Given its long-standing ties with numerous retailers, Pepsi should be able to help give any new music the star might release a marketing push at least as big as the campaigns that powered *Born This Way* and *Red*.

However, relying on allies also has downsides, as the collapse of Lady Gaga's deal with Target illustrates. Adopting and executing a brand-partnership strategy is hard: partners, after all, will bring their own brands and their own goals to the collaboration. These different and often competing agendas create numerous challenges. One is to ensure that a star's brand connection with a company is credible; in the case of Lady Gaga and Target, political differences ultimately made that impossible. Another challenge is matching timelines with corporate partners. Carter described how this affected team Gaga's planning: "In the music industry, everything is done within months. The corporate world is playing on a different time scale. They often set marketing strategies two years in advance." The need to accommodate these kinds of schedules was a key reason why Carter started crafting his plan for the launch of *Born This Way* several months before work on an album release usually commences.

Structuring the partnership behind Jay-Z's *Decoded* campaign had its challenges, too. Tellingly, the Spiegel & Grau team kept working on what Grau called "Plan B"—a traditional marketing campaign, with book signings and an advertisement in the *New Yorker*—in the event that the Droga5 campaign fell apart. By June 2010, five months before the book was due to be published, conversations between Droga, Essex, Meneilly, and the Microsoft Bing team had led to an initial agreement. Bing would play a major role in underwriting the campaign, bing.com/jay-z would be the central hub for all activities, and Bing's search and maps functionality would be used in both the street and online components of the launch. Jay-Z would lend his name and likeness to the campaign, be intimately involved in the entire process, and personally sign off on all aspects, but he would receive no fee. The Spiegel & Grau team would be responsible for finalizing the text and the book's complex design. They would also keep the Droga5 and Bing teams informed of any changes, since completing the production of the book would overlap with the planning of the campaign. Droga5, meanwhile, would oversee the entire campaign and be responsible for its design and execution. They would also lead the team from

Microsoft. "Bing will not have an independent team working on this," Essex explained. "Their tech guys work under our guidance. We will customize their search and maps technology with their help."

But an early presentation of creative concepts set off a contest of strength between Microsoft and Roc Nation. First, the size of the Bing logo, visible on each of the pages displayed on outdoor and bespoke media, became a source of contention. Microsoft knew it was fighting a familiar battle. "It is the joke of advertising—the client always wants to make their logo bigger," said Mehdi. "Well, the first thing we said after reviewing the materials is 'We want our logo bigger.'" Meneilly was quick to counter. "We can't do anything that overruns Jay-Z," he said. "People already need Bing to play the game. But we should not go too far. Microsoft even wants to put three logos on a billboard on Times Square that consists of three separate panels but is essentially one image! They have to remember that if it weren't for Jay-Z, this whole campaign wouldn't exist." Grau sided with her author: "This is not a Bing campaign—it has to be about the book."

The issues involving the logo foreshadowed a larger debate about who really held the cards in the partnership. "This is our money, so we want the opportunity to say 'We are the approver,'" Mehdi commented. "Of course it has to fit Jay-Z's brand, too, but when the purchase order comes in from Clear Channel for that three-story billboard in Times Square, it is not going to Roc Nation or Random House—it is going to Microsoft." Mehdi added: "We would have not even considered this deal if we believed we were second to anyone: we demand creative control when it comes to our brand. This is about growing the Bing user base." Meneilly disagreed. "In the end, this is Jay-Z's campaign to sign off on. If Microsoft wants a launch event with Jay-Z at the Delano Hotel in Miami . . . they have to come up with a very good reason for him to be there. Jay-Z is not just a billboard. We want creative control. Bing may pay for the campaign, but the key objective is to sell Jay-Z's book—to open at the top of the bestseller list."

These examples illustrate the kinds of obstacles and challenges that need to be overcome in blockbuster launches powered by brand partnerships. It's one thing for stars like Jay-Z to love this kind of deal—the campaign for *Decoded* was a great, free way to draw attention to the book—but why are companies like Microsoft or Target willing to endure the headaches that often come with these partnerships? In this case, too, the answer is math: more often than not, alliances with superstars are worth it. Behind these deals lie many of the same reasons why content producers bet on blockbuster properties and invest in stars, as well as the same reasons why consumer-goods brands are willing to pay handsomely to secure celebrity endorsements. In an intensely competitive and crowded marketplace, engaging in brand partnerships helps companies draw attention to their products and brands, reach new or broader audiences, or otherwise capitalize on the power of stars like Lady Gaga and Jay-Z. All of this translates into a better financial performance for those companies.

In the case of the *Decoded* campaign, Microsoft was looking for a way to break the twelve-year stronghold its rival Google had on the online-search market. When Microsoft launched Bing in 2009, it embarked on a $100 million mass-media advertising campaign to promote its new search engine. One year later, however, Google still dominated the market with a 66 percent share (and upward trends in both volume and share of search), while Bing's share was below 10 percent. To make matters worse, Bing's core users tended to be white middle-aged women in the Midwest. "That's not a growth segment, and it does not help us in being seen as an innovative choice," noted Mehdi. "Young people shape what is next in technology. And they have grown up with Google as the only real choice." As part of an effort to improve Bing's market performance, Microsoft sent a so-called open brief to a number of advertising agencies—including Droga5. The brief challenged the agencies to find ways to grow Bing. The central goal was "to break the Google habit," as Mehdi put it.

Droga5's plans for Jay-Z's campaign seemed a perfect fit: "The beauty of our scavenger-hunt idea was that it seemed on-brief for Bing, and was sure to generate a lot of heat," said Essex. "We also knew they are used to working with celebrities and sponsoring campaigns—more so than Google—and that they've earmarked a substantial marketing budget for such activities." It was Meneilly, Jay-Z's manager, who suggested they reach out to Microsoft. The new Bing search engine not only fit the scavenger-hunt idea, it featured a unique maps function that could actually improve the experience. "I realized this is all about search, and it could showcase Bing Maps. And Microsoft sponsors Jay-Z's annual dinner with LeBron James, so there already is a relationship," Meneilly recalled. Essex recounted what happened next: "So we called them and said 'Hey, we got something for you, and it's pretty cool. We have this idea, and it involves Jay-Z. Do you want to hear more?'"

The Bing group was immediately enthusiastic. "Jay-Z is one of the biggest stars on the planet, so he can drive awareness," commented Mehdi. "He appeals strongly to African Americans and those between eighteen and twenty-four years old, which are underrepresented groups among Bing users. And the campaign zeroes in on the kind of Bing features we want to emphasize most." Mehdi acknowledged that he and his team took quite a leap: "I have learned that sometimes you just have to go with your gut. There is no hard data that tells you that blanketing a pool or putting a jacket in a Gucci store window is going to get you buzz, but at some point you have to swing for the fences." Mehdi is right about the difficulty of predicting results, and even after a campaign it can be hard to prove causal effects. But Microsoft saw Bing reach a 12 percent share during the *Decoded* campaign—its highest since the search engine's launch—and Bing did enter the top 10 of most visited Web sites for the first time.

The involvement of stars like Jay-Z and Lady Gaga can lift the profiles of all the partners involved in a product launch. Droga5 of course also made a sizable gamble that the *Decoded* project would bring in new clients—forgoing profits on a $2 million project was quite a bet given that the company at the time had modest annual revenues of $24 million. And actual costs for one-off projects such as this one are hard to assess beforehand, as Essex knows all too well. "This isn't like we are going to shoot a television commercial, where we know how much it is going to cost," he explained. "But that is the beauty of doing something unique—some of us were saying, 'This is going to be costly,' and others were saying, 'It will be worth it.'" Droga5 hasn't looked back since—in late 2012, in fact, the advertising industry's preeminent trade magazine *AdWeek* selected Droga5 as its Agency of the Year.

Starbucks works with musicians on an ongoing basis, so it's not surprising that it expressed interest in being involved in Lady Gaga's *Born This Way* launch. Each month, the coffee company features three or four new albums in its seventy-five hundred stores in the United States and Canada. According to Holly Hinton, entertainment category manager at Starbucks, the choice of which records to promote comes about after "lots of listening" by the Starbucks team members who are responsible for curating content. "There is a bunch of music fans making these decisions," Hinton said. "We have conversations all the time about liking the Alabama Shakes' record, or loving the new Katy Perry." This is how *Born This Way* ended up on a counter display labeled "The Handpicked Sound of Starbucks"—right next to the biscotti and chocolate. Starbucks's impressive retail footprint makes this kind of product placement a coup for any artist seeking to drive sales, and it explains why music-industry insiders work hard to get a foot in the door. In Lady Gaga's case, Hinton recalled that the star's producer made a big impression when he previewed *Born This Way* for the company's team of curators. "Vince Herbert came to our Starbucks offices with a stereo system and played music louder in here than I think anyone has ever played music," she said.

But Starbucks went far beyond "business as usual" with Lady Gaga. The company also planned a daylong Lady Gaga "takeover" of the Starbucks Digital Network, which is accessible through the free Wi-Fi in stores. This initiative involved giving away a limited number of downloads of her song *The Edge of Glory*, and streaming both the album and an exclusive video for free. Taking a page from the "Decode Jay-Z" playbook, Starbucks even launched a scavenger-hunt-like game called SRCH (pronounced as "search") around the time of the album's launch. By distributing clues through QR codes on banners and posters in its stores—smartly, the *My Starbucks* iPhone app had an embedded reader of such codes—the company led players around the Internet (including Starbucks-operated pages on Twitter and Facebook) in search of prizes.

For Lady Gaga, the partnership provided the obvious benefit of significant marketing and distribution support. But the deal offered important advantages for Starbucks, too. It enabled the company to build relationships with Lady Gaga's "little monsters," a large group of current or future coffee drinkers. It also allowed Starbucks to integrate its in-store and online experiences, showing customers the value of both. "This was the first time we played Gaga in our stores," remarked Alex Wheeler, vice president of global digital marketing for Starbucks. "We were trying to bring an experience to our retail stores where customers could come in and just hear the music, purchase the CD and engage, go online and watch the exclusive video, or get involved in the game. We wanted to bring an experience that we thought only Starbucks could, and we wanted to drive people into our stores so they could experience it." The company also used the SRCH game banners to promote its Frappuccino, using the buzz around Lady Gaga to draw extra attention to a seasonal offering that appeals to a younger audience.

Perhaps most important, Starbucks found the wide-scale, blockbuster launch extremely attractive because of what it would do for the company's brand. "This was about being part of an important cultural, global moment," explained Wheeler. "A Lady Gaga record coming out—it was a big deal." And Lady Gaga's star power was key. "Like our brand she is innovative, she is very digitally connected, and she has a passionate fan base," said Wheeler.

Starbucks approaches these kinds of alliances with great care. "Brand partnerships are a bit snowflake-like, and each one has to be special," said Wheeler. "We look for the right kind of opportunities." But in Gaga's case, the company felt that the expected rewards outweighed the risks. "We knew that she could be polarizing, and we prepared our organization for what that might look or feel like," Wheeler recalled. "But we all felt it was the right risk to assume." And she has no regrets: Wheeler looked back on the collaboration as her favorite among other activities her team had undertaken.

Executives at Zynga are also very positive about their partnership with Lady Gaga. In advance of the release of *Born This Way*, *FarmVille* users were given a chance to expand their game-playing to a Lady Gaga–themed virtual farm community with items such as crystals, unicorns, and, in a play on the album cover art, leather-clad sheep riding motorcycles. In the week leading up to the record's launch in May 2011, users could earn early access to its songs. They could also purchase special prepaid $25 Zynga game cards at Best Buy (a third partner in the deal) that included a free download of the album, as well as exclusive bonus tracks and virtual goods.

No money changed hands between Zynga and Carter's Atom Factory, but Zynga did pay Lady Gaga's record company Interscope for the rights to the music. For Lady Gaga, the complex partnership deal helped drive album awareness and sales. For Zynga, too, the deal offered many benefits. Anders Klemmer, then Zynga's global director for business development, told me: "We always looked for ways to inject pop culture into our games to make them more relevant to what is happening in the lives of our players, to keep them engaged and coming back for more."

Around the time of the album's release, *FarmVille* attracted forty-six million players every month, but usage was down sharply from a year before, when nearly twice as many people played the game. "We are a hits-driven business, and we need these popular artifacts in our game," remarked Klemmer, who described the partnership as a "high-water mark" for Zynga. Lady Gaga's audience appeal was a big reason for the deal, he explained: "At the time, Gaga was by far the biggest, most talked-about artist in the world. We wanted to work with her. And our analytics told us that there was a great overlap in who played *FarmVille* and who liked Gaga on Facebook." Zynga had earlier worked with the hip-hop artists Dr. Dre and Snoop Dogg on another game, *Mafia Wars*. "That performed well above the baseline," said Klemmer, "so we thought, 'Well, what if we went with a really strong name?' It takes a special kind of artist to support a promotion like we did with Gaga."

All in all, it makes sense to invest in blockbusters and superstars. The advantages of such bets are hard to deny. Advances in digital technology create exciting new content distribution and marketing opportunities, but can also seriously hamper existing business models, making blockbuster strategies more difficult and risky to execute. But both effects do nothing to lessen the need for big bets—in fact, blockbusters only gain power in a digital landscape.

Partnerships between content producers and other types of companies make perfect sense in this new world. Such alliances are not a one-size-fits-all solution for every product in every setting, of course, but brand partnerships can help content producers gain distribution and marketing power and help them make better use of the wealth of possibilities that digital media offer. Two of the world's biggest superstars, Jay-Z and Lady Gaga, have led the way in books and music, but there is no reason why other sectors of the entertainment industry can't and won't follow. Corporations crave opportunities to be associated with the strongest, most engaging brands, and many entertainment products fit that bill.

Precisely because partnerships allow for a "meeting of the best brands"—each partner selects the other based on brand strength and fit, after all—the growth of brand alliances may further fuel a winner-take-all trend in the entertainment business. We will soon see even bigger launches for the biggest bets involving the biggest superstars on the planet—backed by campaigns that skillfully capitalize on the dramatic changes that have transformed the media landscape.

NO BUSINESS LIKE SHOW BUSINESS?

Sometimes, it seems, the best way to put your latest blockbuster bet to the test is by throwing an epic launch party. Nightlife impresarios Jason Strauss and Noah Tepperberg knew they had done just that as they looked out over a crowded dance floor where hundreds of revelers were enthusiastically ringing in the rebirth of their famed New York City–based nightlife establishment Marquee. The co-founders and co-owners had chosen this night in early January 2013 for a spectacular reopening after a costly, six-month-long renovation that, they hoped, would again place Marquee among the country's most sought-after venues. If anyone could bring back the magic, it was the two of them: before Marquee temporarily closed its doors, the club had been going strong for almost nine years—an eternity for a venue in one of the world's most competitive nightlife markets, where most clubs were over within a mere eighteen months.

Strauss and Tepperberg, who had both started as promoters at age fifteen, had already built up impressive résumés in the hospitality industry by 2003, when they set out to convert an old, five-thousand-square-foot Manhattan garage into a new nightclub that would become Marquee. "When we started, it wasn't much of a neighborhood—just a lot of warehouses and housing projects across the street," said Strauss. "But we thought that we would be strong enough to create a destination, and we saw the vision of the room, so we took out a lease on an old, broken-down garbage truck garage that had no plumbing, no electricity, and a roof that was partially open with pigeons and leaks going through it like you wouldn't believe." Tepperberg recalled their confidence: "We felt we knew what a clubgoer wants. . . . We knew how much bar space we wanted, how big the dance floor needed to be, where we had to have a coat check, where the bathroom needed to be—all the details that matter."

Marquee quickly became a magnet for clubgoers. The venue was notoriously difficult to get into, with a crowd of cars and people often blocking several lanes of traffic and a line of hopefuls usually stretching around the block. "Only the fashionable, famous, or financially secure need apply," observed one insider. Over the next few years, Marquee's neighborhood would see an influx of new and revamped clubs—so much so that it became known as "club row," described as a "one-stop party shop" and "an amusement park for adults." Strauss and Tepperberg were well aware of the club's impact. "A whole neighborhood has erupted," Strauss told me in 2007. "Everything from restaurants to galleries to a dozen other nightclubs trying to feed off of the energy that we brought to the area."

By then, the owners had Marquee's operations down to a science. Each night, two managers, a doorman, six bartenders, six cocktail waitresses, thirteen other staffers, and twelve security people served Marquee's customers. On a busy evening, the club admitted up to twelve hundred people. Of these, four hundred "bottle customers"—socialites, bankers, models, celebrities, and other jet-setters—would pay handsomely for the right to sit at any of the thirty-six tables. They were asked to purchase at least two or three bottles of top-shelf liquor, with prices ranging from $350 for a bottle of Absolut Vodka (which retailed for $25 at a local liquor store) to $900 for Cristal champagne. (For that price, customers got to mix their own drinks; juice, tonic, and an ice bucket

were included.) The remaining customers—the "filler crowd"—
paid a $20 cover charge to gain entrance, ordered their drinks from
the bar, danced on the main floor, and moved around the establishment's different rooms, perhaps hoping for a chance to rub el-
bows with a celebrity or VIP. "The filler crowd creates the energy,"
said Strauss.

By the time it closed for renovations in 2012, Marquee's run had
been a tremendous success. Strauss commented: "Eight and a half
years is almost unheard of in New York City nightlife. We've had
iconic events, top celebrities, and great press, and we think we've
made a significant contribution to the nightlife culture. Marquee
really was the staple. If we were open five nights a week, people
were going out five nights a week."

Even while operating Marquee, Strauss and Tepperberg had
also significantly expanded their portfolio of clubs, having launched
three new establishments in New York City—Avenue, LAVO, and
PH-D at the Dream Downtown hotel—while also managing the
popular TAO, TAO Beach, LAVO, and a second Marquee in Las
Vegas, and even launching a Marquee in Sydney, Australia. Located
in the new $4 billion Cosmopolitan Hotel, the $50 million, sixty-
two-thousand-square-feet Marquee Las Vegas with a capacity
crowd of three thousand people in particular was a huge bet—and
an undeniable success. In 2011, its first full year, it became the
highest-grossing club in North America, with an estimated $80
million in revenues. A departure from the New York City–based
Marquee, it embraced electronic dance music and featured a high-
profile DJ every night.

"We already had two clubs in Vegas, and didn't want to compete with ourselves," said Strauss, an early believer in the growth
of the electronic dance music genre. For Marquee Las Vegas, the
Cosmopolitan shelled out $3 million for a top-notch lighting and
sound system. "The room is designed to give it a festival feel, in a
coliseum-like setting, with sight lines to the DJ booth," explained
Strauss. "We created a throne for our DJs—in a way, we said, 'Let's
give [superstar DJ] Kaskade a Maybach to drive.'" Tepperberg
added: "There wasn't a club that had well-known electronic DJs

every night. Everyone told us we were crazy to try. Within a month, a major competitor had switched to headlining electronic DJs, too. The market exploded—now, Vegas is all about the DJs."

Their success in Las Vegas led the two nightlife entrepreneurs to set their sights on a new goal: they wanted to bring the model of focusing on electronic dance music and star DJs to Marquee New York City. "We want to make it less about who is who, about seeing and being seen, and make it more about the show—about who is playing," Tepperberg commented. "There is so much competition for bottle service now—everyone has copied our model." Renovating the old space had cost nearly $3.5 million (one especially expensive change was—literally—raising the roof), but a focus on star DJs would have high ongoing expenses, too. "Well-known DJs make up to four hundred thousand dollars a night," said Tepperberg—a sizable sum given Marquee's capacity. But he believed in the new model: "If you are open three nights a week, or a hundred and fifty nights a year, it is difficult to make each night special. DJs are a way to program a venue. The idea is to open when we have content." Strauss reflected on the task in front of them: "Being in the hospitality industry is about doing good work. We know how to manage the operations side. The challenge is to remain relevant."

Could it be that the hospitality industry is putting down big bets on potential blockbusters and superstars, too? Although we might not readily associate nightlife establishments with the film, television, publishing, music, sports, and other entertainment businesses examined in this book, they have much more in common than may be immediately apparent. The same is true for many other sectors of the economy. Pharmaceutical companies, for instance, have long been known for their blockbuster products; in fact, the term is common parlance in that industry. But features of the entertainment industries transfer to a wide variety of other sectors, and each day new examples emerge.

The nightlife industry deserves a closer look first. Anyone with a serious inclination to party will have heard of at least one of the clubs managed by Strauss and Tepperberg. But even some of the most hard-core revelers might not appreciate exactly how successful the two men are as entrepreneurs. In the business of nightlife, clubs can go from being "hot" to "not" in a heartbeat. The best clientele will only go to of-the-moment clubs—a distinction each venue by definition can hope to have for only a matter of time. Much like word of mouth for a movie or a new album, the sizzle can quickly subside. As a result, although revenues for clubs can start at a high level, they usually quickly taper off, leaving the owners to scramble to recover their high up-front costs.

Not so in the case of Strauss and Tepperberg's clubs, though. Both Marquee New York City and Marquee Las Vegas beat those odds in a big way. Revenues for Marquee New York City even trended upward in its first years, from just under $10 million in 2004 to more than $15 million, and a net income of around $2.5 million, three years later. Although revenues declined in subsequent years, the club remained profitable throughout its run. And yet, with their renovation of Marquee New York City, Strauss and Tepperberg are significantly altering their formula, inching ever closer to the practices of some of the world's biggest entertainment businesses.

The new model developed by the two entrepreneurs promises to transform the nightlife business from one that is all about selling high-priced alcohol delivered to table customers seated at hot spots, to one that is at least as much about selling tickets to heavily marketed events featuring superstar DJs. Marquee Las Vegas was their first big foray into that new era—and it certainly proved the value of the concept. In part, the move may have been driven by the recession, which didn't exactly help grow the bottle-customer market. (In the old Marquee New York City, bottle customers accounted for a third of all customers but as much as 80 percent of revenues.) But Strauss and Tepperberg's decision to focus on electronic dance music was a clever bet on a trend that emerged years ago in Ibiza (still the bastion of that music genre), conquered most of Europe next, and is now taking over the United States.

"They were recognizing something that no one else in Vegas was recognizing yet," said Pasquale Rotella, who each year hosts the Electric Daisy Carnival, an international electronic dance music festival. After securing space in a new hotel development on the Vegas strip financed by Deutsche Bank—"the world's largest bank took a gamble on a seven-year-old brand, Marquee, and we as operators gambled on a new model," said Strauss—the impresarios decided to cater to customers who enjoyed dancing to music spun by high-profile DJs rather than, say, expect nightlife mainstays like Paris Hilton and Kim Kardashian to draw bottle customers and filler crowds.

In the old days, Strauss and Tepperberg focused much of their time on building relationships with high-end clients. With their new content-centric model, the entrepreneurs have become major buyers in the market for DJs, so cultivating relationships with both established and up-and-coming DJs is now another major priority. The DJ market has a few winners and thousands of also-rans—much like those for movie and television actors, authors, athletes, and other creatives. The hottest DJs have seen their fortunes rise sharply in recent years: they now play stages and stadiums once reserved for only the most successful rock, pop, and hip-hop musicians. In 2012, Ryan Raddon, better known as Kaskade, sold out a concert at Los Angeles's Staples Center—a feat that was previously unheard of for a DJ in North America. Strauss and Tepperberg shrewdly banked on the star power of top DJs to draw crowds to their new Vegas club. They even convinced Kaskade, described by industry magazine *DJ Mag* as being "among the vanguard of electronic musicians," to sign on to a yearlong "residency" that required him to commit to a dozen performances in Marquee's first twelve months.

Relying on DJs has all the advantages that come with bets on superstars in media and sports. And because popular DJs often have a strong presence in social media, they are good at mobilizing their audiences. "DJs have a vested interest in people showing up, so they have incentives to market events," said Lou Abin, along with Marc Parker and Richard Wolf a partner in Strauss and Tepperberg's umbrella company, TAO Group. "If we book Tiësto for two hundred thousand dollars, thousands of customers will want to buy a ticket in advance," said Tepperberg, adding, "Some DJs bring bottle-service customers, some bring in ticket buyers, and some do both."

But betting on superstar DJs also means having to deal with their power. Because they have such a strong hold on audiences, well-known DJs often earn rewards that are on par with the dazzling fees for top performers in other entertainment domains. Top spinners like Avicii, Deadmau5, David Guetta, and Tiësto can earn well over $1 million for a festival appearance and as much as $10 million for a high-profile Las Vegas nightclub residency. By some estimates, the world's ten highest-paid DJs collectively earned $125 million annually in the 2011–2012 season—more than the Los Angeles Lakers' payroll. Top DJs, keen to keep track of how they stack up, closely watch their rankings. "Every year there is a new guy who makes it onto the scene and onto the list," Kaskade told me in late 2012, adding: "Last year it was Skrillex. And the year before that it was Deadmau5. This year Avicii will get a high spot."

DJs with clout often drive a hard bargain in their negotiations with nightlife impresarios. "For actresses and rappers, appearances in clubs are just a side thing. But for DJs, this is what they do—this is how they make their money," explained Tepperberg. With agents and managers intent on getting the most lucrative deals for their clients, club owners face a difficult challenge, explained Rotella: "Everyone wants certain guys, and lots of people are now trying to jump into the business of hosting events. That is driving up the fees." Strauss, based in Las Vegas, experiences those dynamics firsthand. "Stupid operators spend stupid money," he said. "For some, it is just about market share. They ruin the market for us."

Under the old model, a club's "promoters," hired to attract a crowd that fit the image of the club, drove costs up. "If you run a nightclub, you know that the longer you are open, the higher your costs will be," Tepperberg told me. "The rent goes up every year, and payroll and promotional fees are going up even faster." Fees paid to promoters, who brought in around a third of the bottle customers and a fifth of the filler crowd for the old Marquee New York

City, were the biggest drivers of cost increases for that club. "Promoters hold the crowd, create the energy, and give the place a certain look," said Tepperberg. "They are the hosts." At the old Marquee New York City, each promoter had his or her own approach to finding desirable patrons: some drew heavily on their own network of friends, whereas others relied on acquaintances from their day job. An average promoter made hundreds of dollars a night. (Knowing many fashion models and other good-looking people pays dividends in lots of ways, it seems.)

A popular club's costs can go up drastically when promoters realize how important they are to securing the right crowds and then begin to ask for higher fees. Tepperberg knows the problem all too well: "Here in New York City, promoters usually started at a low rate, but as their crowd developed, and as they started to bring in more and more people, other clubs offered them higher salaries, or higher commissions. They then came to us, saying, 'Hey, you need to pay me more if you want me to stay.' We make an effort to develop our own promoters, but as they get more successful, it ends up costing the club more money." Laughing, he added, "We create monsters."

Ironically, with their move from a promoter-driven model to a DJ-driven model, Strauss and Tepperberg may find that DJs and their representatives have become even bigger monsters that need taming. That certainly would fit the experiences of many entertainment businesses that rely on superstars.

The more nightlife entrepreneurs focus on programming their nights, the more the practices of the best entertainment businesses will become useful in their world, too. So far, Strauss and Tepperberg seem to be making all the right moves. First, just as athletes want to play in stadiums and for teams that allow them to showcase their talents, the impresarios recognized the value of investing in excellent conditions for DJs. The design of the venue plays a key role here. Strauss and Tepperberg made sure DJs love to play at Marquee Las Vegas. "Right now it's the premier club in North America. It's the best thing we have in this country," said Kaskade.

"Their sound and lights are amazing. And the way the room is designed, with that tiered half-dome around the DJ booth, it's really cool, because the most die-hard fans are right in front of me. That's where the energy is, and that's where it should be."

A high fee alone isn't sufficient, Kaskade told me: "If the room isn't conducive to my performances, I will not do the deal, regardless of the money involved." Tepperberg is well aware of what DJs look for in a club and seeks to provide just that: "They want the right crowd, a great sound system, a good overall production, and great marketing around their shows—a story in the *New York Times* that helps build their brand." With DJs knocking on the door seeking an opportunity to play the venue and fans knowing they'll get the best possible experience, club managers face fewer challenges in attracting the most popular DJs and filling rooms to capacity. What initially seem risky investments to cater to DJs therefore become ways to help the club contain ongoing costs and maximize revenues.

Second, just as with media production and distribution, scale brings advantages. It's no coincidence that Marquee Las Vegas's square footage is among the largest for clubs in Vegas, or that it operates not just a nightclub but also a dayclub on the premises— the scale allows Strauss and Tepperberg to make bigger bets on superstar DJs and other performers. For the same reason, the two men added capacity to the renovated Marquee New York City. Scale also manifests itself in the number of clubs under the TAO Group umbrella: the company's expanding portfolio helps Strauss and Tepperberg to gain leverage over DJs and other partners, much as MLB and the NFL rely on the diversification of their distribution channels to gain power.

Residencies such as the one Strauss and Tepperberg set up with Kaskade are also enabled by scale. When a nightclub owner secures a commitment from a high-profile DJ to play anywhere from eight to twelve nights, he or she is behaving much like a Hollywood producer signing up talent for sequels or a record label executive offering longer-term deals to musicians. Residencies help the nightclub impresarios better manage the risks inherent in investments in top talent. These deals up the size of the bet, of course—$10 million is hardly small change—but they also increase the likelihood of a solid payoff, just like Hollywood's tent-pole movies featuring A-list stars.

Third, borrowing a page from the best media and sports companies, Strauss and Tepperberg understand the importance of balancing superstar acquisition and talent development. "Jason and Noah are smart because they are not booking all the big DJs," explained Rotella. "They have Kaskade and a few others star DJs. Some clubs are booking every big name but don't see even close to the regular volume of customers when they do not have established DJs. Noah and Jason have up-and-coming DJs on those nights that are just as talented." Rotella added: "You can't ever be at the mercy of the acts. You have to own the experience." Strauss and Tepperberg are careful to avoid getting caught up bidding higher and higher for superstar DJs. Recognizing that their venues can be a valuable platform to grow new stars, they are building relationships with newer, lesser-known performers who have genuine talent but need time to grow a fan base—not unlike, say, *Saturday Night Live* does with comedic talent. The more Marquee, TAO, LAVO, and Strauss and Tepperberg's other clubs are recognized as brands in themselves—as places where great DJs play and where customers have a memorable experience—the more such talent development becomes possible.

Of course, none of this means that the renovated Marquee New York City will be as big a success as Marquee Las Vegas; just as any Hollywood blockbuster can flop at the box office or any Broadway play can bomb, things could go wrong here. After all, there is inherent uncertainty about market outcomes in this sector, too, and the competition is fierce. Staying on top with Marquee Las Vegas will be no small feat, either. But it appears Strauss and Tepperberg's strategy of making major events out of their blockbuster bets and being strategic about their investments in superstars is sound. With their shift to the content business—they have become, in a way, concert promoters as much as nightlife promoters—they live by the same rules that media companies do.

"The market has changed," observed Tepperberg. "People want more for their money, they want a show, a real production—they don't just want to look at each other, or look at the pretty people. We saw what worked in Las Vegas, and now want to bring that to New York City." There's no reason their content has to be limited to electronic dance music and the DJs that create it, either. "In our new venues, we can do other things, too: a performance by a hip-hop star, a celebrity night, or a Cirque-du-Soleil-type show," said Tepperberg. "DJs, live music, performance art—we can accommodate all those different types of content."

When you look close enough, the principles and practices of "show business" can be found in a wide cross section of companies and sectors in our economy—and increasingly so. The hallmarks of blockbuster strategies and bets on superstars are visible throughout the hospitality industry, from the rise of celebrity chefs and cooking shows to the evolution of cruise lines and hotel concepts that seek to create unique customer experiences. (And in some ways, the Las Vegas Strip is nothing but an ongoing series of blockbuster bets on new hotel developments.) But the practices of entertainment businesses also apply outside the hospitality sector.

In consumer electronics, for example, Apple has long used what looks an awful lot like a blockbuster strategy to compete with its rivals. And I don't mean in its media business (where Apple makes 30 cents on every dollar's worth of music, video, or other software sold through its iTunes and App stores—a multibillion-dollar business in itself), but rather in its approach to selling desktop and laptop computers, displays, smartphones, and other hardware. Consider this: Apple releases fewer products and product variations than virtually all of its competitors in computer hardware. The MacBook Pro, for instance, only comes in two or three different screen sizes and allows for far less customizing than laptops made by manufacturers such as Sony and Lenovo (which also carry a much wider assortment of machines—Lenovo, for instance, offers seven series of its ThinkPad alone, each consisting of a number of different models). Apple makes only a few bets each year: it focuses its production efforts on a small number of the most likely blockbusters.

The same is true for the company's marketing efforts. Apple puts all its weight behind each product launch, carefully planning the release date and the rollout of product information, all in an attempt to drum up as much free publicity as possible and create broad awareness of the launch. The approach works beautifully: each product announcement is discussed—and indeed dissected—by established news media and blogs alike. (By contrast, it's hard to recall the last time the news media came out in full force to report on the launch of a new laptop by, say, Dell, Hewlett-Packard, or Sony.) And when a new Apple product hits the stores, the company often appears to deliberately create a sense of scarcity, fostering a "must buy" or "can't miss" feeling and prompting people to form the kinds of lines in front of Apple Stores that are also often seen for big movie premieres and other entertainment events. Perhaps Apple's former leader Steve Jobs learned a thing or two during his time at Pixar and his tenure on the Walt Disney Company's board of directors.

Although it may seem to have little in common with the world of computing, the market for underwear has seen its fair share of blockbuster-like marketing tactics, too. Victoria's Secret, for instance, purposefully turns its annual fashion show into a media spectacle, so as to attract maximum attention and awareness for its collection of bras, panties, and other women's clothing and accessories. Broadcast in more than 180 countries, the $12 million show serves as the main form of advertising for the lingerie brand.

In 2012, the event saw dozens of beautiful women showcase Victoria's Secret product lines by walking the runway, just as one would expect with any fashion show. But the show also highlighted live performances by A-list pop stars such as Rihanna, Bruno Mars, and Justin Bieber (who, dancing among the models, presumably invited the envy of millions of other eighteen-year-old males). And it prominently featured a group of superstar models who have signed on with the brand to become Victoria's Secret

"Angels," including Alessandra Ambrosio, Doutzen Kroes, and Candice Swanepoel, even following them behind the scenes. (The footage mostly suggested the models engage in a lot of pacing around, and are stalked by at least three dressers at all times, but that's beside the point.) In the United States, where CBS licenses the show for more than $1 million, over nine million viewers tuned in. The one-hour show aired in a prime-time slot on December 4—timed perfectly to coincide with the start of the Christmas holiday shopping season—and was designed to send viewers to Victoria's Secret retail outlets or its e-commerce operations. The blockbuster bet, which absorbs a significant chunk of the brand's advertising budget, is tremendously effective in creating buzz around the company's brand in the mass market every year.

Beyond the fashion show, Victoria's Secret—which generates over $5 billion in net sales annually for its parent company, Limited Brands—appears to get a lot of mileage out of its superstars. The models who sign on as Angels serve as brand ambassadors throughout the year, making appearances, participating in interviews, or attending publicity events on behalf of Victoria's Secret. And these elite models benefit, too. Not only does being an Angel pay handsomely—reportedly up to $5 million a year—but the association with Victoria's Secret also helps these superstars further enhance their reputations, much more so than any regular endorsement deal. Just being selected is a huge career boost: it's perhaps roughly equivalent to the benefits that befall a soccer player being recruited by Real Madrid or Manchester United. Becoming an Angel gives the models tremendous exposure. "It puts millions of dollars of advertising behind you," according to a senior vice president of IMG Models, which represents many Victoria's Secret Angels. These mutual benefits help explain why the brand's strategy works so well.

The advent of digital technology is helping to bring a wide range of companies a huge step closer to media businesses and the rules they play by. Think back to Starbucks: in addition to procuring recorded music for sale in stores, it is investing in its Starbucks Digital Network—and both initiatives help the coffee company provide its consumers with content that speaks to the brand. Or take Red Bull, which seems to be transforming itself into a media company. The energy-beverage brand is well-known for unusual stunts, such as its air show and cliff-diving competition. But it took things to new heights with Red Bull Stratos, which involved sky-diver Felix Baumgartner jumping out of a capsule twenty-four miles above the earth's surface. That widely promoted event allowed Red Bull to reach a worldwide audience of tens of millions of viewers—including eight million with its own live stream on YouTube. The company seems committed to becoming a real player in entertainment, whether by selling content to consumers, licensing the rights to sports events, or building an advertising business around its YouTube channel. None of these tactics are guaranteed to help sell more cans of its energy drink, but they all cleverly speak to the brand's "Red Bull gives you wings" slogan.

Or consider a company in yet another sector: the one-and-a-half-century-old British retailer Burberry, among the world's leading luxury brands, and famous for its blockbuster product, the trench coat. When I interviewed Burberry's chief executive officer Angela Ahrendts in the fall of 2012, she described her firm not as a clothing company but as a "digital-media company." It may be startling to hear her use that description—Burberry makes decidedly analog products, after all—but the statement actually makes perfect sense considering the way in which Ahrendts has reinvented the company since her arrival in 2006.

In an effort to woo younger consumers and truly connect with them, Burberry has recently made a strong push in digital channels, effectively becoming a content producer. Media expertise is now essential to the company's direction. "If you look at the composition of our board of directors, you'll see it includes individuals who have served as the CMO of Time Inc. and the CEO of BBC Worldwide," said Ahrendts. "Everything you see on Burberry.com, we shoot that in-house. We have a creative media team of a hundred people." Burberry has live-streamed its runway shows since

September 2010 (a first in fashion, apparently), allowing millions of viewers at home to view the shows online and post comments in real time. The brand continues to innovate, for example by simulcasting runway shows in 3D globally, and by offering online customers the opportunity to buy directly from the runway.

Burberry has also focused heavily on populating its Facebook and Twitter accounts with useful content; it now has more fans and followers than any other luxury brand. And the company has launched several online destinations. At artofthetrench.com, for instance, consumers can submit photos of themselves in its iconic rainwear. "Nothing is for sale; it is just a site to connect people," explained Ahrendts. At Burberry Acoustic, which falls under Burberry.com, people can find songs recorded exclusively for the brand by British artists who have been handpicked by Burberry's chief creative officer. All these efforts stem from Ahrendts's zeal for engaging customers and building communities of fans. Her strategy is working: in the seven years since she came to Burberry, the company's annual sales have nearly tripled to more than $3 billion.

Perhaps it shouldn't be all that surprising to see more and more companies, from a wide variety of sectors, adopt strategies that are successful in the business of entertainment, or even move into content production and distribution themselves. Every strong brand has a story to tell, after all, and entertainment businesses are masters at getting people to view, read, or listen to their stories. The best content producers have a keen understanding of how they can do so over and over again—how they can have lasting success in reaching and engaging audiences. So it's only natural that those businesses would lead the way in a world that is increasingly connected and in which there is intense competition for people's attention.

Strategies that are effective in the entertainment business are also highly relevant to other sectors and, if current trends are anything to go by, best practices will increasingly pervade those industries. Many business leaders will find themselves competing in winner-take-all markets where being "average" is not good enough and scale is critical, where smart firms make blockbuster bets and put all their weight behind making those bets catch on with consumers, and where top-ranked individual performers—true superstars—are critical to success and may capture most of the rewards that are up for grabs. All in all, it is time to rewrite Irving Berlin's 1954 blockbuster *There's No Business Like Show Business*—the business world at large, it turns out, can learn quite a bit from the entertainment industry.

NOTES

In this book, I draw on hundreds of in-depth interviews I have conducted with entertainment executives, talent, and other personalities over the course of nearly a decade. Many of these interviews were a part of the case studies I developed in my role as a professor at the Harvard Business School; some interviews were conducted exclusively for the book. As is standard procedure with Harvard Business School cases, the interviewees have had a chance to review their quotes. The detailed notes below refer to the individual case studies.

I also rely on my analyses of sales and other quantitative data on the entertainment industry. Some of my findings have been published in scholarly articles in academic journals. The notes below provide information on both the data sources and the corresponding journal articles, and often provide additional details on the analyses.

Prologue: Show Business—a Business of Blockbusters
1   as Horn put it, "really pursued it as a strategy": Unless otherwise indicated, I obtained the quotes in this book from personal interviews.
3   "He's earned the respect of the industry for driving tremendous: Dawn C. Chmielewski, "Alan Horn Could Revive Walt Disney Studios' Magic," *Los Angeles Times*, June 1, 2012.
3   One rival executive labeled Zucker "a case study in the most destructive: Maureen Dowd, "The Biggest Loser," *New York Times*, January 12, 2010.
7   to crow about "an electricity in the building" at the company's headquarters: James B. Stewart, "NBC Finds a Winner in 'The Voice,'" *New York Times*, March 2, 2012.

Chapter One: Betting on Blockbusters
15   In June 2012, less than two weeks after the news of: This section is partly based on: Gary Pisano and Alison Berkley Wagonfeld, "Warner Bros. Entertainment," Harvard Business School Case 610-036. I identify each quote used from this case separately, but I think a wider acknowledgment of their work is appropriate. My own

interviews with Alan Horn, which are the source for the large majority of his quotes in the book, were conducted before he commenced his new role at Disney Pictures.

15 Disney Pictures had posted disappointing box-office results: Ryan Nakashima, "Disney Says 'John Carter' to Lose $200 million," *Associated Press*, March 19, 2012.

16 Described as "a consensus builder," Horn went to great lengths: Patrick Goldstein, "Alan Horn: Can Disney's New Boss Reinvent the Studio?," *Los Angeles Times*, 24 Frames blog, June 1, 2012.

16 The results proved the wisdom of his strategy: Warner Bros. press releases, boxof ficemojo.com.

17 "Making monster projects into profit centers is no slam-dunk: Merissa Marr, "Warner's Event Movie Bet," *Wall Street Journal*, June 1, 2004.

17 Detractors of event-film strategies also loved to point to the western: Steven Bach, *Final Cut: Dreams and Disaster in the Making of Heaven's Gate* (New York: William Morrow & Co., 1985); "Review of 'Heaven's Gate,'" *Chicago Sun-Times*, January 1, 1981.

17 "In a good year, a major studio is happy to bat .500: Gary Pisano and Alison Berkley Wagonfeld, "Warner Bros. Entertainment," Harvard Business School Case 610-036.

18 "It is such a gut-level decision that it is impossible to define": The last sentence of this quote comes from ibid.

19 The studio released twenty-two films that year, spending about $1.5 billion: I estimated production budgets mentioned in this section using a variety of sources, including interviewees and other industry experts, boxofficemojo.com, the-numbers .com, imdb.com, annual reports, and trade magazines. Assessing production budgets is unavoidably an inexact science, though, so the numbers cited should be regarded as approximations. I obtained (proprietary) data on advertising spending from Kantar Media; I did not receive such data directly from Warner Bros. or any other studio.

20 "We have made a conscious decision at Warner Bros.: Gary Pisano and Alison Berkley Wagonfeld, "Warner Bros. Entertainment," Harvard Business School Case 610-036.

20 Although the top three biggest bets only accounted for a third: I obtained domestic box-office data from Rentrak, and international box-office estimates from boxoffice mojo.com.

20 At the other extreme, the four least expensive movies released in 2010: Several of these movies were only distributed by Warner Bros. and not produced by Warner Bros. And although a twenty-third film, *Pure Country 2*, was a part of its slate that year, too, I have excluded it here because it saw virtually no theatrical release and was largely distributed in DVD format. Including the film would make the distribution of revenues and profits across films even more skewed.

21 The figure plots each of the 119 films that Warner: To construct the sample, using data provided by Rentrak, I first compiled a listing of all Warner Bros. movies that were theatrically released in the five-year window from January 1, 2007, through December 31, 2011, and then excluded rereleases and IMAX movies. I used various sources to compile the necessary data: domestic box-office revenues from Rentrak; foreign box-office revenues from boxofficemojo.com; and production-budget estimates from interviewees and other industry experts, boxofficemojo.com, the numbers.com, imdb.com, annual reports, and trade magazines.

22 *The Blind Side, The Hangover*, and *Gran Torino*: *The Blind Side* was distributed by Warner Bros. but produced by Alcon Entertainment.

23 The figure shows how much the 119 movies, when grouped: To illustrate the basic relationship between costs and revenues, I define "surplus" as the difference between worldwide box-office revenues and production expenditures. The metric is

not meant to be taken literally as the profits that flow to the studio; note, for instance, that the metric does not account for the studio's advertising expenditures and the revenue share that the studio pays the theater.

24 "The advertising expenditures for a movie that cost $150 million to make: The same is true for distribution costs, which in the film industry come in the form of prints (or copies of the film): a more expensive film may be distributed more widely, meaning more prints are needed, but, again, distributing a more expensive film will be more cost efficient. When films are fully digitally distributed, making extra copies will be very inexpensive. This further increases the relative advantage of bigger releases.

25 The figure shows, for Warner's 2010 movie slate: I obtained data on advertising expenditures from Kantar Media. The data cover advertising expenditures across a range of media, including newspapers, magazines, network and cable television, radio, and outdoor.

28 "We intend to relax risk aversion policies: "Paramount Sees Its Future in the Stars," *New York Times*, March 31, 2004.

28 The latter was one of the biggest box-office disasters of all time: As estimated by boxofficemojo.com.

28 One of the most daring bids in the world of book publishing: I have earlier discussed some of these arguments in an article on blockbuster bets in book publishing: Anita Elberse, "Blockbuster or Bust," *Wall Street Journal*, January 3, 2009.

29 His charming, unassuming personality easily made up for it: This section is based on: Anita Elberse, "Grand Central Publishing," Harvard Business School Case 508-036.

29 Author advances in the tens of thousands: For more information on the structure of such contracts and the publishing industry more generally, see: Albert N. Greco, *The Book Publishing Industry*, 2nd ed. (Hillsdale, NJ: Lawrence Erlbaum, 2005); The Book Industry Study Group, "Book Industry Trends 2006"; *The Bowker Annual Library and Book Trade Almanac*, 51st ed., edited by Dave Bogart (Medford, NJ: Information Today, Inc., 2006); and Standard & Poor's "Industry Surveys: Publishing," March 8, 2007.

29 *Marley & Me* had garnered critical and commercial success: "Competitors Bark at Heels of 'Marley's' Success," *USA Today*, April 29, 2007.

30 William Morrow, a HarperCollins imprint, had paid: Ibid.

30 "It's stunning, the advances being paid: Motoko Rich, "Iowa Library's Cat Has a Rich Second Life as a Biography," *New York Times*, April 4, 2007.

30 According to Kosztolnyik's records, Peter Gethers' *The Cat Who Went to Paris*: These data are from Nielsen BookScan, the most comprehensive source of information on industry sales. BookScan does not cover all retailers, though; Walmart is an example of a retailer that is excluded.

31 A publisher's front list is its catalog of new books: Standard & Poor's, "Industry Surveys: Publishing," March 8, 2007.

31 Grand Central chose to compete this way in a sector where: The Association of American Publishers (AAP) collects monthly and annual data on book returns.

32 The sixth-highest-selling book (fiction or nonfiction) of 2006: I am indebted to Al Greco for his help in securing these Nielsen BookScan data.

34 and when a no-name filmmaker with a minuscule budget: *The Blair Witch Project* cost only $60,000 to produce and generated close to $250 million in worldwide box-office revenues. *Paranormal Activity* cost only $15,000 to produce and generated nearly $200 million at the box office worldwide. Even *Paranormal Activity 4*, made for $5 million, generated five times its production budget in its opening weekend alone.

35 Many movie lovers lament the offerings: These nine films were *Harry Potter and the Deathly Hallows: Part 2*, *Transformers: Dark of the Moon*, *The Twilight Saga: Breaking*

Dawn—Part 1, The Hangover Part II, Pirates of the Caribbean: On Stranger Tides, Fast Five, Mission: Impossible—Ghost Protocol, Cars 2, and *Sherlock Holmes: A Game of Shadows.*

36   "Sometimes this industry is like the mafia: Gary Pisano and Alison Berkley Wagon-feld, "Warner Bros. Entertainment," Harvard Business School Case 610-036.

37   When, in the mid-2000s, a brave producer: This paragraph is based on: Anita El-berse, "Xanadu on Broadway," Harvard Business School Case 508-062.

37   Described by influential film critics as "the epic failure: Roger Ebert, "Xanadu" Re-view, *Chicago Sun-Times,* September 1, 1980; Clark Collis, "Why People Love 'Xan-adu,'" *Entertainment Weekly,* July 6, 2007.

38   "As soon as you say *Xanadu,*" he remarked: Clark Collis, "Why People Love 'Xan-adu,'" *Entertainment Weekly,* July 6, 2007.

38   When Ahrens approached Douglas Carter Beane: John Berman and Ted Gerstein, "Can Broadway Fix 'Xanadu'?," *ABC News,* July 9, 2007.

40   Literary agent Jonny Geller joked that his agency: *Sex Story: Fifty Shades of Grey,* Documentary, Channel 4, United Kingdom.

42   The above figure plots each of the sixty-one hardcover books: These data came directly from Grand Central Publishing; the sample covers all books on the pub-lisher's fall 2006 front list.

42   because of the economies of scale involved in advertising campaigns: In video games, Activision Blizzard is an interesting example. Its three key franchise titles—*Call of Duty, World of Warcraft,* and *Skylanders*—accounted for approximately 73 percent of its net revenues and, according to the game publisher, "a significantly higher percentage" of its operating income in 2011. (Source: Activision's 2011 An-nual Report.)

43   The figure shows how much the fall 2006 hardcover titles: Here, "costs" include the author's advance and royalty payments, printing and binding, freight and ship-ping, and marketing. "Net sales" are the net copies sold multiplied by the cover price, and taking into account any retailer discounts. "Gross profits" are the net revenues (which cover net sales and any subsidiary rights) minus paper, printing and binding, freight and shipping, marketing, and total author earnings.

44   Called *Dewey: There's a Cat in the Library,* it sold 106,000 copies: Again, I am indebted to Al Greco for his help in securing these Nielsen BookScan data.

44   At one point, there was even talk of a movie adaptation: Michael Fleming, "Meryl Streep to Star in 'Library Cat': Actress Purrs for New Line's 'Dewey,'" *Variety,* No-vember 12, 2008.

45   Additionally, a larger number of products often leads to volume discounts: Savings on advertising are especially likely if studios can buy television advertising time on the so-called up-front advertising market (as opposed to the "scatter market"). A larger scale facilitates such media buys.

46   Large media producers may buy advertising time on television months in advance: Most television advertising is sold on the up-front market, which takes place in May each year, when the networks present their program lineups for the upcoming season.

48   In August 2009, Disney announced a $4 billion purchase: This section is based on: Anita Elberse, "Marvel Enterprises, Inc.," Harvard Business School Case 505-001.

48   As Disney's purchase of the company came together: "Marvel May Need Heroic Help," *Wall Street Journal,* June 29, 2004; "Shareholder Scoreboard: Leaders and Lag-gards in the Rankings," *Wall Street Journal,* March 8, 2004.

50   In 2005, Marvel made its first strides toward that goal: Marvel Enterprises, "Marvel Launches Independently Financed Film Slate with Closing of $525 Million Non-Recourse Credit Facility," press release, September 6, 2005.

51   "This treasure trove of over 5,000 characters offers Disney: David Goldman, "Disney to Buy Marvel for $4 Billion," *CNN Money*, August 31, 2009.

55   the first films to come out of the company's deal with Paramount: Marvel Enterprises, "Marvel Launches Independently Financed Film Slate with Closing of $525 Million Non-Recourse Credit Facility," press release, September 6, 2005.

55   Disney gained further control of the Marvel portfolio by buying Paramount: Pamela McClintock, "Move for Marvel Rights," *Variety*, October 18, 2010.

Chapter Two: Launching and Managing Blockbusters

56   Standing backstage at a sold-out concert in Boston's TD Garden: This section is based on: Anita Elberse and Michael Christensen, "Lady Gaga (A)," Harvard Business School Case 512-016; Anita Elberse and Michael Christensen, "Lady Gaga (B)," Harvard Business School Case 512-017.

57   Born as Stefani Joanne Angelina Germanotta in New York City: "Bio," www.lady gaga.com; "Lady Gaga: Biography," *Rolling Stone*. Both accessed May 31, 2011.

57   In 2003, she was one of twenty students given early admission: Vanessa Grigoriadis, "Growing Up Gaga," *New York Magazine*, March 28, 2010.

58   "May you always have soft cuticles while tweeting: Mawuse Ziegbe, "Lady Gaga Thanks Fans for Twitter Crown," MTV.com, August 22, 2011.

61   *My Big Fat Greek Wedding* is a classic example: For more information on this and other limited releases, see: Anita Elberse, John A. Quelch, and Anna Harrington, "The Passion of the Christ (A)," Harvard Business School Case 505-025; Anita Elberse, John A. Quelch, and Anna Harrington, "The Passion of the Christ (B)," Harvard Business School Case 505-026.

62   In the book business, the initial launch of E. L. James's mega-seller: Peter Osnos, "How 'Fifty Shades of Grey' Dominated Publishing," *Atlantic*, August 2012.

63   Carter and his team arranged for fifty popular music bloggers: Simon Owens, "The Secrets of Lady Gaga's Social Media Success," *The Next Web*, March 15, 2011.

63   *Just Dance* broke into major charts for dance airplay and club play: Jonathan Cohen, "Lady GaGa Dances to the Top of Hot 100," *Billboard*, January 8, 2009.

65   Spending ramps up dramatically in the six to eight weeks before release: In a 2007 academic article, I present data for a sample of 280 films in which 91 percent of spending takes place in the four weeks before release, 81 percent in the final three weeks, 62 percent in the final two weeks, and 34 percent in the final week. For more information, see: Anita Elberse and Bharat N. Anand, "The Effectiveness of Pre-Release Advertising for Motion Pictures: An Empirical Investigation Using a Simulated Market," *Information Economics and Policy* 19, nos. 3–4 (October 2007): 319–43.

65   In 2011, for example, the top hundred films, from *Harry Potter*: I conducted this analysis using rankings and box-office-revenues data pulled from boxofficemojo.com.

65   That, in turn, follows from the very nature of entertainment products: The economist Richard Caves has an in-depth examination of how properties of creative industries and creative goods drive business strategy: Richard E. Caves, *Creative Industries: Contracts Between Art and Commerce* (Cambridge, Mass.: Harvard University Press, 2000). Whereas Caves considers industrial-organization and contracting issues, my focus is on strategic marketing challenges.

66   For media products, initial success breeds further success: These ideas are explored in considerable detail in Robert H. Frank and Philip J. Cook, *The Winner-Take-All Society* (New York: Free Press, 1995).

66   When Disney's $250-million-budget *John Carter* generated a disappointing: Pamela McClintock, "Box Office Report: 'John Carter' Earns Weak $30.6 Mil Domestically, $101.2 Mil Globally," *Hollywood Reporter*, March 11, 2012.

67   Even products that have no discernible quality differences: Matthew J. Salganik, Peter Sheridan Dodds, and Duncan J. Watts, "Experimental Study of Inequality and Unpredictability in an Artificial Cultural Market," *Science* 311 no. 5762 (February 10, 2006): 854–56; Matthew J. Salganik and Duncan J. Watts, "Leading the Herd Astray: An Experimental Study of Self-Fulfilling Prophecies in an Artificial Cultural Market," *Social Psychology Quarterly* 71, no. 4 (2008): 338–55.

68   The ultimate success of an entertainment product, Watts and his colleagues: Duncan J. Watts, "Is Justin Timberlake a Product of Cumulative Advantage?," *New York Times*, April 15, 2007.

69   In the movie industry, study after study has shown: See, for instance: Anita Elberse and Bharat N. Anand, "The Effectiveness of Pre-Release Advertising for Motion Pictures: An Empirical Investigation Using a Simulated Market," *Information Economics and Policy* 19, nos. 3–4 (October 2007): 319–43; Anita Elberse and Felix Oberholzer-Gee, "Superstars and Underdogs: An Examination of the Long Tail Phenomenon in Video Sales," *Marketing Science Institute* 4 (2007): 49–72; Jehoshua Eliashberg, Anita Elberse, and Mark Leenders, "The Motion Picture Industry: Critical Issues in Practice, Current Research, and New Research Directions," *Marketing Science* 25, no. 6 (November–December 2006): 638–61; Anita Elberse and Jehoshua Eliashberg, "Demand and Supply Dynamics for Sequentially Released Products in International Markets: The Case of Motion Pictures," *Marketing Science* 22, no. 3 (Summer 2003): 329–54.

69   Higher advertising expenditures help, too: Anita Elberse and Jehoshua Eliashberg, "Demand and Supply Dynamics for Sequentially Released Products in International Markets: The Case of Motion Pictures," *Marketing Science* 22, no. 3 (Summer 2003): 329–54. (One study even finds that we have to look to screens to explain why co-financed movies do better. The idea is that when two studios co-finance a movie, they release their other movies further apart from the opening weekend of the movie on which they collaborate. That leads to softer competition, clearing the way for the co-financed film to play in more theaters. See Ronald L. Goettler and Philip Leslie, "Cofinancing to Manage Risk in the Motion Picture Industry," *Journal of Economics and Management Strategy* 14, no. 2 [2005]: 231–61. Incidentally, Warner Bros. engaged in relatively few of such co-financing deals with other studios; it seemed to prefer to partner with third-party players such as Village Roadshow and Legendary Pictures.)

69   In the music industry, radio airplay: See, for instance: Wendy W. Moe and Peter S. Fader, "Modeling Hedonic Portfolio Products: A Joint Segmentation Analysis of Music CD Sales," *Journal of Marketing Research* 38, no. 3 (2001): 376–83; Alan L. Montgomery and Wendy W. Moe, "Should Music Labels Pay for Radio Airplay? Investigating the Relationship Between Album Sales and Radio Airplay," Working Paper, August 2002.

70   With so much money tied up in their projects: Richard E. Caves, *Creative Industries: Contracts* (Cambridge, Mass.: Harvard University Press, 2000). Higher interest rates exacerbate the importance of recovering investments in a timely manner.

70   experienced entertainment executives will favor a big launch: As explained earlier, advertising campaigns for wide releases can be relatively cheap. For instance, the cost per advertising exposure tends to be lower under national media buys than under a series of local media buys cobbled together in a limited release.

71   Amazon sold an estimated 440,000 units for just 99 cents: Glenn Peoples, "How Many Millions Did Amazon Lose on Two Days of 99 Cent Lady Gaga Sales?," *Billboard*, May 27, 2011.

71   during the same period, eighteen million copies: Nielsen SoundScan, accessed December 2012.

72   James Diener never was your typical record-label executive: This section is based on: Anita Elberse and Elie Ofek, "Octone Records," Harvard Business School Case 507-082; Anita Elberse, Elie Ofek, and Caren Kelleher, "A&M/Octone Records: All Rights or Nothing?," Harvard Business School Case 511-031.

72   rose to the position of vice president of A&R/Marketing: A&R stands for "Artist & Repertoire."

75   Smaller and larger content producers are different: Some general information on the music industry discussed here draws from Donald S. Passman, *All You Need to Know About the Music Business*, 6th ed. (New York: Free Press, 2006).

82   *Moves Like Jagger*, which became the ninth best-selling digital single: International Federation of the Phonographic Industry, "IFPI Digital Music Report 2012: Key Facts and Figures."

Chapter Three: Investing in Superstars

83   In June 2009, Florentino Pérez, president of renowned Spanish soccer club: This section is partly based on John A. Quelch, José Luis Nueno, and Carin-Isabel Knoop, "Real Madrid Club de Fútbol," Harvard Business School Case 504-063; and Anita Elberse and John A. Quelch, "Real Madrid Club de Fútbol in 2007: Beyond the Galácticos," Harvard Business School Case 508-060. I identify each quote used from the case that I did not co-author.

83   Completing what Pérez described as a "dream move: Daniel Taylor and Jamie Jackson, "Manchester United Accept £80m Cristiano Ronaldo Bid from Real Madrid," *Guardian*, June 11, 2009. All foreign currencies listed in this section have been converted into dollars using the historical currency rate for the midpoint of the relevant month.

83   Real Madrid purchased the twenty-four-year-old Ronaldo for a record transfer fee: I compiled all player transfer fee estimates in this section from www.transfermarket.de, and converted them to dollar amounts using the average exchange rate in the corresponding month (or months). Sherwin Rosen, "The Economics of Superstars," *American Economics Review* 71 (December 1981): 845–58.

84   The UK's *Sun* newspaper, meanwhile, set up a help line for distraught British fans: Stefano Hatfield, "As Becks Suits Up for Spain, Real Action Happens in Stores," *Advertising Age*, July 21, 2003.

86   "We began to think of ourselves as content providers: The quotes in this paragraph stem from: John A. Quelch, José Luis Nueno, and Carin-Isabel Knoop, "Real Madrid Club de Fútbol in 2007: Beyond the Galácticos," Harvard Business School Case 508-060.

86   a couple of important features of the market for creative talent: Robert H. Frank and Philip J. Cook, *The Winner-Take-All Society* (New York: Free Press, 1995).

87   In 1995, Jim Carrey famously became the first star: "Pact Mentality," *Variety*, October 16, 2006.

87   Tom Cruise reportedly earned more than $70 million: Edward Jay Epstein, *The Big Picture: The New Logic of Money and Power in Hollywood* (New York: Random House, 2005).

87   Most members of the Screen Actors Guild: According to data reported by the Screen Actors Guild itself. Granted, this covers not just actors who cannot find sufficient work, but also those who refuse work, or those who have moved on to other careers entirely but have kept up their membership dues. Also see: "Don't Forget the Middle People," *New York Times*, June 30, 2008.

87   When David Beckham joined the Los Angeles Galaxy: Five players of the LA Galaxy had a base salary below $20,000 that year. See: Major League Soccer Players Union, "2007 MLS Player Salaries, By Club," www.mlsplayers.org, August 31, 2007.

88   In these markets, the efforts of only a small number of people: In the 1980s, the economist Sherwin Rosen used the term *superstars* to describe the "relatively small numbers of people" who "earn enormous amounts of money and dominate the activities in which they engage."

88   but when entire teams of creative workers come together: Economists call these "complex creative goods."

88   why would anyone consider paying tens of millions of dollars: Several of the factors mentioned are adapted from Robert H. Frank and Philip J. Cook, *The Winner-Take-All Society* (New York: Free Press, 1995).

90   And since people are drawn to winners: Academic research provides lots of evidence for people's "taste for winners." For instance, psychologists have demonstrated people's need to "bask in reflected glory" by communicating their associations with successful others: R. B. Cialdini, R. J. Borden, A. Thorne, M. R. Walker, S. Freeman, and L. R. Sloan, "Basking in Reflected Glory: Three (Football) Field Studies," *Journal of Personality and Social Psychology* 34 (1976): 366–75: C. R. Snyder, M. Lassegard, and C. E. Ford, "Distancing After Group Success and Failure: Basking in Reflected Glory and Cutting Off Reflected Failure," *Journal of Personality and Social Psychology* 51, no. 2 (1986): 382–88.

91   A reliance on popularity also characterizes the industry players: This phenomenon is even affecting on-the-field choices in sports, where, for instance, it could lead to the less-than-optimal tendency to give star players the clutch shot at the end of basketball games. Milwaukee Bucks assistant coach Jim Boylan once explained it as follows: "You're down one. There are 15 seconds to go. You come down the floor, make a few passes. Somehow your best player ends up not getting the ball. Now there are five seconds left, four, three, two . . . boom. Got to shoot. You miss. After the game, everyone asks, 'Why didn't your best player, your highest-paid player, get the basketball? This is why he's here. We're paying him to get the ball at the end of the game and win it for us.' As a coach, you're stuck." Henry Abbott, "Hero Ball," *ESPN The Magazine*, March 19, 2012.

91   In some cases, however, the concentration of rewards: Another example here is the market for art. In auctions for art pieces, a few deep-pocketed buyers can really move the needle on fees for certain artists.

93   in each season since 2000, the team has spent significantly more: These are my conclusions from an analysis of data obtained from www.transfermarket.de.

93   Pérez pursued the strategy from the moment he arrived: John A. Quelch, José Luis Nueno, and Carin-Isabel Knoop, "Real Madrid Club de Fútbol in 2007: Beyond the Galácticos," Harvard Business School Case 508-060.

93   as one club executive put it, "the best players pay for themselves": Ibid.

94   total revenues had risen to over $600 million: In fairness, currency exchange rates contribute to the growth as reported in US dollars. However, when expressed in euros the data show impressive growth, too: revenues increased from 138 million euros in 2000–2001 to 292 million euros in 2005–2006 (with marketing revenues nearly tripling from 39 million euros to 117 million euros), to 442 million euros in 2009–2010.

94   Real Madrid sold some 350,000 jerseys in Britain alone: Emma Daly, "Real Madrid Learns to Win off the Field," *International Herald Tribune*, August 15, 2003.

95   the 2011 winner of the European Champions League, for example: Deloitte Sports Business Group, "Fan Power: Football Money League," February 2012.

95   Ashton Kutcher a reported $700,000 per episode: "Who Earns What: TV's Highest Paid Stars," *TV Guide*, 2011; "Ashton Kutcher's 'Two and a Half Men' Contract Is Only One Year (Report)," *Hollywood Reporter*, May 22, 2011.

96   "The responsibility here is divided among multiple players: John A. Quelch, José Luis Nueno, and Carin-Isabel Knoop, "Real Madrid Club de Fútbol in 2007: Beyond the Galácticos," Harvard Business School Case 508-060.

96 "The greatest players aspire to play with Real Madrid: Ibid.

96 "The fans are part of the show: Ibid.

97 Real Madrid itself is struggling with a sizable debt: Much has been written about the debt of Real Madrid (and FC Barcelona and Manchester United, for that matter) in the popular sports press. While debt is obviously not desirable, most of those reports seem to overstate the severity of the situation. For a comprehensive analysis of the clubs' debt problem, see: the *Swiss Rambler*, "The Truth About Debt at Barcelona and Real Madrid," swissramble.blogspot.com, April 30, 2012.

98 For Real Madrid, that figure was as much as 90 percent: Real Madrid annual reports.

98 When British newspaper the *Observer* asked readers: This section is based on: Anita Elberse, Alberto Ballve, and Gustavo Herrero, "Club Atlético Boca Juniors," Harvard Business School Case 508-056.

98 "The rivalry between Boca and River Plate is the most intense: Gavin Hamilton, "50 Sporting Things You Must Do Before You Die," *Observer*, April 4, 2004.

99 Juan Román Riquelme, one of Boca's former stars: "Riquelme Doesn't Rule Out Returning to Argentine team," Goal.com, February 24, 2007.

99 Boca Juniors is the most popular club in soccer-mad Argentina: Based on data supplied by Octagon, adapted from TNS Gallup 2004.

100 "I'm comfortable here," he stated: "Palacio Option Tougher Than Ever," Goal.com, January 4, 2007.

101 Over the decade in which Macri was in charge: I compiled data from Deloitte's "Football Money League," February 2007; BBDO's "Brand Equity Ranking of European Football Clubs," September 2007; individual clubs' annual reports; and www.forbes.com. For more information, see: Anita Elberse, Alberto Ballve, and Gustavo Herrero, "Club Atlético Boca Juniors," Harvard Business School Case 508-056.

102 Real Madrid alone made $90 million from selling broadcast rights: "Soccer: Real Madrid Agrees to Sell TV Rights for €1.1 billion," *International Herald Tribune*, November 20, 2006.

102 Similarly, Brazil's soccer industry would quickly: "S. America Soccer Relies on Player Sales for Profit, Study Says," *Bloomberg*, December 22, 2006. The article describes the results of a proprietary study by Deloitte & Touche LLP.

102 Real Madrid was rumored to have offered Fernando Gago: "Not the New Maradona, but the New Redondo," *Guardian*, November 29, 2006.

105 "Lorne has had a seismic impact on comedy: Both Conan O'Brien and Tina Fey are quoted in: Stacey Wilson, "A Rare Glimpse Inside the Empire of 'SNL's' Lorne Michaels," *Hollywood Reporter*, April 22, 2011.

106 Many children hoping for a career in show business: Neil Swidey, "What Does It Take to Become a Disney Star?," *Boston Globe*, May 27, 2012.

107 the journalist Peter Bogdanovich disclosed some years ago: Peter Bogdanovich, "SNL's Killer Contract," *New York Observer*, August 16, 1999.

107 Under the contract described by Bogdanovich: Ibid.

108 "I challenge you to name a network, much less a show, that has created: Ibid.

109 "Would she be in a position to play in front of: John Jurgensen, "The Lessons of Lady Gaga," *Wall Street Journal*, February 5, 2010.

110 In the end, Boca Juniors did indeed sell Fernando Gago: I obtained estimates from www.transfermarket.de.

111 The club currently occupies second place in the "football money league": FC Barcelona and Real Madrid's annual reports; Deloitte's "Football Money League," February 2012.

111 "For lovers of the "beautiful game," Barça's onslaught: Jimmy Burns, "Who's the Greatest of Them All? Barcelona!," *Newsweek*, June 13, 2011.

111 The performance owed much to FC Barcelona's youth academy: "A Different Perspective: More Than a Club, but Also More Than a Business," *Pictet Report*, Winter 2012; ESADE, "Carles Folguera, Director of Barcelona FC's La Masia," December 20, 2011.

112 Messi has star power, too: when he joined Facebook: Alana Fisher, "Lionel Messi Joins Facebook, Reaches 6.7 Million Fans, Gains 40,000 Interactions in a Few Hours," *Brand New Directions*, April 7, 2011.

112 The club invests heavily in its youth program: "A Different Perspective: More Than a Club, but Also More Than a Business," *Pictet Report*, Winter 2012; ESADE, "Carles Folguera, Director of Barcelona FC's La Masia," December 20, 2011.

113 "That is why giving them an education is so essential": ESADE, "Carles Folguera, Director of Barcelona FC's La Masia," December 20, 2011.

113 "in the choice between buying talent or growing it in-house: "A Different Perspective: More Than a Club, but Also More Than a Business," *Pictet Report*, Winter 2012.

113 In the five seasons before the summer of 2011: All player transfer fee estimates in this paragraph were compiled from www.transfermarket.de and converted to dollar amounts using the average exchange rate for July 2011.

113 In fact, Barça is estimated to be the world's best-paying sports team: "200 Best-Paying Teams in the World," *ESPN The Magazine*, May 2, 2011.

114 "too high for the club to be able to dictate its future": "A Different Perspective: More Than a Club, but Also More Than a Business," *Pictet Report*, Winter 2012.

114 "We won't always win, so our challenge: "Faus: 'We've Reduced the Debt, but the Situation Is Delicate,'" www.fcbarcelona.com, September 14, 2011.

114 Long the undisputed leader in building its business globally: "The World's Most Valuable Soccer Teams," *Forbes*, April 18, 2012; "The World's 50 Most Valuable Sports Teams," *Forbes*, July 16, 2012.

115 Real Madrid's executives have explicitly said that they modeled their approach: See: John A. Quelch, José Luis Nueno, and Carin-Isabel Knoop, "Real Madrid Club de Fútbol in 2007: Beyond the Galácticos," Harvard Business School Case 508-060.

115 But much of the credit for the club's achievements goes to one man: This section is based on: Anita Elberse and Tom Dye, "Sir Alex Ferguson: Managing Manchester United," Harvard Business School Case 513-051. Ferguson is Europe's most decorated manager.

116 In the past decade, one in which Manchester United has won: Based on an analysis with data I pulled from www.transferleague.co.uk that covers the ten seasons from 2001–2002 through 2010–2011. On this metric, Manchester United even outperforms Arsenal, which is known for investing in young talent.

116 he outperformed the typical short life cycle of a coach: In England, 30 percent of coaches survive less than a year in the job, and more than half less than two years, while records in most other European countries are even worse.

Chapter Four: How Superstars Use Their Powers

118 In November 2006, movie star Tom Cruise: This section is based on: Anita Elberse and Peter Stone, "Metro-Goldwyn-Mayer (MGM) and Tom Cruise," Harvard Business School Case 508-057.

119 "Tom Cruise, in 10 months, for Paramount Pictures, generated: "Mission Improbable: Tom Cruise as Mogul," *New York Times*, March 4, 2007.

119 "It's nothing to do with his acting ability, he's a terrific actor": "Sumner Redstone Gives Tom Cruise His Walking Papers," *Wall Street Journal*, August 23, 2006.

121 These contracts typically lasted seven years: Edward Jay Epstein, *The Big Picture: The New Logic of Money and Power in Hollywood* (New York: Random House, 2005).

121 The studio system was brought to a standstill by legal challenges: Ibid.

122 My own research, most notably a study that examined: Anita Elberse, "The Power of Stars: Do Star Actors Drive the Success of Motion Pictures?," *Journal of Marketing* 71, no. 4 (October 2007): 102–20. Of course no academic researcher can convince a studio head to produce two versions of a $100 million movie, one with a certain star and one without, just to understand the difference. So researchers hoping to understand the power of stars have to be creative. In my study, I examined how casting decisions impacted traders on an online artificial market in which the goal was to predict movies' box-office results as well as traders of "real" stocks of movie studios listed on the New York Stock Exchange. It may sound far-fetched, but such "event studies" are a common research tool; it turns out that, collectively, traders are pretty good at assessing the financial impact of any kind of announcement. (See, for instance: James Surowiecki, *The Wisdom of Crowds* [New York: Anchor Books, 2005]. In his book, Surowiecki discusses some of my earlier work involving prediction markets.)

122 My study is just one in a large stream of research: For example, in an earlier study on the relationship between star involvement and film profitability, S. Abraham Ravid concludes that "stars capture their economic rent," meaning that they capture the value they add: S. Abraham Ravid, "Information, Blockbusters, and Stars: A Study of the Film Industry," *Journal of Business* 72 (October 1999): 463–92. If stars indeed fully capture their "rent"—the excess of expected revenue over what the film would earn with an ordinary talent in the role—ordinary talent and stars are equally valuable for a studio that aims to maximize shareholder value rather than revenues. For more information, see: Richard E. Caves, "Contracts Between Art and Commerce," *Journal of Economic Perspectives* 17 (Spring 2003): 73–83. I have borrowed the term *the curse of the superstar* from another study in this area: Arthur De Vany and W. David Walls, "Motion Picture Profit, the Stable Paretian Hypothesis, and the Curse of the Superstar," *Journal of Economic Dynamics and Control* 28 (March 2004): 1035–57.

123 Tellingly, not one of the top movies released by MGM: I performed this analysis using data from imdb.com and boxofficemojo.com. For more information, see Anita Elberse and Peter Stone, "Metro-Goldwyn-Mayer (MGM) and Tom Cruise," Harvard Business School Case 508–057.

123 Sloan's experiment was essentially an attempt to, as he put it: "Mission: Rescue Operation," *New York Times*, November 3, 2006; "Mission Improbable: Tom Cruise as Mogul," *New York Times*, March 4, 2007.

123 Sloan's choice of the dormant United Artists as the vehicle: "UA Started with Artists in Lead Role," *Hollywood Reporter*, November 3, 2006.

125 In July 2004, at the tender age of seventeen, Maria Sharapova: This section is based on: Anita Elberse and Margarita Golod, "Maria Sharapova: Marketing a Champion (A)," Harvard Business School Case 507-065; Anita Elberse and Margarita Golod, "Maria Sharapova: Marketing a Champion (B)," Harvard Business School Supplement 507-066.

125 the highest-paid female athlete in the world: "The International 20," *Sports Illustrated*, July 27, 2006.

126 she was also the tenth-highest-paid overall: Ibid.

126 Estimates put her income from endorsing such brands: As estimated by *Forbes*. Max Eisenbud has stated about these estimates: "I have no idea how they estimate these numbers. They are always a few million dollars short and keep quoting the same numbers year in year out."

128 The chart on the left shows the ages of all players starting: Using a Web crawler, I pulled these data from ESPN's English Premier League Web site, "ESPN FC" (soccernet.espn.go.com). Player ages are rounded to the nearest whole year. The

"player starts" figure shows the distribution of the ages of players starting each match; the "goals scored" figure shows the distribution of the ages of players scoring each goal in each match, but excluding own goals.

129   The chart on the left shows the ages of all finalists in the four men's: I collected information on Grand Slam finalists from various sources, including the tournaments' own web sites, and information on player ages from the ATP (Association of Tennis professionals) and WTA (Women's Tennis Association) web sites. Ages are calculated as of the day of each final and rounded to the nearest whole year.

129   Based on a sample of the 675 movie actors and actresses listed: I pulled these data from boxofficemojo.com. Ages are rounded to the nearest whole year.

130   what economists call "path dependencies" or "positive feedback effects": Robert H. Frank and Philip J. Cook, *The Winner-Take-All Society* (New York: Free Press, 1995).

131   And Cruise has starred in more movies that collected at least: For an overview, see Anita Elberse and Peter Stone, "Metro-Goldwyn-Mayer (MGM) and Tom Cruise," Harvard Business School Case 508–057.

132   This theory, first described in the context of the creative industries: Richard E. Caves, *Creative Industries: Contracts Between Art and Commerce* (Cambridge, Mass.: Harvard University Press, 2000).

135   The actor Will Smith, for one, is known to be especially shrewd: See for instance: Rebecca Winters Keegan, "The Legend of Will Smith," *Time*, November 29, 2007.

136   agencies like IMG are thought to receive an average of: Also see: Bharat N. Anand and Kate Attea, "International Management Group (IMG)," Harvard Business School Case 702-409.

137   My own study of hundreds of endorsements by athletes: Anita Elberse and Jeroen Verleun, "The Economic Value of Celebrity Endorsements," *Journal of Advertising Research* 52, no. 2 (June 2012): 149–65.

138   "You are waving their dream in their face: Peter Bogdanovich, "SNL's Killer Contract," *New York Observer*, August 16, 1999.

139   The adult cast members of ABC's *Modern Family* did just that in 2012: Matthew Belloni, "'Modern Family' Cast Sues 20th TV as Contract Renegotiation Turns Ugly (Exclusive)," *Hollywood Reporter*, July 24, 2012.

140   Worth more than $90 million before he even graduated from high school: This section is based on: Anita Elberse and Jeffrey McCall Jr., "LeBron James," Harvard Business School Case 509-050.

141   He had coached James's summer league team and was working for Nike: "LeBron Inc.: The Building of a Billion-Dollar Athlete," *Fortune*, November 28, 2007.

141   Taking basketball legend Michael Jordan's billion-dollar brand: Ibid.

143   quarterback Tim Tebow, for instance, jumped on the bandwagon: J. Goodman, "Team Tebow Marketing Arm, XV Enterprises, a Long Time in the Making," *Gator Clause, Miami Herald* blog, September 8, 2010.

143   "We interviewed the top 15 marketing agencies in the world: Ibid.

148   Robert Downey Jr. reportedly received $50 million: Matthew Belloni, "Marvel Moolah: Robert Downey Jr. 'Avengers' Pay Set to Hit $50 Million," *Hollywood Reporter*, May 15, 2012.

149   50 Cent's endorsement deal with vitaminwater is: Zack O'Malley Greenburg, "50 Cent's Next Move: Get Rich, or Feed the Poor Trying," *Forbes*, September 20, 2011.

149   an eight-year, $70 million agreement with longtime sponsor Nike: Danielle Rossingh, "Sharapova Said to Renew Nike Contract for 8 Years, $70 Million," *Bloomberg*, January 11, 2010.

Chapter Five: Will Digital Technology End the Dominance of Blockbusters?

150 How do you change the fortunes of a company: This section is partly based on: Anita Elberse and Sunil Gupta, "YouTube: Time to Charge Users?," Harvard Business School Case 510-053. The statements can be found in: "Best Inventions 2006," *Time*, December 2006; "The 10 Biggest Tech Failures of Last Decade," *Time*, May 14, 2009. The section also draws heavily on John Seabrook, "Streaming Dreams: You Tube Turns Pro," *New Yorker*, January 16, 2012.

150 Co-founders Steve Chen, Chad Hurley, and Jawed Karim: Ellen Lee, "YouTube Video's Boom 'a Social Phenomenon,'" *San Francisco Chronicle*, October 10, 2006.

151 The video quickly went viral, ultimately collecting five million views: Anita Elberse and Sunil Gupta, "Hulu: An Evil Plot to Destroy the World?," Harvard Business School Case 510-005.

151 "We're in the middle of a shift in digital media entertainment: Ellen Lee, "YouTube Video's Boom 'a Social Phenomenon,'" *San Francisco Chronicle*, October 10, 2006.

151 Advertisers remained wary of the vast amount of user-generated content: A *New York Times article*, "YouTube Videos Pull in Real Money," December 11, 2008, estimated that only 3 percent of the videos were ad-supported, while a report by Bernstein Research, "Web Video: Friend or Foe . . . and to Whom?" October 2009, suggested about 10 percent of videos were monetized.

151 the average YouTuber only spent a paltry fifteen minutes: The fifteen-minutes estimate is stated in John Seabrook, "Streaming Dreams: YouTube Turns Pro," *New Yorker*, January 16, 2012. Other estimates put this statistic between six and twenty-four minutes. See for instance: "Web Video: Friend or Foe . . . and to Whom?," Bernstein Research, October 2009.

151 Industry insiders expressed strong doubts about YouTube's: "Web Video: Friend or Foe . . . and to Whom?," Bernstein Research, page 43; "Google Inc.: Potential Ways to Monetize YouTube," Piper Jaffray Company Note, July 16, 2009.

152 YouTube's "Partners Program," splitting advertising revenues with the site: "Google in-Depth Part 2: YouTube—the Super Bowl of Online," Piper Jaffray Company Note, June 2, 2008.

152 "What we do is commission channels," declared Kyncl: John Seabrook, "Streaming Dreams: YouTube Turns Pro," *New Yorker*, January 16, 2012.

153 "People went from broad to narrow . . . and we think they will continue: Ibid.

153 "For example, there's no horseback-riding channel: Ibid.

154 Every manager in the entertainment industry should be acutely aware: For a more comprehensive treatment, see: Anita Elberse, "Should You Invest in the Long Tail?," *Harvard Business Review* 86, nos. 7–8 (July–August 2008): 88–96.

156 in 2012, YouTube claimed it had eight hundred million users: YouTube, "Press Statistics," accessed December 18, 2012.

157 the central tenet of a best-selling book, *The Long Tail*: Chris Anderson, *The Long Tail: Why the Future of Business Is Selling Less of More* (New York: Hyperion, 2006).

157 Anderson's beliefs "influence Google's strategic thinking in a profound way: Ibid.

159 Anderson goes on to predict that "fickle customers" will "scatter: Ibid.

159 According to Nielsen: Copyrighted information ©2011, 2012, of The Nielsen Company, licensed for use herein. Nielsen SoundScan is the leading source for recorded-music sales data in North America. The data cover major and independent labels, and even unsigned artists, as long as they are properly registered and set up with identifiers like UPC barcodes.

161 For instance, nearly 6 million titles—74 percent of all unique titles: Source: Nielsen SoundScan®, 2011.

162   For instance, 513,000 titles—58 percent of all unique titles: Source: Nielsen Sound-Scan®, 2011.

162   But the large majority of products in the tail were not: In line with this view, the extreme concentration of sales is present in both "current" and "catalog" sales, with the latter representing titles eighteen months or older.

163   now that online consumers can cherry-pick the most popular: My research on unbundling in the music industry shows that independent artists with weaker track records are especially hard hit by the unbundling of albums. They are overrepresented in the tail. For more information, see: Anita Elberse, "Bye-Bye Bundles: The Unbundling of Music in Digital Channels," *Journal of Marketing* 74, no. 3 (May 2010): 107–23.

163   These statistics for the recorded music industry are no fluke: Some research is discussed in more detail in: Anita Elberse, "Should You Invest in the Long Tail?," *Harvard Business Review* 86, nos. 7–8 (July–August 2008): 88–96. For academic research on long-tail trends in video sales data, see: Anita Elberse and Felix Oberholzer-Gee, "Superstars and Underdogs: An Examination of the Long Tail Phenomenon in Video Sales," *Marketing Science Institute* 4 (2007): 49–72. For a more recent study on video rentals, see: Anita Elberse and David Schweidel, "Popularity Profiles: How Customers' Use of a Long-Tail Assortment Relates to Their Retention," Working Paper, Harvard Business School, January 2011.

164   the sociologist William McPhee in the early 1960s: William N. McPhee, *Formal Theories of Mass Behavior* (New York: Free Press of Glencoe, 1963).

164   over 98 percent of iPhone users had at the time shown: According to data published by appsfire on its *Appsfire Blog*: Appsfire team, "100k Apps, Announced Today (Only) by Apple. Not a Word on the VERY Long Tail," blog.appsfire.com, November 4, 2009.

165   "I would like to tell you that the Internet has created such: James Manyika, "Google's View on the Future of Business: An Interview with CEO Eric Schmidt," *McKinsey Quarterly* (September 2008).

166   "In fact, it's probable that the Internet will lead to larger: Ibid.

168   In late 2012, YouTube doubled down on its investment: Peter Kafka, "Changing Channels: YouTube Will Pull the Plug on at Least 60 Percent of Its Programming Deals," *All Things Digital*, November 11, 2012.

168   Meanwhile, among the ten most popular channels in early 2013: *Advertising Age*, "YouTube Original Channels Tracker," adage.com/youtube/most-popular-channels. This statement is based on the rankings as of February 4, 2013.

168    $100 million on its own television series *House of Cards*: Nancy Hass, "And the Award for the Next HBO Goes to . . . ," *GQ*, February 2013.

168   "They're huge budgets shows, they're doing things: Andrew Wallenstein, "Netflix Series Spending Revealed," *Variety*, March 8, 2013.

169   "the largest Internet video distribution network ever assembled: "NBC Universal and News Corp. Announce Deal with Internet Leaders AOL, MSN, MySpace, and Yahoo! to Create a Premium Online Video Site with Unprecedented Reach," press release, March 22, 2009.

169   "started out of frustration that other people were using our video: "Free, Legal and On-line: Why Hulu Is the New Way to Watch TV," *Wired*, September 22, 2008; "NBC CEO Jeff Zucker: Hulu Will Start Breaking Even 'Soon,' " *All Things Digital*, May 28, 2009.

169   "Old media guys don't 'get' the Internet": "Old Media Strikes Back," *Newsweek*, March 2, 2009.

170   "Name this thing fast, before 'Clown Co.': Michael Arrington, "Dear ClownCo.: Name This Thing Fast Before It's Too Late," *TechCrunch*, March 23, 2007.

170   "the most promising new way for consumers to view television shows: "Hulu: Five Burning Questions," *Entertainment Weekly*, March 21, 2008.

170 "Happy Birthday Hulu. I'm Glad You Guys: Michael Arrington, "Happy Birthday Hulu. I'm Glad You Guys Didn't Suck," *TechCrunch*, October 29, 2008.

172 True, some studies have shown that illegal downloading: See for instance: Sudip Bhattacharjee, Ram D. Gopal, Kaveepan Lertwachara, and James R. Marsden, "Stochastic Dynamics of Music Album Lifecycles: An Analysis of the New Market Landscape," *International Journal of Human-Computer Studies* 65, no. 1 (2007): 85–93; Sudip Bhattacharjee, Ram D. Gopal, Kaveepan Lertwachara, James R. Marsden, and Rahul Telang, "The Effect of Digital Sharing Technologies on Music Markets: A Survival Analysis of Albums on Ranking Charts," *Management Science* 53, no. 9 (2007): 1359–74.

172 Other researchers, however, have concluded that illegal file sharing: See for instance: Felix Oberholzer-Gee and Koleman S. Strumpf, "The Effect of File Sharing on Record Sales: An Empirical Analysis," *Journal of Political Economy* 115, no. 1 (2007): 1–42.

173 Consider the perspective of free, over-the-air broadcast networks: They can make money in three main ways: through advertising sales on their own stations, through sales of national advertising spots placed on third-party "affiliate" stations, and, in a few cases, through license fees paid by cable operators or the affiliate stations.

173 Networks live and die by so-called CPM rates: In recent years, the lines between broadcast and cable networks have blurred. Major broadcast networks now also receive a monthly fee from cable operators, albeit not as high a payment as, say, ESPN.

174 Hulu's CPM rates have been much higher from the start: In 2009, average CPMs for Hulu reportedly varied between $40 and $50.

174 And several parties participate in these revenues: Content owners receive up to 70 percent of the advertising revenues generated on Hulu, and distribution partners up to 10 percent of the advertising revenues. This means CPMs on Hulu may have to be even higher to create parity.

175 Prime-time CPM rates for original dramatic content: In 2009, rates were estimated to be between $15 and $25, yielding an estimate of well over $1,200 per thousand viewers per hour.

176 Powerful cable operators, which control about 70 percent: Satellite companies account for the remaining 30 percent. Standard & Poor's, "Broadcasting, Cable & Satellite Industry Survey," July 30, 2009.

176 "gets our content out there when and where people want it: "Some Online Shows Could Go Subscription-Only," *New York Times*, March 29, 2009.

177 a whopping quarter of the total online-video advertising revenues: These are data for 2008: Hulu was responsible for 5 percent of video streams and collected about a quarter of the total of $700 million online-video advertising revenues. I obtained data from various sources, including Nielsen VideoCensus and eMarketer. For more information, see: Anita Elberse and Sunil Gupta, "Hulu: An Evil Plot to Destroy the World?," Harvard Business School Case 510–005.

178 Hulu's estimated revenues rose to nearly $700 million in 2012: Jason Kilar, "A Big 2012," Hulu blog, December 17, 2012.

178 In the 2006–2007 season, the Metropolitan Opera: This section is based on: Anita Elberse and Crissy Perez, "The Metropolitan Opera (A)," Harvard Business School Case 509-033; Anita Elberse and Crissy Perez, "The Metropolitan Opera (B)," Harvard Business School Supplement 509-034.

179 Although opera attendance had risen in the 1980s and 1990s: U.S. Census, "Statistical Abstract," 2008; U.S. Census Bureau, "Profile America," February 6, 2006.

179 "My aim is to strip away the veil of elitism: Peter Gelb, Lecture at the Kennedy School of Government, Harvard University, March 3, 2008.

179   The largest independent performing arts company in the world: The Metropolitan
      Opera, 2005–2006 Annual Report; Peter Gelb, Lecture at the Kennedy School of
      Government, Harvard University, March 3, 2008.

179   Gelb said, he wanted to "conceive of it as an event": "As Audience Shrinks, the Met
      Gets Daring," *New York Times*, February 11, 2006.

179   But that didn't come cheap: the simulcasts required substantial investments: Peter
      Gelb, Lecture at the Kennedy School of Government, Harvard University, March 3,
      2008; "Music for the Masses," *Economist*, July 3, 2008.

180   In total, three hundred thousand people turned out for the Met's first season: "Sight-
      ings: The Metropolitan Opera Goes to the Movies," *Wall Street Journal*, March 29, 2008.

180   In April 2007, as audiences settled into their seats: Boston Opera representative;
      Peter Gelb, Lecture at the Kennedy School of Government, Harvard University,
      March 3, 2008; "Man Behind the Curtain," *New Yorker*, October 22, 2007; "Music for
      the Masses," *Economist*, July 3, 2008.

182   "Just as sports teams have discovered that fans still: Peter Gelb, Lecture at the Ken-
      nedy School of Government, Harvard University, March 3, 2008.

182   Over the past twenty years, only twenty-six different operas: Opera America, "Most
      Produced Works," www.operaamerica.org, accessed on April 30, 2008.

183   Early evidence emerging from surveys offers an explanation: Opera America,
      "Metropolitan Opera Live in HD Survey," prepared by Shugoll Research, July 2008.
      Survey results are summarized in: Anita Elberse and Crissy Perez, "The Metropoli-
      tan Opera (B)," Harvard Business School Supplement 509-034.

183   In the early 2000s, there were close to 180 American opera companies: U.S. Census
      Bureau, "2002 Economic Census." (This is the last available data point before the
      launch of the Met's Live in HD program.)

183   Attendance figures and revenues were quite concentrated: I received these data
      from Opera America; for a full overview, see: Anita Elberse and Crissy Perez, "The
      Metropolitan Opera (B)," Harvard Business School Supplement 509-034.

184   "one in 15,000 opera singers makes it": "Divas in Training," *Wall Street Journal*, April
      24, 1996.

184   Luciano Pavarotti, reportedly earned $100,000 for a recital: "In Final Twist, Ill Pava-
      rotti Falls Silent for Met Finale," *New York Times*, May 12, 2002.

185   "they are invading our space, to put it bluntly": "Verdi with Popcorn, and Trepida-
      tion," *New York Times*, February 15, 2009.

185   San Francisco Opera, has called the Met's innovations "a bombshell": "Met Opera to
      Expand in Theaters Across Globe," *New York Times*, August 9, 2007.

185   the Met collected a record-high $182 million in private donations: Daniel J. Wakin
      and Kevin Flynn, "A Metropolitan Opera High Note, as Donations Hit $182 Mil-
      lion," *New York Times*, October 10, 2011.

Chapter Six: Will Digital Technology Threaten Powerful Producers?

187   "I like the people at our record company,: This section is based on: Anita Elberse
      and Jason Bergsman, "Radiohead: Music at Your Own Price (A)," Harvard Busi-
      ness School Case 508-110; and Anita Elberse and Jason Bergsman, "Radiohead:
      Music at Your Own Price (B)," Harvard Business School Supplement 508-111. Thom
      Yorke is quoted in: Josh Tryrangiel, "Rebels Without a Contract," *Time*, March 19,
      2007.

187   By 2007, Radiohead's six albums collectively had sold over eight million copies: I
      obtained recorded-music sales data from Nielsen SoundScan and *Billboard*. The
      quote can be found in: Jon Pareles, "With Radiohead, and Alone, a Sweet Malaise,"
      New York Times, July 2, 2006.

188 "The first time we did *All I Need*, boom! it was up on YouTube: Jon Pareles, "Pay What You Want for This Article," *New York Times*, December 9, 2007.

188 Bricks-and-mortar record stores accounted for just over 30 percent: As reported in: e-Marketer, "Recorded Music: Digital Falls Short," November 2007. For more information, see: Anita Elberse and Jason Bergsman, "Radiohead: Music at Your Own Price (A)," Harvard Business School Case 508-110.

188 files were traded at an estimated ratio of twenty illegal downloads: International Federation of the Phonographic Industry, "IFPI Digital Music Report 2008," January 24, 2008.

188 Radiohead retained all rights to the album, and worked out: Lars Brandle, "Radiohead in Direct-Licensing Deal for New CD," *Billboard*, October 9, 2007.

189 Describing traditional strategies as a "decaying business model: Josh Tryrangiel, "Rebels Without a Contract," *Time*, March 19, 2007.

189 "You can say we've earned the privilege to do things our way": Gerald Marzorati, "The Post-Rock Band," *New York Times*, October 1, 2000.

189 For instance, *OK Computer* was introduced with a single, *Paranoid Android*: Paul Sexton, "Capitol, Parlophone Are Confident in Radiohead," *Billboard*, May 10, 1997.

189 For *Kid A*, the band's fourth album, Radiohead eschewed a traditional promotional approach: Paul Sexton, "Radiohead Won't Play by Rules," *Billboard*, September 16, 2000; Charles Goldsmith, "Radiohead's New Marketing: Videos—and Singles to Disappear Completely," *Wall Street Journal*, September 18, 2000.

189 "want[ed] to find other ways of doing what has to be done: Gerald Marzorati, "The Post-Rock Band," *New York Times*, October 1, 2000.

190 A small group of fans pushed the average price up: Additionally, one in every twenty-five transactions was for a deluxe box set, at $80; the deluxe album alone thus yielded $3.20 in revenues per transaction.

190 240,000 people downloaded the album for free over BitTorrent: "Free? Steal It Anyway," *Forbes*, October 16, 2007.

194 $2.7 billion in A&R and another $1.8 billion in marketing in 2011: International Federation of the Phonographic Industry, "Investing Music: How Music Companies Discover, Nurture, and Promote Talent," IFPI, 2012.

195 Described as "the darling of the self-publishing industry: Sarah Millar, "How a Failed Author Made $2 Million from e-Books," *Toronto Star*, March 3, 2011.

195 By 2011, she had seven books on *USA Today*'s bestsellers list: Dianna Dilworth, "Amanda Hocking Is Second Self-Published Author to Sell a Million Kindle eBooks," Mediabistro.com, November 9, 2011.

195 Held up as an example of an author who had shrewdly: Ibid.; Julie Bosman, "Noted Self-Publisher May Be Close to a Book Deal," *New York Times*, March 21, 2011.

195 she shopped a new four-book paranormal series, *Watersong*: Julie Bosman, "Noted Self-Publisher May Be Close to a Book Deal," *New York Times*, March 21, 2011.

196 "I want to be a writer," she wrote in her blog: Ibid.

196 Self-publishing is "easier to get into but harder to maintain: Amanda Hocking, "Some Things That Need to Be Said," AmandaHockingBlogspot.com, March 3, 2011.

196 of the top one hundred albums on the *Billboard* chart in 2012: According to data by Nielsen SoundScan. In September 2012, the merger between Universal and EMI was completed, leaving only a "big three."

197 St. Martin's had to overcome several other major publishers' bids: Julie Bosman, "Self-Publisher Signs Four-Book Deal with St. Martin's," *New York Times*, March 24, 2011.

198 "In terms of digital income, we've made more money: "Estimates: Radiohead Made Up to $10 Million on Initial Album Sales," Wired.com, October 19, 2007.

198   "We can safely say that the experiment really worked: Louis CK, "A Statement from Louis CK," buy.louisck.net, December 13, 2011.

198   Total sales of the special are now reportedly well above $1 million: Louis CK, as told to Jimmy Fallon, on *Late Night with Jimmy Fallon*, December 21, 2011.

199   "It only works for us because of where we are": "David Byrne and Thom Yorke on the Real Value of Music," *Wired*, December 18, 2007.

200   The iTunes Store has a larger share of the online music market: According to press releases by the NPD Group. See, for instance: NPD Group, "iTunes Continues to Dominate Music Retailing," press release, September 18, 2012.

201   When a special request comes in from Apple's highest echelons: This section is based on: Anita Elberse and Brett Laffel, "Major League Baseball Advanced Media: America's Pastime Goes Digital," Harvard Business School Case 510-092.

202   the URL MLB.com directed visitors to a Philadelphia law firm: Will Leitch, "MLB's Digital Dominance," *FastCompany*, March 20, 2008.

202   an idiotic suggestion, co-workers would respond with "Japanese audio!": Steven Levy, "Covering All the Online Bases," *Newsweek*, June 25, 2007.

203   *Newsweek* called BAM "the grand-slam online leader among major sports": Ibid.; Mark Newman, "MLB.TV Continues to Raise the Bar," MLB.com, February 3, 2010. (The number one selling iPhone app was Navigon AG's *MobileNavigator North America*, priced at $89.99.)

204   in the 2009 season, seventy-three million tickets to live games were sold: I consulted data reported in: *Forbes* ("The Business of Baseball," April 22, 2009; "The Business of Basketball," December 9, 2009; "The Business of Football," September 2, 2009; "The Business of Hockey," November 11, 2009); and MLB, NFL, NBA, and NHL (National Hockey League) press releases. For a complete overview, see: Anita Elberse and Brett Laffel, "Major League Baseball Advanced Media: America's Pastime Goes Digital," Harvard Business School Case 510-092.

206   The contract with ESPN, owned by Disney, was worth $2.4 billion: These statistics are based on data reported in: "ESPN to Add Monday Night Baseball in New Deal," ESPN.com, September 14, 2005; "MLB, Fox Reach Seven-Year Extension," MLB.com, July 11, 2006; "Fox Reups MLB TV Deal," *Mediaweek*, July 11, 2006; "MLB's Squeeze Play: League Struggles to Renew TV Rights Deals," *Brandweek*, February 13, 2006.

209   They have taken a hard line against cable networks: When, in March 2010, Comedy Central pulled *The Daily Show with Jon Stewart* and *The Colbert Report*, along with a handful of Viacom library shows, from Hulu, pressure from cable operators on Comedy Central was rumored to have contributed to the decision.

210   In late 2009, the NFL was wrapping up its biggest season: This section is based on: Anita Elberse, Kelsey Calhoun, and Daven Johnson, "The NFL's Digital Media Strategy," Harvard Business School Case 511-055.

211   Cable channel ESPN annually paid the league well over $1 billion: "Sports Business Resource Guide & Fact Book: Digital Media Rights," *SportsBusiness Journal*, 2010.

213   Verizon would pay the NFL $720 million over four years: John Ourand and Terry Lefton, "Verizon-NFL Deal: Convergence Is Here," *SportsBusiness Journal*, March 15, 2010.

214   "the biggest overlap between a sponsorship and media deal": Ibid.

216   satellite radio network Sirius; wireless carrier Verizon: Sirius is now known as SiriusXM.

216   "We are keeping our eyes on this. It's starting to nibble at the edges": John Ourand and Terry Lefton, "Verizon-NFL Deal: Convergence Is Here," *Sports Business Journal*, March 15, 2010.

217 over 70 percent of all Americans proclaim themselves football fans: I received data
     from: ESPN Sports Poll 2009, Nielsen, and OTX Weekly Tracker. For an overview of
     the data, see Anita Elberse, Kelsey Calhoun, and Daven Johnson, "The NFL's Digi-
     tal Media Strategy," Harvard Business School Case 511-055.
217 In fact, as of early 2013, four Super Bowls belong: The top five are: 1. Super Bowl
     XLVI (2012) with 111.3 million viewers; 2. Super Bowl XLV (2011) with 111.0 million
     viewers; 3. Super Bowl XLVII (2013) with 108.4 million viewers; 4. Super Bowl XLIV
     (2010) with 106.5 million viewers; and 5. *M*A*S*H* finale (1983) with 106.0 million
     viewers. (Source: Nielsen ratings.)
218 more of a guarantee of success than if you've got Brad Pitt, George Clooney: Sean
     Leahy, "NFL TV Ratings Soar; Dick Ebersol Says League's Dominance Has Been
     Mind-Numbing," *Huddle*, October 9, 2009.
218 in 2013, they reportedly paid as much as $3.8 million: Brian Steinberg, "Who Bought
     What in Super Bowl 2013," *Advertising Age*, February 1, 2013.

Chapter Seven: The Future of Blockbuster Strategies

220 When Shawn Carter—better known as hip-hop megastar Jay-Z: This section is
     based on: Anita Elberse and Kwame Owusu-Kesse, "Droga5: Launching Jay-Z's
     Decoded," Harvard Business School Case 513-032.
220 a "lyrical memoir" that explained the hidden meanings behind: Michiko Kakutani,
     "Jay-Z Deconstructs Himself," *New York Times*, November 22, 2010.
223 won Droga5 several of the advertising industry's most prestigious awards: Among
     other awards, the campaign won Droga5 a Golden Effie 2012 (in the "Media Innova-
     tion" category), a Titanium Lion, an Integrated Grand Prix, an Outdoor Grand Prix,
     and a Direct Gold at the Cannes Lions International Festival of Creativity.
223 The agency released the book in the form of two hundred placements: Many illus-
     trations spread out over two pages and were distributed as one placement.
224 Some of these placements were true works of art: Droga5's campaign video, which
     shows many other examples, can be viewed at: www.droga5.com/#/casestudies
     /bingcs.
225 Priced at $35, the book sold three hundred thousand copies: I obtained data from
     Nielsen BookScan.
225 Warner Bros. teamed up with 42 Entertainment to develop an ARG: I compiled this
     information from the 42 Entertainment web site (www.42entertainment.com) and
     various campaign videos.
226 Lionsgate won accolades for its digital-marketing campaign for *The Hunger Games*:
     A useful summary of the campaign can be found here: Ari Karpel, "Inside 'The
     Hunger Games' Social Media Machine," *FastCompany*, www.fastcocreate.com, ac-
     cessed on December 1, 2012.
227 In my own research, I have examined how movie and video game trailers: Anita
     Elberse, Clarence Lee, and Lingling Zhang, "Viral Videos: The Dynamics of Online
     Video Advertising Campaigns," Working Paper, Harvard Business School, January
     2013. The study is based on data provided by Visible Measures.
227 they turn out in force primarily for the biggest brands: Anita Elberse, Clarence Lee,
     and Lingling Zhang, "Viral Videos: The Dynamics of Online Video Advertising
     Campaigns," Working Paper, Harvard Business School, January 2013.
230 the star had amassed a net worth of over $450 million: Forbes Staff, "The Forbes
     400: America's Billionaires in the Making," *Forbes*, September 24, 2010.
230 he is also an extremely capable businessman: Various articles provide insight into
     Jay-Z's business interests: Jeff Leeds, "In Rapper's Deal, a New Model for Music
     Business," *New York Times*, April 3, 2008; Stuart Elliot, "A New Venture for Jay-Z, on

Madison Avenue," *New York Times*, February 8, 2008; Daniel Gross, "Jay-Z's $450 Million Business Empire," *Yahoo!*, March 25, 2011; Mike Snyder, "Jay-Z and Eminem Spin a Musical Game Out of 'DJ Hero,'" *USA Today*, May 31, 2009.

232 Which outcome is more likely depends on how groups of consumers differ: The economics and marketing literature on bundling has traditionally emphasized one critical determinant of the payoff of a bundling strategy: the variance in so-called reservation prices across and within consumers. According to Schmalensee in his seminal 1984 paper, bundling "operates by reducing the effective dispersion in buyers' tastes," which will "enhance profits by permitting more efficient capture of consumers' surplus" as long as people's reservation prices are not perfectly positively correlated. The basic idea is that when reservation prices vary, a bundle can be designed to appeal (and more profitably sell) to consumers who would otherwise buy only one or a few items at prices below their reservation prices. I discuss the literature in my paper: Anita Elberse, "Bye-Bye Bundles: The Unbundling of Music in Digital Channels," *Journal of Marketing* 74, no. 3 (May 2010): 107–23. For more information, see: Richard Schmalensee, "Gaussian Demand and Commodity Bundling," *Journal of Business* 57 (January 1984): S211–30.

233 My own research shows that unbundling has had a strong negative impact: Anita Elberse, "Bye-Bye Bundles: The Unbundling of Music in Digital Channels," *Journal of Marketing* 74, no. 3 (May 2010): 107–23.

233 Although albums by the biggest stars with the strongest track records: In the study, track records were measured by the number of an artist's albums that had previously appeared in the *Billboard* Album Top 200.

234 HBO president Richard Plepler used just one word: "math": Richard Plepler, Q&A at the Harvard Business School, December 4, 2012.

235 responsible for well over 60 percent of legal digital music downloading: NPD Group, "iTunes Continues to Dominate Music Retailing," press release, September 18, 2012.

235 now used by some 425 million people: "Survival of the Biggest," *Economist*, December 1, 2012.

235 now responsible for nearly 30 percent of total book sales: For the estimates of Amazon's overall share and the relative size of the e-book market, see: Jim Milliot, "E-books Market Share at 22%, Amazon Has 27%," *Publishers Weekly*, November 5, 2012. For the estimate of Amazon's share of the e-book market, see: David Streitfeld, "Little Sign of a Predicted E-Book Price War," *New York Times*, December 23, 2012.

235 The company's vast range of products generated $48 billion in revenues: According to Amazon.com Inc.'s income statement for the year 2011.

237 How many brand partners does it take to launch one hit album?: This section is based on: Anita Elberse and Michael Christensen, "Lady Gaga (A)," Harvard Business School Case 512-016; Anita Elberse and Michael Christensen, "Lady Gaga (B)," Harvard Business School Case 512-017.

237 "undeniably unique" and likely to "attract fashionistas far": Jasmine France, "Heartbeats by Lady Gaga Headphones from Monster—Editor's Review," CNET.com, December 18, 2009.

238 "Lifestyle, music, art, fashion! I am so excited to extend myself: "Lady Gaga Named Creative Director for Specialty Line of Polaroid Imaging Products," Polaroid press release, January 5, 2010.

239 "Jay-Z doesn't do straightforward endorsement deals": I am unsure whether Jay-Z's partnership with Duracell is a deviation from this path. In 2012, Jay-Z appeared in television commercials for the brand that are suggestive of a more standard endorsement deal.

240 Procter & Gamble started funding programs as early as: Procter & Gamble, "Procter & Gamble Entertainment: History," www.proctergambleproductions.com.

240 Lexus paying a share of the production costs for a special episode: "Lexus Bankrolls Extra Episode of Food Network's 'Restaurant Impossible,'" *Advertising Age*, December 7, 2012.

241 In late 2012, when she released her album *Red*, Swift did so: Glenn Peoples, "Why Taylor Swift's 'Red' Is Absent from Subscription Services," *Billboard*, October 23, 2012.

242 "We're always looking at, 'How can we create more doors?': Andrew Hampp and Phil Gallo, "How Taylor Swift's 'Red' Is Getting a Boost from Branding Mega-Deals," *Billboard*, October 22, 2012.

242 *Red* debuted at the top of the *Billboard* album chart: Ibid.

242 more than four hundred thousand units were sold at Target: Brian Mansfield, "Taylor Swift Goes No. 1 with Million-Plus 'Red' Sales," *USA Today*, October 31, 2012.

242 In late 2012, she closed a $50 million brand partnership with Pepsi: Pepsi, "Pepsi and Beyoncé Partnership Fact Sheet," PepsiCo, December 10, 2012.

245 Google still dominated the market with a 66 percent share: Microsoft internal documents.

246 Microsoft saw Bing reach a 12 percent share during the *Decoded* campaign: Ibid.

247 *AdWeek* selected Droga5 as its Agency of the Year: Gabriel Beltrone, "Agency of the Year: Droga5's Delicious World," *AdWeek*, December 10, 2012.

249 *FarmVille* attracted forty-six million players every month: Miguel Helft, "Zynga Does a Deal with Lady Gaga," *New York Times*, May 10, 2011.

Epilogue: No Business Like Show Business?

251 Sometimes, it seems, the best way to put your latest blockbuster bet: This section is partly based on: Anita Elberse, Ryan Barlow, and Sheldon Wong, "Marquee: The Business of Nightlife," Harvard Business School Case 509-019.

251 most clubs were over within a mere eighteen months: Although solid numbers are hard to come by, the typical life span of the 129 legally operating nightclubs in Manhattan is thought to be about eighteen months. And of the ten American nightclubs in the "Hot Clubs Around the World" list published in a 2006 *Forbes* report on the "Business of Nightlife," three (Amika in Miami, Crobar in New York City, and Ice in Las Vegas) had closed their doors by 2008. For more information, see: "Flaming Out Never Felt So Good," *Forbes*, August 22, 2006; "The Science of a Sizzling Club," *Forbes*, August 22, 2006.

252 "Only the fashionable, famous, or financially secure need apply: "Club Stays Hot at Ripe Old Age of 2," *New York Times*, November 3, 2005.

252 described as a "one-stop party shop": "The Short, Drunken Life of Club Row," *New York Magazine*, February 11, 2007.

253 with an estimated $80 million in revenues: According to estimates by *Nightclub & Bar*, "Nightclub & Bar Top 100 2012," www.nightclub.com.

256 being "among the vanguard of electronic musicians: According to rankings by *DJ Mag*, "DJ Top 100: The Full 2012 Results," www.djmag.com/top-100-djs.

257 Top spinners like Avicii, Deadmau5, David Guetta, and Tiësto: Ben Sisario, "Electronic Dance Concerts Turn Up Volume, Tempting Investors," *New York Times*, April 4, 2012.

257 the world's ten highest-paid DJs collectively earned $125 million: Zack O'Malley Greenburg, "The World's Highest-Paid DJs, 2012," *Forbes*, August 2, 2012.

261 are visible throughout the hospitality industry: In fact, seemingly taking a cue from entertainment businesses, restaurants such as Grant Achatz's Next (based in Chicago) are experimenting with ticketing models.

262   Apple makes only a few bets each year: In his biography of Steve Jobs, Walter
      Isaacson recalls how, upon his return to Apple in the mid-1990s, Jobs introduced
      this much more narrow product focus. "Deciding what not to do is as important
      as deciding what to do," Jobs is quoted as saying. At the time, Apple had a dozen
      versions of the Macintosh; Jobs cut 70 percent of them, and urged the Apple em-
      ployees to focus on just one consumer and one professional product in both the
      desktop and portable market. Source: Walter Isaacson, *Steve Jobs* (New York: Si-
      mon & Schuster, 2011).

262   Broadcast in more than 180 countries, the $12 million show: Marisa Guthrie, "How
      'Victoria's Secret Fashion Show' Turns $12 Million into $5 Billion in One Hour,"
      Hollywood Reporter, November 28, 2011.

263   CBS licenses the show for more than $1 million: Yvonne Villarreal, "Victoria's Se-
      cret Helps Lead CBS to Victory," *Los Angeles Times*, December 5, 2012.

263   reportedly up to $5 million a year: Marisa Guthrie, "How 'Victoria's Secret Fashion
      Show' Turns $12 Million Into $5 Billion in One Hour," *Hollywood Reporter*, Novem-
      ber 28, 2011.

264   the brand's "Red Bull gives you wings" slogan: John Jurgensen, "The New Produc-
      ers," *Wall Street Journal*, December 21, 2012.

264   famous for its blockbuster product, the trench coat: In early 2013, Ahrendts wrote in
      a *Harvard Business Review* article: "Today 60% of our business is apparel, and outer-
      wear makes up more than half of that." A focus on the core product was and contin-
      ues to be a critical element of her strategy to improve the retailer's fortunes, she
      wrote: "Now every major new initiative has the trench coat front and center."
      Source: Angela Ahrendts, "Burberry's CEO on Turning an Aging British Icon into a
      Global Luxury Brand," *Harvard Business Review*, January–February 2013.

264   she described her firm not as a clothing company: All quotes by Angela Ahrendts
      in this paragraph originate from: Angela Ahrendts, Q&A at the Harvard Business
      School, November 28, 2012.

265   Burberry Acoustic, which falls under Burberry.com: Nancy Hass, "Earning Her
      Stripes," *Wall Street Journal*, September 9, 2010.

ACKNOWLEDGMENTS

It's amazing how surprising life can be. I knew I was in for an adventure when I joined the Harvard Business School as a newly minted PhD in 2003, but I didn't quite expect it to be *this* thrilling. If you had told me back then that ten years later I would have been named a chaired professor, would have had the opportunity to study some of the entertainment business's biggest stars and most successful executives, and would have been given a chance to describe my ideas in a book released by a major publishing house, I would have responded that you'd make for an excellent screenwriter in Hollywood—but only if you were to add a healthy dose of realism to your stories.

Yet, here we are. *Blockbusters* is the culmination of a decade-long exploration of my passion, the worlds of entertainment, media, and sports. When I first toyed with the idea of focusing on these sectors in my bid to earn a tenured position at Harvard, I knew it was the road less traveled. Several colleagues told me I was crazy to focus on what seemed such frivolous sectors of the economy, and they were probably right. It certainly appeared very risky to try to launch a Harvard MBA course that revolved entirely around the entertainment business, let alone to dedicate the lion's share of

my time to developing case studies for that course even though I
was trained as an empirical researcher who tackled large-scale
data sets. You could say I made a blockbuster bet on my research
program: if the research had not caught on with students, fellow
academics, and executives, my career likely would have stopped
dead in its tracks.

But beautiful things happened once I decided to go for it anyway. I learned that what initially had seemed quite a gamble wasn't
nearly as risky as everyone thought. The moment I went all in,
many joined in to help. Executives and celebrities gave me unprecedented access and shared their secrets to success and, truly ad-
mirably, explained their failures. Many colleagues collaborated on
research projects. And students enrolled in the course even when
they had no idea exactly what they signed up for. Before I knew it,
one incredible opportunity after another opened up and, as they
say, the rest is history. I hope that with my work I have done justice
to those opportunities and to the efforts of everyone who helped
along the way.

I have numerous people to thank. First, I am deeply grateful to
the many entertainment industry insiders who agreed to participate in my case studies, who granted interviews specifically for
this book, or who otherwise were very generous with their time
and knowledge. The full list of those who feature prominently in
Blockbusters is long, but I count myself among the luckiest people
on this planet to have been able to work with such a remarkable
group of accomplished individuals, so I would like to acknowl-
edge them all here once more:

> Alan Horn; Karen Kosztolnyik, Peter McGuigan, Vicki
> Myron, and Jamie Raab; Avi Arad, Peter Cuneo, and Isaac
> Perlmutter; Steve Berman, Bobby Campbell, Troy Carter,
> Arthur Fogel, Stefani "Lady Gaga" Germanotta, and Vin-
> cent Herbert; Ben Berkman, David Boxenbaum, and James
> Diener; Ramón Calderón and Florentino Pérez; Mauricio
> Macri; Sir Alex Ferguson; Tom Cruise, Harry Sloan, and
> Paula Wagner; Max Eisenbud and Maria Sharapova;

Maverick Carter and LeBron James; Alex Carloss; JP Colaco, Andy Forssell, and Jason Kilar; Peter Gelb; Bob Bowman; Brian Rolapp and Hans Schroeder; David Droga, Andrew Essex, Shawn "Jay-Z" Carter, Julie Grau, Chris Jackson, John Meneilly, and Yusuf Mehdi; Holly Hinton, Anders Klemmer, and Alex Wheeler; Lou Abin, Ryan "Kaskade" Raddon, Pasquale Rotella, Jason Strauss, and Noah Tepperberg; and Angela Ahrendts, Garth Ancier, Scooter Braun, and Richard Plepler.

Thank you all—it was a joy to work with you and learn from you.

Countless other people who are not mentioned by name in this book were just as crucial to the end result. Special thanks go to Jason Ferguson, Andrew Goldberg, Lee Gomes, Michelle Horowitz, John Maatta, Martin O'Connor, Lex Suvanto, Judy Tepperberg, Page Thompson, and Blair Westlake.

By now, nearly a thousand students have signed up to take my Harvard Business School course *Strategic Marketing in Creative Industries* (sadly, for all my talk about not playing it safe in my career, when I launched the course I didn't quite have the guts to opt for the infinitely cooler sounding *Show Business*). Those students were an invaluable source of insights and ideas. Thank you, my dear SMICIs. You have a special place in my heart—even if I gave you a "3"—and you are the primary reason why what I do is far too much fun to be called "work." I'm so impressed by you, and I can't wait to see how you'll change the world for the better in the years to come.

Fifteen students had an even greater impact on the book by helping to write the case studies featured here: Thank you, Ryan Barlow, Jason Bergsman, Kelsey Calhoun, Michael Christensen, Tom Dye, Margarita Golod, Daven Johnson, Caren Kelleher, Brett Laffel, Jeffrey McCall, Kwame "DJ K.Kess" Owusu-Kesse, Crissy Perez, Peter Stone, Kimball Thomas, and Sheldon Wong, for all your prized contributions.

For all the deep insights that case studies can bring, I continue to analyze quantitative data to understand market trends, and some of those analyses found their way into the book, too. I am grateful to the many individuals and companies that over the years have given me proprietary data to work with. Here, I'd like to especially thank The Nielsen Company's Hugh Anderson, Howard Appelbaum, and David Bakula as well as Rentrak's Bill Livek. Hugh, Howard, David, and Bill, I appreciate your generosity and willingness to help.

I am forever indebted to my academic mentor and collaborator Jehoshua Eliashberg at The Wharton School, whose pioneering work inspired my PhD dissertation on the film industry, and who has been a trusted adviser ever since. Thank you, Josh, for always being there for me—Kalderon forever! Several other colleagues in academia were coauthors on research projects that found their way into *Blockbusters*: I am grateful to Bharat Anand, Gustavo Herrero, Sunil Gupta, Felix Oberholzer-Gee, Clarence Lee, Elie Ofek, John Quelch, David Schweidel, Jeroen Verleun, and Lingling Zhang for all their wisdom. And thank you, Julia Kirby, for teaching me so much about writing for practitioners.

More generally, I owe all my colleagues at the Harvard Business School a great deal of gratitude for their encouragement over the years, for creating a wonderful work environment, and for never giving up on the challenge to be relevant to management practice. Thank you, Dean Jay Light, for stimulating me to, in your words, "think big," and thank you, Dean Nitin Nohria, for all your guidance and support.

Without my rock-star literary agent Chris Parris-Lamb, I probably would have never taken the step of packaging my research into what you are reading at the moment. "Do you think there's a book there?," he asked me in an out-of-the-blue e-mail now nearly five years ago. Chris, thank you for asking the question I could only answer in the affirmative—and for expertly shepherding our project ever since. You are awe-inspiringly brilliant.

Of course *Blockbusters* also never would have seen the light of day without the star-studded team at Henry Holt. John Sterling, my fabulous editor, was instrumental throughout the book-writing process. John, thank you for having faith in this project, and for having faith in me. I know I made your life difficult at times, but I have no doubt that your sublime efforts made the book much better than it otherwise would have been. You taught me many writing lessons that will stick with me, and I will never be able to thank you enough. Steve Rubin, thank you for making a (blockbuster!) bet on my book. I was honored by the extraordinary vote of confidence. Emi Ikkanda, thank you for tirelessly and patiently working behind the scenes to keep everything on track. Patricia Eisemann, Emily Kobel, Katie Kurtzman, Jason Liebman, and Maggie Richards, thank you for plotting a blockbuster-worthy promotional strategy. Gretchen Crary and Dee Dee De Bartlo, thank you for jumping on board so enthusiastically. Finally, Michael Bierut, thank you for designing such a stunning cover.

I can't believe how many other friends and colleagues helped with the book in other ways. Chris Satti, thank you for making me a higher priority than the mayor of Boston. James Allworth, I am convinced you are Australia's very own superhero. I owe you many, many dinners. Chris Allen and Marc Lubbers—thank you for your beautiful design work. And Anthony Accardo, Jyoti Agarwal, Shane Bills, Barbara Cleary, Nick Krasney, Minal Mehta, Jann Schwarz, Rena Wang, Calvin Willett, Carter Williams, and the dozens of others who have kindly offered to help shape or promote the book—you showed that the Harvard Business School community always steps up to a challenge. I promise to return the favor by throwing a spectacular launch party.

But most of all, I want to thank my family, my dog, Moseley, for having the wisdom to never contradict me, and my husband, Michael, for making Brad Pitt look decidedly mundane and for being the best friend and most supportive partner I could ever imagine.

—Anita Elberse

INDEX